KINSHIP, HONOUR AND MONEY IN RURAL PAKISTAN

NORDIC INSTITUTE OF ASIAN STUDIES

Recent Monographs

63. SURVIVAL AND PROFIT IN RURAL JAVA
Sven Cederroth
64. THE STATE AND ITS ENEMIES IN PAPUA NEW GUINEA
Alexander Wanek
65. MISSION AND TAMIL SOCIETY
Henriette Bugge
66. FOLK TALES FROM KAMMU – V: A YOUNG STORY-TELLER'S TALES
Kristina Lindell, Jan-Öjvind Swahn and Damrong Tayanin
67. ISLAM AND POLITICS IN AFGHANISTAN
Asta Olesen
68. EXEMPLARY CENTRE, ADMINISTRATIVE PERIPHERY
Hans Antlöv
69. FISHING VILLAGES IN TOKUGAWA JAPAN
Arne Kalland
70. THE HONG MERCHANTS OF CANTON
Weng Eang Cheong
71. ASIAN ENTREPRENEURIAL MINORITIES
Christine Dobbin
72. ORGANISING WOMEN'S PROTEST
Eldrid Mageli
73. THE ORAL TRADITION OF YANGZHOU STORYTELLING
Vibeke Børdahl
74. ACCEPTING POPULATION CONTROL
Cecilia Nathansen Milwertz
75. MANAGING MARITAL DISPUTES IN MALAYSIA
Sharifah Zaleha Syed Hassan and Sven Cederroth
76. SUBUD AND THE JAVANESE MYSTICAL TRADITION
Antoon Geels
77. FOLK TALES FROM KAMMU – VI: A STORY-TELLER'S LAST TALES
Kristina Lindell, Jan-Öjvind Swahn and Damrong Tayanin
78. KINSHIP, HONOUR AND MONEY IN RURAL PAKISTAN
Alain Lefebvre
79. THAILAND AND THE SOUTHEAST ASIAN NETWORKS OF THE VIETNAMESE REVOLUTION, 1885–1954
Christopher E. Goscha
80. INDIAN ART WORLDS IN CONTENTION
Helle Bundgaard
81. CONSTRUCTING THE COLONIAL ENCOUNTER
Niels Brimnes
82. RELIGIOUS VIOLENCE IN CONTEMPORARY JAPAN
Ian Reader

KINSHIP, HONOUR AND MONEY IN RURAL PAKISTAN

SUBSISTENCE ECONOMY AND THE EFFECTS OF INTERNATIONAL MIGRATION

ALAIN LEFEBVRE

CURZON

Nordic Institute of Asian Studies
Monograph Series, No. 78

First published in 1999
by Curzon Press
15 The Quadrant, Richmond
Surrey TW9 1BP

Typesetting by the Nordic Institute of Asian Studies

Publication of this volume was assisted by a grant from the Danish Council for Development Research (Danida)

British Library Catalogue in Publication Data

Lefebvre, Alain

Kinship, Honour and Money in Rural Pakistan : subsistence economy and the effects of international migration. - (NIAS monographs ; no. 78)

1.Men - Employment - Pakistan - Punjab 2.Labour mobility

3.Labour policy - Pakistan - Punjab 4.Punjab (Pakistan) - Economic conditions 5.Punjab (Pakistan) - Social conditions 6.Punjab (Pakistan) - Economic policy

I.Title

331'.09545

ISBN 0-7007-0984-3

To my parents
and Gunilla

CONTENTS

Figures

Maps

Tables

PREFACE

This study explores the social and economic situation encountered in two villages of the Pakistani Punjab during the 1980s. It analyses the interrelationships between subsistence economy and international labour migration as they are perceived at village level.

Sixteen years after the peak of the migration flow in 1983 and eight years after the Gulf War, which transformed the regional political-economic scene, Pakistani villagers still cannot make a living solely from the incomes of their traditional occupations. They continue to rely upon sources of revenue external to the village. Their economic strategies and the subsequent effects upon the social life of the village community nowadays resemble those experienced in the 1980s. The 'Dubai Syndrome' has not become obsolete.

ACKNOWLEDGEMENTS

I would like to thank the Department of Economics of the Quaid-i-Azam University in Islamabad for assistance and, more particularly, Nigar Ahmed, Tariq Javed, Ijaz Navi and Ali A. Ercelawn, whose research in different Punjabi villages helped me to choose the village with rainfed agriculture. Concerning the selection of the village in an irrigated area, I was assisted by Faiz Bilqueez, Mohammed Irfan, Munawar Iqbal, and Ghulam Mohammad Arif, all working at the Pakistan Institute of Development Economics in Islamabad.

I also wish to mention the late Mohammed Rauff, Chairman of the Department for Anthropology at the Quaid-i-Azam University, Islamabad, to whom I am grateful for his support, and his help in providing the aid of a female Pakistani anthropologist, Shahida Haque. I am much indebted to Shahida Haque, since without her profound knowledge of Punjabi rural society, her strenuous work and her friendship, the fieldwork could not have become a reality.

Moreover, I want to thank Klaus Ferdinand of the Institute of Ethnography and Social Anthropology at Aarhus University, Denmark and Sofus Christiansen of the Institute of Geography at Copenhagen University for their encouragement and advice during the course of this study, as well as Jean-Pierre Digard of the Ecole des Hautes Etudes en Sciences Sociales, Paris.

Last but not least, I have a special debt to all the villagers who most heartily accepted me and patiently answered my many questions whilst treating me as their friend.

ACKNOWLEDGEMENTS

The Danish Research Council for Development Research and the French Centre National de la Recherche Scientifique generously provided the grants for the realization of this work. Completion of this monograph has been possible thanks to the scholarly and material assistance of the Centre for Development Research in Copenhagen.

I would also like to thank the Nordic Institute of Asian Studies for its support for transforming the manuscript into a book, especially Gerald Jackson for his editing suggestions and Liz Bramsen, Janice Leon and Leena Höskuldsson for their work on the typescript.

Units of measurement

2 *bigah* = 1 acre = 0.4 ha.
1 *choha* = 1.75 kg.
1 *dropa* = 4 *seers* = 3.7 kg.
8 *kanal* = 1 acre = 0.4 ha.
20 *marla* = 1 acre = 0.4 ha.
1 *maund* = 40 *seers* = 37 kg.
1 *seer* = 0.93 g.
1 *tola* = 12 g.
1 *topa* = *ca.* 2 kg.

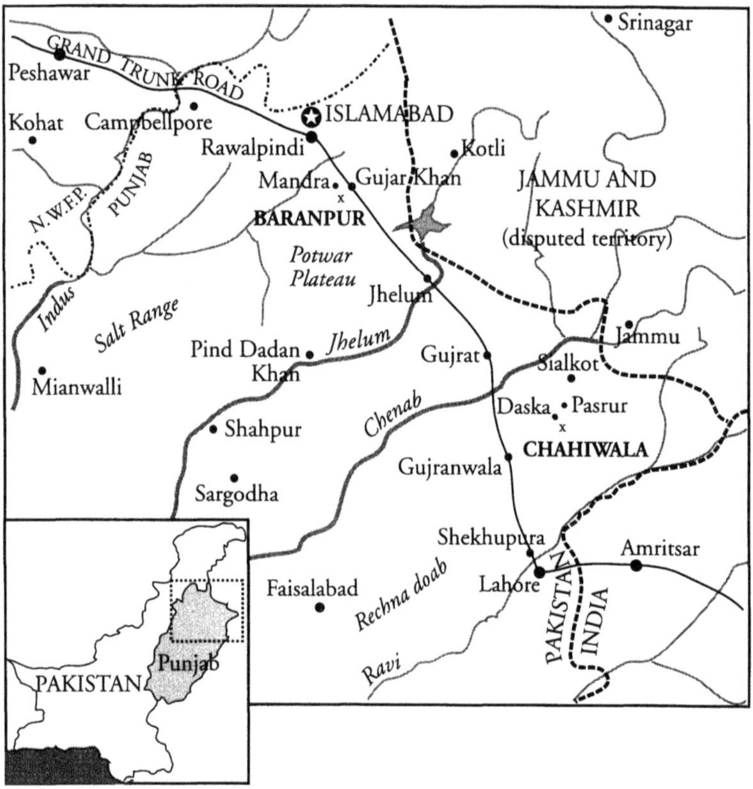

Map 1: The northern area of the Punjab showing the placement of Chahiwala and Baranpur

INTRODUCTION

The history of the expansion of capitalism is characterized, among other factors, by the peasants' and craftsmen's departure from their traditional system of production and from their economic equilibrium in order to sell their labour. The process by which colonial exploitation is established on the basis of subsistence agriculture is not, however, a question of a simple movement of population from a traditional living area to a new area opened up to migration. Any analysis made only in terms of the passage from one zone to another, the propulsion away from the zone of departure, and the attraction to the zone of arrival would not give a complete picture of the phenomenon.

In this monograph, migration is considered as an element of the international economic order with its concomitant distribution of capital and its organization of the international division of labour as they occurred at the time of the study in the 1980s.

On the one hand, the transnationals invest in Asia, South America and Africa where strategic natural resources are available and their procurement is facilitated by favourable tax policies and other economic advantages such as cheap manpower. On the other hand, industrialized and/or oil-producing countries are recruiting vast numbers of semi-skilled and unskilled workers from poorer countries in order to have a cheap labour-force reserve, often without access to the same rights as Western workers. This practice is economically profitable both for the employers and the national governments because of the lower living expenses of workers from poorer countries and their families: they do not have to pay for their education and retirement, and for their families' social insurance.

Pakistan is one of these countries of the South where emigration and overseas employment are considered as solutions to pressure on jobs at home and where the remittances sent back home by Pakistanis overseas have become a fundamental factor in the Pakistani national economy. Since 1971, when the Bureau of Emigration and Overseas Employment was created, the Pakistani government has partly organized the departure of its citizens and tried to channel them, particularly towards the countries of the Persian Gulf. However, most departures are organized through private recruitment agencies.

Migration Research in Pakistan

Labour migration from Pakistan to the Gulf countries has been the subject of increasing research since the 1980s (J. Addleton 1984 and 1992; A. S. Ahmed 1984 and 1990a; H. Alavi 1989; F. Arnold and N. Shah 1984; R. Ballard 1987 and 1989; S. J. Burki 1980; C. Clarke, C. Peach and S. Vertovec 1990; S. E. Guisinger 1986; ILO/UNDP 1993; M. S. Karim and W. C. Robinson 1986; O. Noman 1991; I. Tsakok 1986; M. Weiner 1982; P. Wickramasekara 1993). It has, in most cases, focused on the general characteristics of the relationships between oil-rich and population-rich countries, and the impact of the phenomenon upon the Pakistani politics, economy and social structure from a national perspective. In Pakistan, economists at the Pakistan Institute of Development Economics have conducted many research projects on this issue (among others one can mention M. Akbar n.d.; R. Amjad 1986; I. Gilani *et al.* 1981; M. Iqbal *et al.* 1981; M. Irfan *et al.* 1979, 1981a and 1981b; S. Kazi 1989 and 1993; I. Nabi 1986; K. Sarmad 1985). Through the use of neo-classical economic theory, their analyses establish a cost-benefit framework so as to determine the net cost or benefit of labour migration to the economy. The mobility of labour is mostly reduced to an analysis of its quantified forms. This approach does not give a complete picture of the phenomenon because on the one hand, important variables are not quantifiable, and on the other hand, factors subject to measurement cannot be adequately quantified because of data scarcity and imperfections. Moreover, the migratory phenom-enon is not considered in relation to other important factors, such as the historical development of Pakistan's economy and specific regional situations. Attention is only focused on the assumption that an individual is a rational actor or a universalized *homo oeconomicus* who calculates how to improve his well-being, or at least to maintain his standard of living within varying sets of constraints. This assumption cannot be disregarded but other elements have to be introduced if we are to arrive at an adequate understanding of their social action.

Other Pakistani social scientists – like E. Ahmad 1973; F. Ahmed 1975 and 1976; M. A. Chaudhary 1978 and 1979; J. Rashid 1980 and 1986 – try to explain the pattern of migration through the use of imperialist theories by reference to Pakistan's relationships of dependency at the world level.

Feroz Ahmed writes:

> Imperialist domination of South and South-West Asia resulted in arresting productive forces there and in preventing a harmonious development of economic relations between the various entities of the region by separately linking each of them with the centres of world capitalism ... While advanced technology, military material, machinery, consumer durables and high-level expertise for the Gulf States had to be imported from the United States and other imperialist countries, it was economically inexpensive and politically prudent to import intermediate technology, skilled manpower, agricultural products, light manufactures, personal services, and military personnel and expertise from the countries in the region (F. Ahmed 1976: 19, 20–21).

However, such global analyses do not present a picture of what really happens at the grassroots level. They do not take into consideration the social and cultural components of the villages from where the bulk of the migrant labourers originate, and their relations to the labour force mobility.

An Anthropological Analysis

The analysis of labour migration at the village level from an anthropological angle can bring a supplementary understanding to the phenomenon through its focus upon the local factors which are otherwise underestimated by macro-oriented studies (T. H. Aase 1979 and 1992; A. Lefebvre 1984, 1985, 1989, 1990a and 1990b; F. Selier and M. S. Karim 1986).

Pakistan and the Punjab Province are highly heterogeneous entities in a number of domains. The Pakistani being is moulded by a pre-Islamic past, by the influence of Islam in each sphere of the society, by contacts with Hinduism, by British colonization, by the difference in social organization according to ethnicity, by the actual unequal economic development and allocation of resources between the five main areas of the country, etc. It is vital to remember this multiple identity and at the same time to consider the possible unity of all these components. The anthropological method allows scrutiny of how the social and cultural differences of the local populations can be combined with the sense of national identity and consensus demanded by the state power.

In other words, the anthropological approach can explain the villagers' mode of behaviour by taking into account both the particular worldview that constrains their social actions and the political-economic space within which their actions actually occur.

Works on labour migration conducted by Pakistani anthropologists have identified three main aspects of its impacts. The first type of impact refers to negative effects like the socio-economic difficulties in readjusting to the rural environment (Z. Hussain 1986), or to the increase in female-headed households and its concomitant adverse affect on agricultural production (A. Khurshid 1982; Naveed-i-Rahat 1986; M. A. Rauf 1982 and 1984).

The second type of impact is the transformation to some aspects of the social organization, such as the replacement of the traditional family system by the nuclear family system (M. H. Chaudhry 1982; A. Khurshid 1982; F. Bashir 1981; A. Un Nisa 1984) or the disequilibrium occurring in the traditional status competition between households through the migrant's ability to increase expenditure on marriages and other ceremonies of the life-cycle and religious festivals (M.H. Chaudhry 1982).

The third type of impact concerns the migrant's entrepreneurial initiatives (N. Imdad 1978; Naveed-i-Rahat 1981; F. Bilquees and S. Hamid 1981).

It is the aim of this study to provide supplementary empirical data in order to assess more precisely the economic significance of migration in villages. It will try to identify the economic causes of the villagers' departure from their community. It also tries to answer questions related to the way in which the traditional organization of the agricultural production and of the craftsmen's activities have been affected by the economic transformations since Partition in 1947, especially during the Green Revolution. One of the hypotheses of this study was whether it is possible to establish a causal relation between the level of development of agriculture and the international migration. Has the rural scene improved or become poorer? Which non-agricultural activities are available to the villagers?

The other purpose of this study is to examine the immediate and long-term effects of the international migration on the village's domestic economy. What are the foreign remittances by the migrants used for? Are productive investments made in agriculture or other economic sectors of the village? If this is the case, does this process assist in transforming the relations of production? More globally, are the social relations found in the village – at the level of the household, the family, the lineage and the social classes – transformed by the existence of new economic resources? Is the division of labour between genders modified? And when the emigration has become an inevitable necessity, which socio-economic problems are bound to it?

At the outset of this monograph, it should be mentioned that the heterogeneity of the country (as mentioned above) means that the conclusions derived herein, which are based on two specific villages, cannot be taken as necessarily representative of other villages. Similar anthropological studies should therefore be made as a point of comparison to this study.

Methodology

The aim of this study is thus to analyse the international labour migration from two Punjabi villages with differing forms of agriculture, and to determine the relationship between the level of their economic development and the compulsion to take a job abroad. For the sake of comparison, one of these villages has an irrigated type of cultivation, the other a rainfed agriculture.

The choice of the two villages was also determined by other criteria. First, their population had to range between 100 and 250 households; second, at least 20 households should have experienced migration, either currently or in the past. The size of the population and of the migrant sample was dictated, on the one hand, by the necessity of obtaining a deep insight into each household and, on the other, by the importance of not generalizing from a limited sample.

The villages were chosen in collaboration with staff members of the Pakistan Institute for Development Economics who had participated in a World Bank study about labour migration from Pakistan in 1980. From the World Bank report I selected the villages where interviews had been conducted and which were located in areas with either rainfed or irrigated agriculture. I then had a shortlist of 25 villages from which to make a selection. I followed this up with a visit to the Bureau of Census to find villages with appropriate populations. This left four villages on my list. With the help of local officials who advised where my Pakistani counterpart and I could best be accommodated, the villages Chahiwala in the Sialkot district and Baranpur in the Rawalpindi district were selected.

During the fieldwork, the household was used as the basic unit of analysis. It is the first frame of reference which villagers mention in the self-perception of their identity, followed in the second place by the patrilineage (*biraderi*). The household is a unit of production, a unit of consumption, and the location of socialization and ritual life. By unit of production, I do not mean a self-sufficient and autarkic cell but rather an economic matrix depending on multiple sources of income. It is composed of all the people who are socially and economically related to one another and who share residence, although some of the male members live in another town in Pakistan or work abroad. These physically absent individuals must nevertheless be included since their remittances are crucial to the economy of the household. Members of a household are always related through consanguinity or marriage. The only difference between the structure of households is the existence of nuclear family and extended family households.

The apparent similarities of the roles and functions of households should not, however, lead to their consideration as identical units. The household obtains a more sophisticated analytical relevance if it is perceived as an entity where individuals also have the power to choose between different actions, especially in crisis situations. The structural position of each member might not automatically overlap individual interests. The nature of the relationships between a household's members – harmonious or conflictual – and the individuals' attitudes towards the patriarchal norms and values of the society influence the household's strategies. However, on the surface, the dominant discourse is the one expressed by the male household leader, even when women and youths may have other opinions on certain daily matters.

The collection of data was carried out over two periods. First, I contacted Pakistani scientists who had worked on this topic in order to avoid repetition and to acquaint myself with their results. I studied reports, publications, papers and monographs concerning Punjab's economic history, the rural and international migration, and Pakistan's agricultural and industrial policy (see Appendix 1 for the consulted organizations). After reading these documents, I was able to improve the content of the questionnaire which was used in both villages. The driving idea behind its formulation was to collect basic socio-economic information from each household before inquiring about the international migration.

The second work period entailed a nine-month stay in two villages in collaboration with a female Pakistani anthropologist, Shahida Haque. From the very start we insisted on working together throughout the day and sharing the practical activities in order to get the villagers used to our collaboration. Through S. Haque's rural origin and our previous field-work experience, we were rapidly able to gain the people's confidence. Almost 80 per cent of the socio-economic information concerning the households was obtained from women during the day while their husbands were absent from the house.

The village with irrigated agriculture is called Chahiwala.[1] We stayed there for four months, from the middle of September to the end of January (i.e. during the periods of rice harvest and wheat sowing). We were also in Baranpur – the village with rainfed agriculture – for four months, from March to June (the period of wheat harvest).

The data were collected in each village through anthropological research methods, i.e. participant observation, use of questionnaires, structured and open conversations with key and representative informants of both genders. The gathering of data was accomplished in different phases.

The first part of the work was to fill in the questionnaires – one for every household – 351 in total. At the same time, a detailed map of the village was drawn with measurements (see Chapter 2) and a questionnaire number was allocated to each household. Starting the inquiry in this way offered several advantages. It accustomed the villagers to our presence in their everyday life and it also rapidly allowed the visualization of the networks of relationships.

In fact, the actual village setting reproduces spatially the initial settlement: blocks of houses reflect the actual distribution between social categories, the cohesion of the extended family, the factions, and other social relationships. Moreover, a comparison of traditional dwellings with recently built houses (financed by the migrants' remittances) helps to reveal changes in kinship ties and relations of production.

The second part of the work consisted of the collection of data about the history of the villages, particularly the economic history. This information was gathered through interviews with local government officers and with elderly people living in each village and its surroundings, and through consulting the following official records:

- The local records of the Agriculture Department
- The local records of the Agriculture Development Bank

- The Crime Register Book of the village
- The Village Crime Notebook
- The Land Revenue books
- The Land Settlement books
- The Consolidation of Land books
- The Register for Annual Winter/Summer Crops since 1933.

The third part of the work was devoted to the deeper investigation of households selected as representatives of each socio-economic group, i.e. for each lineage of landless villagers, and for each category of landowners according to the size of their landholding.

In order to compare the results of the analysis with other studies about migration and agriculture made in Pakistan, I used the same size-class (S.C.) tenure of cultivated areas as the ones established in 1980 by the World Bank research programme and the Department of Economics of the Quaid-i-Azam University in Islamabad.

These tenures correspond to different acreages for rainfed and irrigated areas. It is usual to equate one irrigated acre with two rainfed acres. One then has the following five size-classes (in acres):

Table 1.1: Division of landholdings in both villages (in acres)

Size-class	Rainfed	Irrigated
1	0.10–12.49	0.10–7.49
2	12.50–24.99	7.50–12.49
3	25.00–49.99	12.50–24.99
4	50.00–99.00	25.00–49.99
5	100 and above	50.00 and above

This form of measurement is acceptable for the two villages because there are no extreme cases of rainfed land with a very high productivity due to well irrigation, or irrigated land with a very low productivity due to waterlogging and salinity.

Since the majority of cultivators in the village with rainfed agriculture belongs to size-class 1, this category was divided into seven sub-groups to arrive at a more detailed analysis:

Table 1.2: Sub-division of landholdings in the village with rainfed agriculture

Size-class sub-group	Landholding (in acres)
S.C.1.1.	0.00–0.99
S.C.1.2.	1.00–1.99
S.C.1.3.	2.00–2.99
S.C.1.4.	3.00–3.99
S.C.1.5.	4.00–4.99
S.C.1.6.	5.00–5.99
S.C.1.7.	6.00–12.49

Finally, case studies and genealogies were also collected. The genealogical data were not aimed at analysing the kinship system, and were therefore limited to a time period of only four generations. The purpose was rather to explain the economic activities of the kinship system, such as land ownership, flow of goods through bride prices and wedding compensation (*mehr*) in order to reconstruct the different phases of emigration.

Every household with a migrant was visited several times in order to obtain a more accurate response to the general questionnaire.

S. Haque daily reported on what she heard and saw in the villages when we were not together. In this way I could also follow the evolution of the social activities, conflicts and intimate events among the female community.

Note

1 For the villagers' protection, the names of places and people are fictitious.

1 PAKISTAN AND INTERNATIONAL LABOUR MIGRATION

It would be a mistake to consider the two studied villages as isolated, self-centred and self-sufficient communities, lacking an internal dynamic and without the possibility of tackling external transformations. They have always been an integral part of a regional entity, which in turn is influenced by the national policy of the state.

The state inducement for exporting the national workforce is part of the economic strategy followed by the Pakistani rulers. This choice is not only governed by the state of Pakistan's internal economic situation, it is also conditioned by the geographical position of the country in the international division of labour. More specifically in the scope of this study, the international labour migration from Pakistan is the result, on the one hand, of Pakistan's articulation with the politico-economic system of the Gulf States and Saudi Arabia, and, on the other hand, of the domestic development policy of the country.

In this chapter, we shall look at the overall characteristics of this export of labour and at the internal Pakistani features which have caused it.

International Labour Migration and Capital Accumulation

The general theoretical framework which has guided this research is based on theories of imperialism as they were discussed at the time of the inquiry. They do not limit themselves to an understanding of the unequal exchange of commodities in the relations between centre and periphery, but also focus upon the perception of the labour force in countries of the South as a form of industrial reserve army. The international movements of labourers are here perceived as components of the accumulation of capital.

It was through reading works written by French Africanists in the 1970s, such as C. Meillassoux (1975 and 1979) and P. P. Rey (1976 a and b), together with research carried out on the South African apartheid by M. Legassick (1974), M. Morris (1976) and H. Wolpe (1972), which helped to focus this theoretical frame.

Labour Migration in the World Economy

The mobility of international labour is a means of adaptation by the labour force to the requirements of capital. It is not a new phenomenon. Only the forms of exploitation have changed throughout history. The entire period of the development of capitalism has necessitated the existence of a cheap labour-force reserve. As an example, we can briefly look at the case of Western Europe.

The passage from feudalism to capitalism was characterized by the eviction of ruined peasants and destitute artisans from the rural areas where they had lost their livelihood because of competition with the new capitalist methods of production. As long as it was possible, the peasants kept ties with their plots of land and families left behind since the wages earned in the towns did not allow them to become self-sufficient. With the expansion of capitalism, the labour force became more of a commodity and the ties with the rural areas were broken.

Simultaneously with this rural–urban migration, overseas migration also took place. From 1815 to 1914, 35 million Europeans left for the USA in successive waves. The demographic pressure in Euope was high and the industria-lization process was too slow to absorb the increase of labour from the rural areas. These migrants were also the victims of numerous social troubles such as wars, revolutions, religious persecution and the like.

The two world wars and the 1929 economic crisis brought a change to the form of capitalist expansion, so as to give another orientation to labour migration. From being mainly a movement from Europe to the USA, it became a south–north movement from the semi-industrialized areas of European Mediterranean countries and from the poor areas of

Asia, Africa and South America towards the highly indus-trialized and capitalist metropolises of northern and western Europe. In this part of Europe, the period 1945–65 was characterized by an important industrial expansion. At that time the native population was insufficient because of war casualties and the low birth-rate between the two world wars for some countries such as France. Moreover, the effects of longer schooling and better professional training were noticeable. The workers became more demanding regarding work conditions and salary expectations. Meanwhile, the managers looked for a cheap and docile labour force to avoid spending too much on investments and wages. As a result, industrialized countries were forced to look elsewhere to meet their workforce needs. Consequently, after World War II, the large and unemployed labour force of southern Europe and of the European colonies was called upon to assist in rebuilding the economy of the most industrialized European countries. The migration movement was rapidly gaining momentum, without control, planning or preparation of social infrastructures. The sole aim was the rapid utilization of workers for unskilled tasks within industry, the construction sector and services.

In other words, Europe based its development after World War II upon – among other factors – the exploitation of a large number of foreign workers. The transformation of the international economic situation entailed a concomitant transformation of the migration policies conducted by European countries.

In 1965 politicians began to take notice of the socio-cultural and political consequences of an uncontrolled migration policy. In fact, the working class paid a high price for this economic development, especially the foreigners. Slums, work casualties, racism, school discrimination and illness were some of the evils which they had to face. The politicians were also concerned by the arrival on the work market of the large generation of young people born after 1945.

The so-called energy crisis from the end of 1973 was the catalyst for changing the immigration policy in the majority of north and west European countries. The main receiving countries successively reduced the entry of foreign workers, seemingly without harmony of action.

However, it is wrong to believe that the European countries no longer need a foreign labour force. The latter is, in fact, a necessary structural element of the production process. Its behaviour and management are just as important for the capitalist class and the governments as the maintenance of the production apparatus. Its use fluctuates in the same direction as the national economies. In periods of economic expansion and full employment, it is a means to limit wage increases as well as to reduce or postpone investment in factory equipment. On the other hand, when the economic situation is unfavourable, the foreign workers are the first to be fired. They serve as scapegoats for the crisis in order to reduce the social and political consequences of the national workers' dissatisfaction.

This need for a foreign labour force is related to the difficulties of the most developed economies in maintaining the integrality of the process of formation of the value within their political territories because of the high cost of the productive forces, and because of the workers' level of political combativeness. When the capitalist social formation has reached the stage of monopolist capitalism, it may become necessary to internationalize the production according to the evolution of the class struggle. The solution consists of finding areas where the rate of exploitation is higher, either by importing labourers from or by exporting a part of the production process towards those countries where the labour force is both specialized and cheap because of the lesser development of the legislative and social coverage of the workers. The migration of foreign workers is thus the result of the inequalities in development of political and economic forces between different areas of the world.

The Reserve Army of Labour

It is essential for a capitalist system to recruit workers who do not cost too much. The cheap labour-force reserve has previously been made up of people within the surviving pre-capitalist zones of the industrialized countries or within the categories of the population which were not integrated into the production, i.e. women and young people. When these social groups became less accessible in Europe because of the drying up of manpower reserves and higher manpower costs due to class struggles and their resulting salary increases, an alternative source of manpower was needed. The solution was found in the former colonies, where a huge pool of manpower had been 'liberated' by the decolonization process.

It is necessary to make a distinction between the migration which occurred due to the destruction of the European feudal societies and the migration from countries of the South to the industrialized countries. The former is a type of migration with a definitive character, while the latter is of a cyclical form. In fact, the societies of the Southern countries are not always radically transformed when the capitalist economy becomes dominant.

The politico-economic concept of foreign workers' migration to Europe is based on the principle of dominance between different economic systems: the capitalist economy appropriates a free rent by the inability of the emigrating zones – artificially created – to reproduce themselves without their submissive relations to the receiving capitalist spheres.

Because of competition between capitalist economies, an ever-increasing part of the production costs had to be invested in the modernization of industrial equipment during the first decades after World War II. This meant that their profits tended to fall. There are various means to control this phenomenon and the exploitation of migrant workers is one of them. Such workers are underpaid and less able to defend their interests through trade unions. When they are hired, they have not yet acquired a tradition for class struggle, and, moreover, they are still very much influenced by the ideological systems prior to the capitalist exploitation. They are also very mobile and easy to replace.

The savings made are realized because the cost of reproduction of the migrant worker is not entirely covered within the capitalist sphere of production. This practice is not new. In fact, looking at the colonial policy of the Western powers, one sees that little by little they considered it more profitable not to radically transform the dominated societies but rather to retain their traditional social relations. In fact, their economic production is more collective, and by putting an individual to work, one can exploit not only this labourer but also the social group to which he belongs. Furthermore, a greater part of the labourer's time in these socio-economic formations is not devoted to the production of his subsistence goods but remains free. One has to maintain these two elements in order to exploit them to profit the capital. The exploitation took two forms:

- cash-crop agriculture, intended for export, was developed without considering subsistence activities;
- rotating migrations of labourers were organized in order to provide labour for non-agricultural activities, irrespective of the seasonal cycles of traditional activities.

The same practice is still in use today. The migrant worker and his relatives are regarded by the receiving countries as constituting a homogeneous unit. The former is employed in the capitalist sector while the latter is engaged in subsistence agriculture.

A double profit is then extracted from the foreign worker, even if it appears that surplus value and labour-rent are identical: on the one hand, it extracts from him a surplus value, as it does from any other worker, by a salary which does not correspond to the quantity of produced work; on the other hand it extracts a labour-rent equal to the quantity of unpaid labour furnished by the migrant worker's relatives in the home area in order to assure their own reproduction and maintenance as well as the migrant's when he becomes unemployed, ill or old. C. Meillassoux (1975) calls this double exploitation 'over-exploitation'.

In order to perpetuate the transfer of the value from the pre-capitalist to the capitalist sector, it is essential that the workers return to their home areas during the periods when they are not useful to the capital. Areas of labour force reservation are thus maintained by wholly or partially preserving the subsistence agriculture and the traditional socio-economic relations. Here a worker can assure his reproduction, but only at subsistence level. At the same time, his need for cash makes it necessary for him to go to capitalist areas since he can only obtain it there. It is also important that workers do not become a burden to their employers by the creation of a repressive administrative system. This mechanism reproduces itself once the process of economic dependence of rural areas in the developing country has begun. The foreign worker is thus over-exploited because of his position in the international labour market.

A further form of exploitation by the receiving countries is the distinction made between two kinds of remuneration: the direct salary and indirect wages. The former covers only the immediate reconstitution of the labour power, while the latter assures diverse social benefits such as family allowances, unemployment and sickness benefits, retirement funds, etc. The indirect wages are calculated individually for each worker according to his social situation, which therefore allows for several rates of payment. Here also savings are made through employing migrant workers. In fact, when one looks at the demographic composition of the migrant population, one sees that it is constituted of a high percentage of productive individuals, as opposed to the native population with its retired people, its unproductive youth and its physically and psychologically disabled people. These social categories are very expensive since they do not produce a surplus value. The foreign population, however, which is almost entirely active, compensates for this deficit.

Moreover, by limiting the immigration of the migrant's family, no social payments have to be made to the wife and children. Considerable savings are made on the cost of reproduction of the labour force by this absence of dependants, since new collective facilities such as schools, stadiums and the like do not have to be built. Expenses are also saved on education and professional training.

Both in theory and practice therefore the strategy of the receiving countries is characterized by the over-exploitation of migrant workers. However, we should be aware that the concept of over-exploitation does not describe a situation in which the foreign workers constitute a form of lumpen-proletariat, separated from the national labour class. The rate of exploitation is equal to the ratio surplus value/salary. The highest rate of exploitation is not necessarily suffered by the workers who receive the lowest salaries, but rather by those who produce the highest surplus value, which is not very often in the case of migrant workers, because of their low professional qualifications. Over-exploitation refers more to the wage policy of the receiving country which pays the migrants less than their actual worth, i.e. below what is generally considered necessary for the reproduction of the labour force, but which is enough in their home countries. The work produced is considered as having an inferior value and is therefore a particular aspect of the unequal exchange, since equal hours of labour are exchanged at different rates of value.

Following this introduction of the overall characteristics of the constant need for additional labour forces, we can now turn our attention towards the specific case of Pakistan and the neighbouring oil-exporting countries.

The Political Economy of Labour Migration in the Arab OPEC Countries in the 1980s

Although there are differences in the history of the flow of migrants to the oil producers in the Gulf States and Saudi Arabia because of their respective policies on oil exploitation and differences in their political orientation, the global characteristics of this labour migration correspond to the same logic of foreign labourers' exploitation as found in Western Europe. The main difference is seen in the volume of migration: while foreign workers are in a minority in Western Europe, they constitute up to a third of the population in Saudi Arabia and outnumber the number of nationals in the sparsely populated Gulf States.

The economy of the oil-producing countries is not based on the development of industry or modern agriculture, but on the use of a rent inflow issued from the sale of oil at a price established through complex economic and political mechanisms between the oil owners, the oil producers (i.e. the transnational oil companies), and the consumers. This oil rent is partly distributed in the form of gifts according to the traditional cultural values of the genuine Bedouin society. Although changes occur in the tribal social organization, the sheikh's wealth is still considered as collective, to be shared among the members of the tribe. This diffusion allows the preservation of the tribesmen's political support and the muting of social protests. It is a payment for loyalty and postpones confrontations between antagonistic forces. Another consequence of this redistribution is the suppression of a motivation to work as a wage labourer among the native population.

Another part of the oil rent is used in the domestic economy for the construction of an infrastructure and the import of foreign commodities, including military hardware, from the OECD countries. A third part is invested on international financial markets in the form of bank deposits and short-term securities in the USA and Western Europe.

All in all, the oil-exporting countries have been more and more integrated into a geopolitical and economic context dominated by the West. Their economic difficulties, due to the decrease in the oil prices, show they are not immune to domination from the highly developed countries of the North. Oil becomes a wealth only through the intermediary of the Western and Japanese need for it.

This integration into the world economy means that many of the characteristics specific to labour migration in Western Europe reappear in this new context: the majority of migrant workers are confined to semi-skilled and unskilled jobs, mainly in construction and service sectors. They are paid the least and face the same social problems as their counterparts in Western Europe: illegal entry, unsatisfactory housing conditions, denial of union rights, interdiction of their dependants' migration. Here also the same means are used for the capital accumulation process. Permanent settlers are not wanted in the Gulf States and in Saudi Arabia. The migration is cyclical. The workers are usually hired on a temporary basis with a rate of renewal depending on the country and the worker's vocational qualifications. The few created industrial plants are located in enclaves remote from urban centres. These workplaces, as well as many housing sites, function on a work-camp basis. The isolation and increased control strengthen the exploitation of the workers socially, economically and psychologically. The general intention is to prevent their integration into the local social and political life.

The political aspects of the immigration strategy are closely linked to the economic aspects. In fact, the workers' exploitation is also facilitated by the establishment of a hierarchy of salary and occupation based on a discrimination according to nationalities and religion. Arabs are preferred to non-Arabs and Muslims to non-Muslims by the local governments, and the transnationals compare the ratio professional qualities/wages of each citizenship in their recruitment. Not only the levels of salary are taken into account in this comparison, but also the cost of the fare from the emigration country to the receiving one and the life-style of each community. The cleavage between skilled and unskilled workers is superimposed on that between nationalities. The foreign workers are victims of their own fragmentations at national as well as regional and social levels. The tensions specific to their societies are reproduced and increased through the local rulers' policy of discrimination.

In other words, the Gulf States and Saudi Arabia offer the transnationals a setting where governmental concessions, such as tax relief, are easily obtainable, and a work place exempted from labour regulations. These diverse interests at different levels of the capital accumulation explain why no regional policy of migration exists in the Gulf between population-rich states and oil-rich states.

Pakistan: a Labour-Exporting Country

The Partition of the British Indian Empire in 1947 has entailed enormous displacements of the population between the two new nations, India and Pakistan. Pakistan continued to experience an important rural–urban migration in the two following decades (H. Donnan and P. Werbner 1991). According to J. S. Addleton (1992), this phenomenon expresses a characteristic specific to the Pakistani labour force, namely its mobility. Furthermore the Indian subcontinent has been used as a labour reserve since the seventeenth century (C. Clarke, C. Peach and S. Vertovec 1990). Simultaneously with the post-independence extensive rural–urban migration, Pakistani labourers left the country in several waves since the end of the 1940s, with Great Britain as their preferred choice of destination for several reasons.

In 1948, when the the foundations of the British Empire began to be undermined, the Attlee Cabinet decided to grant British citizenship to all the inhabitants of British colonies and dominions, and with it the possibility of immigration to Great Britain. For many Indian Muslims who arrived in Pakistan as unemployed refugees, emigration to Great Britain was a way of gaining economic security during a period of religious and political conflict.

Throughout the 1950s, the flourishing British economy required a cheap and plentiful labour force. Since this need could only be filled by foreigners, no precise immigration policy was formulated.

With the Commonwealth Immigration Act of 1962, the government began to control immigration for the first time since World War II. During the 18 months between the promulgation and the implementation of this law, immigrants continued to arrive. Most of the Pakistanis involved came in the aftermath of the building of the Mangla dam in Pakistani Kashmir. These migrants were either villagers from the over-flooded area because of the creation of the artificial lake, or labourers from the worksite on the dam. Special agreements were signed between the Pakistani and English governments for facilitating the emigration of these people to Great Britain.

In 1968 a new Commonwealth Immigration Act reinforced control, particularly concerning Asians from East Africa. Despite these restrictions, the foreign population of Great Britain had swollen to 1,300,000 in 1971, representing 2.5 per cent of the total population. Giving way to strong pressure, the government passed the Immigration Act of 1971. In order to enter Great Britain, one not only had to be a citizen of a Commonwealth country, the United Kingdom or one of its colonies, but also had to be born a citizen of Great Britain, or to have British citizenship through naturalization or 'registration', or to have parents or grandparents with British citizenship. For any other applicants the right to immigrate was granted only if they could furnish a special guarantee, i.e. an economic sponsorship by people already living in Great Britain.

Thus through different stages since 1962, immigration into Great Britain has been strictly curtailed. Consequently, Pakistanis started to emigrate to other European countries. Since 1971, migration has shifted from Spain to Greece and from Norway to West Germany, following the contingencies of immigration policies adopted in these countries.

From the middle of the 1970s, strict controls on immigration due to a decline in the economic expansion were established in most European countries. A major cause was the so-called 'energy crisis' of 1973. After the October war against Israel, oil producers from the Middle East increased the price of oil. This was the start of an intense accumulation of capital which created a need for a direct quantitative increase in the labour supply. The Arab OPEC countries were also facing a labour scarcity, induced, on the one hand, by their low demographic resources and level of economic growth (the numbers of national workers were insufficient in all sectors, including the public sector), and, on the other hand, by socio-cultural factors such as the normative impossibility for women to work outside their home in urban and industrial areas and the tendency of the Bedouin population (which constitutes the majority of the indigenous population) to avoid manual occupations because they do not fit their cultural value system. Consequently, labour imports covering the whole occupational range have solved the labour shortage. Until 1975, Arabs provided the majority of migrant workers within the Middle East. But the volume and the rapidity of the demand for extra labour power and political suspicion towards specific communities like the Palestinians meant that the Arab supplying states could not meet this demand. Additional supplies of labour had to come from other places.

This new investment policy of the Gulf States and Saudi Arabia occurred when Pakistan was in the process of showing a greater interest towards the Middle East. In fact, when one looks at Pakistan's foreign policy trends during the 1970s and the 1980s, one sees that since the secession of East Pakistan in 1971, it has increasingly identified itself with the Islamic Middle East rather than with the Hindu-dominated Indian subcontinent. Nevertheless, its strategic outlook is still less influenced by its Islamic links than by its relationship with its traditional enemy, Hindu India.

With over 100 million people at the end of the 1980s and a yearly population growth of 3.7 per cent, Pakistan is the most populous Muslim country between India and the Atlantic Ocean. Its involvement with the other Muslim states of the region in politico-military, economic and ideological spheres is deep and multi-faceted. For instance, the importance of Pakistan's economic links to the Middle East, especially since the oil embargo, can be expressed through commercial exchanges. Twenty-five per cent of Pakistan's imports are supplied by the area, which in turn absorbs about the same amount of its exports. Stepped-up aid from Saudi

Arabia and other Middle Eastern sources figure prominently in the country's financial plans.

The new price control on oil by the OPEC countries appeared at an appropriate time for the Pakistani economy. The country was unable to repay its foreign loans. Its export earnings were declining or remaining stagnant while imports were rising. As a client state the country was obliged to import machinery and military hardware under tied loans. The market in East Pakistan for West Pakistani goods was lost after the cessation of Bangladesh. The oil states appeared to be a new source of financial assistance, and the government encouraged the large-scale export of manpower. With the absence of jobs in rural areas as well as in cities for the rapidly growing population and with the practice of a low-wage policy, the country could offer a politically and economically viable labour supply.

The flow of migrants from India and Pakistan is not in itself a new phenomenon since Indians and Pakistanis have played a role as intermediary clerks and managers in the Gulf for decades through the British colonial apparatus. What is new is the volume of the flow. Most of the estimated 1.4 million Pakistani migrant workers employed abroad are found in the Gulf area and in Saudi Arabia. During the period 1980–91, Pakistanis abroad had on average remitted US$ 2.3 billion yearly through official channels, with a peak of US$ 2.8 billion in 1982–83, followed thereafter by a steady decrease due to the reduction in demand for labour in the Middle East, falling to US$ 1.4 billion in 1991–92 (source: Government of Pakistan [GOP], Finance Division 1991–92, quoted in S. Kazi 1993: 107). Remittances from the Middle East accounted for 74 per cent of the total amount. The importance of the inflow of the remittances can best be evaluated by their role in Pakistan's balance of payments. During the best years, they equalled more than 91 per cent of merchandise exports (ibid.: 104). This share decreased concomitantly with the rise in Pakistan's oil import bill. It also fluctuated with the exchange rate of the Pakistani rupee to the US dollar.

These official figures underestimate the actual amount of remittances because migrants prefer to use informal financial mechanisms to transfer their money. These exchange rates are higher and their efficiency greater when compared with regular banks. Another reason for this underestimation is that migrants bring their savings and consumer purchases with them when they come on leave to Pakistan. An ILO study estimates that 43 per cent of total remittances are not officially recorded (ILO/ARTEP, 1987).

The other new characteristic of this labour migration is the qualitative drain: the most energetic and skilled labour is leaving the country. Some of the migrants are white-collar employees, while the majority of them are semi-skilled craftsmen, such as masons and carpenters, or unskilled labourers. Their qualifications might be modest on an international scale but they are greatly needed by the Pakistani economy. In other words, these migrants represent a decrease in the active workforce of Pakistan; their departure has entailed qualitatively negative consequences for the economic development of the country as a whole through the creation of a vacuum of professionals.

To deal with the domestic shortage of skilled labourers, two simultaneous and yet contradictory policies were followed. On the one hand, employers adopted capital-intensive methods in production processes. This new orientation in turn slowed down the creation of new jobs which are necessary to absorb the rapidly growing workforce. On the other hand, the government has responded by launching a technical skills training programme in order to replace the lost manpower.

From the middle of the 1980s, the number of Pakistani labourers in the Gulf has constantly declined as the oil-producing countries have reduced their demand for foreign labour due to a slowdown in their economies caused by falling oil prices. At the same time, the Gulf States have begun to diversify their sources of labour supply. Far Eastern Asian countries like the Philippines and South Korea have become more attractive than South Asian countries in general, and Pakistan in particular, because they can supply cheaper and better educated manpower. It was in this context of increasing numbers of returning migrants, accompanied by a reduction in remittances, that Pakistan experienced the 1991 Gulf War.

This war brought about the first major changes in the international labour migration pattern to the Middle East. As far as Pakistan is concerned, Iraq has never been a major recipient of its labour force, while Kuwait ranked second behind Saudi Arabia as a source of foreign remittances during the 1980s. The loss of remittances during the crisis was compensated for by a transfer of money from Pakistanis working in other Middle Eastern countries, who were afraid of the geographical extension of the war. Kuwait was also Pakistan's main supplier of petroleum and oil products.

Between August 1990 and February 1991, official figures indicate that about 60,000 Pakistanis were repatriated by the government of Pakistan (source: Overseas Pakistani Foundation, quoted in Farooq-I-Azam, 1993: 130). While humanitarian suffering has been great for the migrants who became refugees overnight, the individual economic losses have been more limited. The majority of Pakistani labourers in Kuwait were able to recover their bank deposits when the war was over. Their average losses were estimated at between 9 months' and 2 years' income (ibid.: 134). When the political situation was stabilized after Iraq's defeat, about 35,000 Pakistanis returned to Kuwait to their former jobs, while the majority of Pakistani migrants went to Saudi Arabia to substitute for the Yemeni and Jordanian workers who had been expelled because of their countries' support of Iraq during the war. In the 1990s, reconstruction of the war damage offered a new opportunity for Pakistani immigrants but competition with Egyptian workers was strong since the Egyptians' language and culture were more compatible with the population of the receiving countries.

In short, if the Pakistani economy has been temporarily affected by the Gulf War, the main conclusion one may draw from this crisis is that it has highlighted the risk to a country when it relies on the export of its workforce to solve its domestic employment difficulties and to restore its balance of payments.

The Politico-Economic Causes of Labour Migration from the Punjab

In order to understand why part of the Pakistani labour force has found it necessary to look for employment abroad, it is relevant to look at the historical reasons which have made it difficult for the rural population to make a living from land cultivation and traditional craftsmanship.

The following section introduces the broad socio-economic status of the country inherited at Partition – more particularly the agrarian situation in the Punjab – and the development policy followed by its rulers since that time. In this regard, it is important to remember that Pakistan is characterized by a very unequal level of development between its five provinces at its creation, and even within the Punjab great variations are found between the different districts. This situation is a result partly of the various ecological conditions and partly of the colonial policy.

The Agricultural Policy of the Colonial Rulers

At its creation, Pakistan inherited an agrarian situation whereby 80 per cent of agriculturalists – petty landowners, share-croppers, landless tenants and agricultural labourers – controlled less than a third of the cultivable area, while the remaining 20 per cent – the big landlords – owned the majority of fertile land. Furthermore, landlord–tenant relations were still governed by the Punjab Tenancy Act of 1887. Two hundred years of British colonial administration were responsible for the structural changes in the rural areas.

Colonial rule was influenced by the philosophical and political debate occurring in Britain throughout the nineteenth century, and by the concomitant readjustment of the imperialist strategy. This ideological controversy raised opinions which opposed the Utilitarian political economic doctrines with their conviction that Britain's role was to transform Indian culture and civilization and introduce *laissez-faire* principles with a limited state intervention, and advocated instead a conservative policy respecting the norms and customs of the pre-colonial period.

The colonial policy followed in the Punjab cannot be considered in isolation from the policy implemented in other areas of British India. Each region was dependent on and supplementary to each other. The functions attributed to the Punjab were both agricultural and strategic.

The Punjab was annexed to the British Empire in 1849 for political and economic reasons. With the suppression of the Sikh rule and the disarmament of its army, the British by entering into the Punjab obtained access to a western border which allowed them to monitor the situation in Afghanistan more accurately and to defend the colony better against threats from Tsarist Russia.

At the time of annexation, the East India Company faced heavy debts and the war in Afghanistan since 1839 had become an additional financial burden. In this situation, the Punjab was economically attractive because of its production of good quality cotton, its natural resources, its potential as a market for British goods, and also as a new border area opened to new settlers from other parts of North India. In other words, the British wanted to develop the socio-economic conditions of the province rapidly. In the rural areas, the main changes experienced by the villagers during the period of British rule had been caused by the transformation of the pre-colonial agrarian structure and of the land revenue policy.

Land Rights

During the first years after annexation and up until 1857, the Utilitarian doctrine with its rent theory conditioned the policy of colonial administration. One of the driving forces of James Stuart Mill's Principles of Political Economy was to suppress the social inequality in the rural areas where a few big landlords exploited a majority of hard-working poor peasants. The private ownership of land was recognized as a fundamental right for every individual and the levy of low taxes from its proprietor was considered to be the best incentive to motivate him to increase agricultural production. In practice this meant that the colonial administration did not take the diversity of right of land ownership prevailing in North India into account and introduced private property in land. The first settlement scheme recorded the landholdings and the village customary rights according to a pattern which assured the cultivators' protection. A sharp distinction was created between land-owner and tenant, and the restrictions on land transactions were removed. Land, like any other private property, could be sold, transferred or mortgaged. In some cases, the cultivators of a landholding at the time of settlement were recognized as landowners. In other cases, the landowner kept his property rights and the peasant who had cultivated his land for 12 continuous years was registered as an occupancy tenant with hereditary and permanent rights. He paid a rent and land revenue fixed by the state. Another category of tenants was created of tenants-at-will, without any legal protection regarding the amount of rent and risk of eviction. The remaining village land was the joint property of landowners.

This policy was one of the causes of the 1857 uprising in which the dispossessed proprietary class tooked part. In the aftermath of this revolt, the Utilitarians' political economy was replaced with the Conservatives' paternalist policy. They perceived the *laissez-faire* principles as a failure in the new context of the Indian subcontinent. Errors of the first settlement were recognized and the necessity to have a deeper insight into the norms and customs of the rural society in order to create a strong Indian capitalism was underlined. From then onwards, the agrarian policy of the British rulers in India, particularly in the Punjab, was characterized by the difficulty in practising a balanced policy between two antagonistic objectives. On the one hand, it strove to establish a capitalist agriculture, the surplus of which was destined to be exported, and on the other hand it tried to ensure that the agrarian transformations necessary for the new economic orientation did not lead to political disorder, owing to an increasing number of opponents recruited amongst dispossessed rural classes. In other words, the British needed both a class of landlords as political allies and a class of entrepreneurial cultivators who could increase the agricultural production of British India. This double aim was not easily achieved since these two agrarian classes did not automatically overlap.

The British tried to regain the support of the landed elite by conducting a more conservative policy which respected the traditional power balance in the villages, and by giving a new role to the village squirearchy. Some landowners were appointed to the position of *lambardars*. They were responsible for levying land tax and dealing with all matters regarding law and order in the village. They were remunerated 5 per cent of the collected tax and received grants in land from the village common ground. In this way, the colonial administration acquired loyal allies between the state and the villagers.

The consequences of the agrarian policy were not what the British expected. The tenancy system was an obstacle to the development of agriculture. Since the rent-paying tenant knew that any increase in output would benefit the landlord, who generally did not bear the costs of cultivation, he had little incentive to raise his production. It was extremely difficult for the tenant to use new agricultural techniques. As a result of the high share of his produce taken from him as rent, he was left with a bare subsistence minimum, with no margin for investment. The Famine Commission noted in 1860 that the tenants-at-will had 'no incentive to thrift or to improvement'. This situation explains the colonial rulers' favourable attitude towards tenants by limiting the rate of rent payable to landlords and by protecting the rights of tenants-at-will. In accordance with this policy, the cultivators' rights of landownership attributed at the time of the first settlement were confirmed by the Punjab Tenancy Act of 1868.

Revenue Policy

An essential purpose for establishing private land property was the need to levy a steady land revenue from the cultivators. Along with the new settlement legislation, the revenue system was modified. Instead of being levied according to the quantity of harvest each year, as was the practice before annexation, the British calculated the rate to be paid by the landowners and agriculturalists on an average based upon several years. The payment had to be in cash instead of kind, as was the case under the Sikh rule, and without flexibility regarding the due date and amount for a period of 20 to 30 years.

It did not take long before the cultivators were unable to pay their assessments for a variety of reasons. First, the state did not take the years of bad harvest or famines into account. Second, the diffusion of new agricultural techniques was very limited and capitalist farming management was not accessible to small landowners. They did not produce cash-crops, or even if they did they suffered from the low market prices. They had then to sell their subsistence crops so as to have the required cash. Third, the price of agricultural inputs increased. Consequently, the cultivators had to rely upon credit for their consumer goods and agricultural expenditures, and to borrow money to pay the arrears. A class of non-agriculturalist moneylenders benefited from the situation by a usury loan policy. In fact, the fixed tax assessment had made landed property into a profitable commodity which was subject to speculation. The indebted landowner, unable to pay back his creditors because of the system of compound interest, first mortgaged his land and was later forced to sell it. The legal system introduced by the British transformed debt disputes into a new means to impoverish the peasantry, since it backed up the creditors to recover their loans through land transfers. These evicted landowners were employed as tenants-at-will on their former holdings or started to work as agricultural labourers. Landed property had become a source of investment for the new rich classes. The colonial policy was making the peasants more and more subject to capitalist exploitation without the protection of hereditary rights and customs.

The British rulers became increasingly anxious about the socially negative effect on the rural population from the transfer of land from the agriculturalist classes to the trading and usurer classes in the final 30 years of the nineteenth century. It was no longer considered to be a temporary effect of the first years of British rule but rather a structural problem. As a remedy to peasant unrests, the Punjab Land Alienation Act was passed in 1900. It forbade the transfer of land to non-agriculturalists and was intended to protect the small proprietors and all categories of agriculturalists from moneylenders. However, it did not try to stop the causes of indebtedness. The tax system continued to function in the same way as previously. The consequence of the Land Alienation Act was to reduce the influence of professional moneylenders and to push the impoverished cultivators into the arms of a new class of creditors, namely the rich landlords. These changes were desired by the colonial government since it could consolidate its position in the countryside through the creation of a class of political supporters. Unlike the professional moneylenders, the landlords had a traditional power base there and dispossessed landowners could not identify them with the colonial rulers. The higher price of crops up until the Great Depression of 1929, coupled with the increasing value of land due to its scarcity, particularly favoured the richest peasants who were the sole producers of commercial crops. All the other agriculturalists only produced food crops for their own subsistence and suffered from the general increase in the price of commodities. They continued to be indebted. It was not until the 1930s that a set of Acts was passed to protect the debtors' situation; however, the sources of credit remained inaccessible to the majority of cultivators.

Investment Policy

The policies of land property rights and a revenue system aimed at the creation of producers and consumers of British manufactured goods were not sufficient to transform the Punjab into a prosperous colony. An insufficient food supply, added to the absence of an adequate means of communication and to an inefficient organization of trade, could not cope with successive deficient harvests due to droughts, archaic agricultural techniques and the growing population. These difficulties led to several famines during the period 1860–1900.

Confronted with these problems, imperialist forces pushed for the building of an infrastructure which could extend cash-crop agriculture and, in return, profit British industry. Perennial irrigation projects and the construction of railways, roads and ports were steps taken by the British to improve the situation.

The creation of the complex hydraulic system fulfilled several targets. First, it created new villages with a more prosperous economy and consequently provided supplementary revenues to the state in the form of diverse taxes. Second, it provided new political allies by the attribution of land grants to the landowning elite. Only old landed families and retired army personnel received large holdings from the state which were tilled by share-croppers or agricultural labourers. There was no change in the traditional relations of labour. Finally, it assured military needs by associating the allocation of landholdings to horse-breeding for the army. In other words, this development policy did not reduce the demographic pressure and the concentration of landownership in the old settlement areas since the poorest agrarian classes still did not have access to the new territories. The methods of farming remained extensive with a limited introduction of new techniques of cultivation. The aims of this policy were more to satisfy the British economic and political interest than to improve the living standards of the population.

In summary, the colonial policy destroyed the traditional economic system based on the complementary cultivator/craftsman relationship and deepened the social stratification in the rural areas. The results were a land concentration in the hands of a landed aristocracy and of non-agriculturalists, and the impoverishment of the bulk of villagers due to the dispossession, subdivision and fragmentation of their holdings. These transformations initiated the rural–urban migration. However, with the exception of the armed forces and the police, especially during the two world wars, the offers of employment in towns and cities were not sufficient to absorb this new labour force.

During the two world wars, the Punjab furnished more than half the total number of army personnel of the British Indian army. Even though many households were able to benefit from the soldiers' remittances, their economy did not dramatically improve because the price of all consumer goods increased during this period, and also because the raising of war loans was a new pressure upon them.

Furthermore, Britain destroyed the existing local urban industry in order to protect its own industry. As a result, a large number of craftsmen moved to the countryside and started to cultivate land as landless tenants. This urban–rural migration, associated with the natural growth of population, increased the pressure on the cultivable areas and promoted the exploitation of the tenants by the landowning class through the payment of a rent consisting of a high percentage of the agricultural product. The impoverishment of the bulk of agriculturalists remained the dominant characteristic of the Punjabi agrarian structure until independence.

Land Reforms

With the situation inherited in 1947, the new government could not improve the economic situation of the bulk of the rural population without a radical transformation of the agrarian structures. This change was/is dialectically related to the other economic sectors of the society and cannot occur independently of class interests and ideologies specific to the different elements that compose the ruling elite.

Already before independence the Muslim League, through its Agrarian Reforms Committee, was concerned by the concentration of land and the high percentage of holdings cultivated by tenants (over 50 per cent), which were two factors incompatible with an efficient agriculture and social justice. In 1949, it proposed recommendations for a land reform. However, because the landlord class was a strong element of the power elite, no agrarian transformations took place on a national scale until the end of the 1950s. Only regional acts (in the Punjab in 1950) for the protection and restoration of the tenants' rights were legislated.

When the military under the leadership of Ayub Khan seized power in 1958, land reforms became a component of the rulers' rhetoric. It was necessary to colour the domestic policy with a populist discourse which could increase the government's popularity and extend its social base. It was also important to reduce the power of some of the biggest landlords. However, the reforms should not be a socially destabilizing factor in the rural areas by favouring the small farmers and the landless classes at the expense of the big landlords, who were still very influential in the country's political life. In addition, due to the close connection between the army and the landed gentry, and to the government's practice of allotting land to army officers and senior civil servants in order to gain their allegiance, the new agrarian policy could not be too radical.

The 1959 land reform took a middle-of-the-road solution by, on the one hand, improving the tenants' security against arbitrary eviction, and, on the other hand, by setting a very high upper ceiling on landholdings – 500 acres on irrigated land and 1,000 acres on rainfed land. Instead of taking the household as a unit of reference, landholdings were based on the individual. A great number of land transfers within the family took place before the implementation of the reform, which drastically reduced the number of big landlords who could fall under the measure of expropriation. The global effects of the reform were also limited by many provisions in favour of landlords and by exemptions regarding ownership of orchards, stud farms and religious institutions.

As a result of this desire to satisfy all sections of rural society, the land reform was more symbolic in nature than significant. A very small amount of land was appropriated, and the holdings, which were sold in lots, were often of a poor cultivable quality. The low price of holdings made the former tenant an eventual buyer but the new owners were not allowed to possess land of a size larger than a subsistence holding. The government's intentions were more determined by political interest through curtailing the power of some big landlords and by favouring the middle-sized farmers than by a desire to improve the economic situation of the poorest classes in the rural areas. The rulers' policy was also benefited by a lack of articulation and political organizations among the poor peasantry which did not control channels to formulate claims.

However, in the 1960s it became clear to the power elite that industrial development could not increase if agriculture continued to rely on traditional techniques of cultivation and to have a stagnated production. The Second and Third Five-Year Plans (1960–65 and 1965–70) created incentives for ambitious big landowners and entrepreneurial cultivators to modernize their methods of farming. The so-called Green Revolution was launched. It improved the agricultural production of the middle-sized cultivators and brought about a change in the agrarian structure by the eviction of many tenants. The number of self-cultivators rose due to the higher costs of agricultural inputs and the landlords became more involved in the total management of their farms. As a result, many tenants became landless labourers or migrated to cities. Simultaneously, the number of smallholdings increased. Instead of changing the unfair distribution of wealth, these technological innovations deepened the economic gap between classes in the rural areas. The skewed agrarian structures were accentuated, and this made the demand for radical reforms even more imperative than ten years before.

Z. A. Bhutto's Pakistan People's Party (PPP) won the parliamentary elections in West Pakistan in 1970, partly owing to its promise of a land reform. The reform was promulgated in March 1972 and was more radical than the Ayub Khan's reform. No compensation was given for the expropriated land and the exemptions concerning orchards, stud farms and religious landed properties were cancelled. The tenant was confirmed in his right not to be expelled by the landlord without good grounds, such as non-payment of rent or improper management of the farm. The share of expenditures for agricultural inputs was modified in the tenant's favour, and payments of taxes and fees became the landlord's responsibility. The appropriated land was redistributed free of charge to occupancy tenants with full proprietary rights. The tenant's free labour was forbidden.

Notwithstanding these positive measures, the real effects of the land reform for the poor agrarian classes remained limited. The upper ceiling of landholding was still too high to provide a redistribution of land on a great scale. It was placed at 150 acres on irrigated land and 300 acres on rainfed land. It also considered the individual as the basic unit of ownership. Once more the promise of land reform had been an essential element of the rulers' populist discourse to achieve power, even though the class composition of the government's supporters was not recruited among the big landowners. The politico-economic interests of the PPP's cadres were different from those of the landed gentry and helped to strengthen the class of market-oriented farmers which emerged thanks to the Green Revolution. However, another Act which extended the 1972 reform was passed in January 1977, shortly before Bhutto's fall. It once again reduced the upper ceiling for the size of landholdings, this time down to 100 acres of irrigated and 200 acres of unirrigated land, although there was compensation for the appropriated land. Protection was extended to all types of tenants.

The aims of the land reforms initiated after independence were guided more by socio-political considerations than by economic criteria. Their results are limited because of the discrepancy between their ideological basis and their enforcement. For example, no taxation mechanisms were initiated to make the ownership of large landholdings unprofitable. They also created a climate of insecurity in the rural area which is not favourable for a peaceful atmosphere between landowners and tenants.

With the new military coup in July 1977, Pakistan entered a political period coloured by Islamic values according to the new rulers' interpretation of Islam. Regarding agrarian relations, General Zia-ul-Haq declared a fatwa, stating that the appropriation of private property is contrary to Islamic prescriptions.

After Zia-ul-Haq's death in 1988, many of the laws and measures taken in the name of Islam by his regime in its search for legitimacy have survived because of the continuing power of the ultra-conservative Muslim politicians.

Pakistan's Industrial and Manpower Policy since 1947

At Partition, both wings of Pakistan were largely agricultural with virtually no industry. It was only in the middle of the 1950s that industrial plants were established, supported by large governmental incentives, in order to create a domestic production of manufactured goods based on agricultural raw materials. The strategy of this industrial policy relied upon import substitution industries, and upon the transfer of resources from agriculture to industry and from East Pakistan to West Pakistan.

A class of industrialists developed which over the years began to occupy a monopolistic position in the economy since it came to dominate not only the industrial but also the banking and insurance sectors. This economic domination, associated with political alliances, entailed an unequal distribution of income and wealth.

Moreover, the strategies of industrial development did not take into consideration the rate of natural population growth and the rate of rural–urban migration due to the Green Revolution. They favoured capital- rather than labour-intensive techniques of production and therefore increased the unemployment and underemployment problems. The emphasis was on rapid growth, and on the denial of welfare legislation for the workers. Even though social measures were taken in the 1960s to change the situation, their implementation was ineffective.

Under the PPP's rule a new economic approach was introduced with nationalization of key industries and banking establishments, and the beginning of a social policy for the workers concerning both their wages and their trade union rights. However, Zia-ul-Haq's takeover of the country's leadership put a stop to these measures and the industrial policy made a radical turn. It was again characterized by an emphasis on private management and an anti-labour strategy with a permanent denial of workers' basic rights and their brutal repression.

In conclusion, since 1947 the industrial policy of Pakistan has favoured the emergence of a bourgeoisie closely allied to the state. The level of wages has remained very low and the labour absorption capacity of the industrial sector has always been accorded a secondary priority in the development schemes. Consequently, the demands of the rural population and of the urban workers have not been satisfied.

From this short introduction of the Punjab's economic history, we shall now turn to the impacts that these economic transformations have made upon the two villages of this study during the last 100 years. We shall see how the villagers are able to choose individual strategies according to their traditional cultural values, even though they are dominated by an exploitative macro-economic system. These opportunities 'to bargain for reality' – not always successfully – have also been illustrated in recent studies on rural–urban migration and on urbanisation within Pakistani society through the analyses of the role played by the informal economy (J. Eades, 1987; K. Nadvi, 1989; O. Noman, 1991; F. Selier, 1988 and 1991; F. Selier and M. S. Karim, 1986; J. van der Linden, 1991).

2 CHAHIWALA AND BARANPUR

TWO VILLAGES OF NORTHERN PUNJAB

After a ten-minute bus ride or half-hour journey by horse-cart from the market-town of Pasrur in the Sialkot district, you reach the stop at a bridge over the Upper Marala–Ravi link canal which serves the village of Chahiwala. From there you walk along sandy paths through the fields and after twenty minutes the first houses and stables of the village come into view.

The Sialkot district mostly consists of an alluvial plain called Rechna *doab*, i.e. the tract between the rivers Chenab and Ravi (see Map 1). It slopes down from the uplands at the foot of the Himalayas to sea level in the south-west. The average altitude is 240 m above sea level. The maximum and minimum mean temperatures are 37.9°c and 25.3°c respectively in summer, and 22.5°c and 7.7°c in winter. Evaporation is rapid in the summer and reduces the effect of the monsoon rains.

Chahiwala is surrounded by many other villages, all of which lie within walking distance via sandy paths broad enough for the passage of horse-carts and oxen-carts. However, its economic activities do not take place directly with these villages, but rather at the marketplaces and cattle-fairs in the nearby towns of Pasrur, Daska, and the district capital Sialkot.

Pasrur is the local administrative centre for the area and boasts a civil court, a large police station, a government Agricultural Department, a hospital, and several banks and post offices.

Figure 1: Entrance to Chahiwala village

Figure 2: General view of Baranpur

Baranpur , the village with rainfed agriculture, is located 5 miles from Gujar Khan, an important market town in the Rawalpindi district (see Map 1). This area is part of the Potwar plateau which B.L.C. Johnson describes as follows:

> The Potwar plateau is a confusion of rocky ridges and basin plains, in many areas thickly covered in Pleistocene times, with a mantle of loess which has become dissected into a fantastic 'bad land' of gullies and loess buttes. (B.L.C. Johnson 1979: 47)

Such conditions make irrigation impractical and consequently the agriculture depends on rain. The rainfall for Rawalpindi (25 miles north-west of the village) reaches a maximum of 960 mm annually, of which 259 mm falls in the winter months from October to March.

Unlike Chahiwala, Baranpur is inaccessible to any vehicle all year round. Mini-buses and buses stop at a petrol station with an adjacent restaurant on the Grand Trunk Road connecting Peshawar to Lahore. From there a path, which is impassable for horse-carts, bull-carts or any other vehicles, leads for 2 miles to the village. Villagers often complain about this inconvenience, for instance when they have to carry sick persons on their backs as far as the Grand Trunk Road.

General Considerations about the Social Organization in Muslim Punjabi Villages

Analyses of the social organization in Muslim communities of the sub-continent have repeatedly discussed the importance of the interaction between Islam and Hinduism. The main issue has been whether the concept of a 'caste system' is a relevant paradigm for understanding the social stratifications among Muslims. In his *Homo Hierarchicus*, Louis Dumont argues that the political Hindu subordination to Muslim rulers over several centuries has altered some orthodox principles of Hinduism. The Brahmanic values, their principles of inequality, the idiom of purity and the strict hierarchical scale were not recognized by the Moghul emperors. However, the caste system influenced the ideal of equality stressed by Islam. According to Dumont, what emerged from this cultural osmosis was the idea that castes are present among Muslims, although in a weakened form because they lack an ideological justification. When Hindus converted to Islam, they did not transform the social order. Moreover, they remained surrounded by Hinduism which continued to dominate the global cultural scene even under the rule of

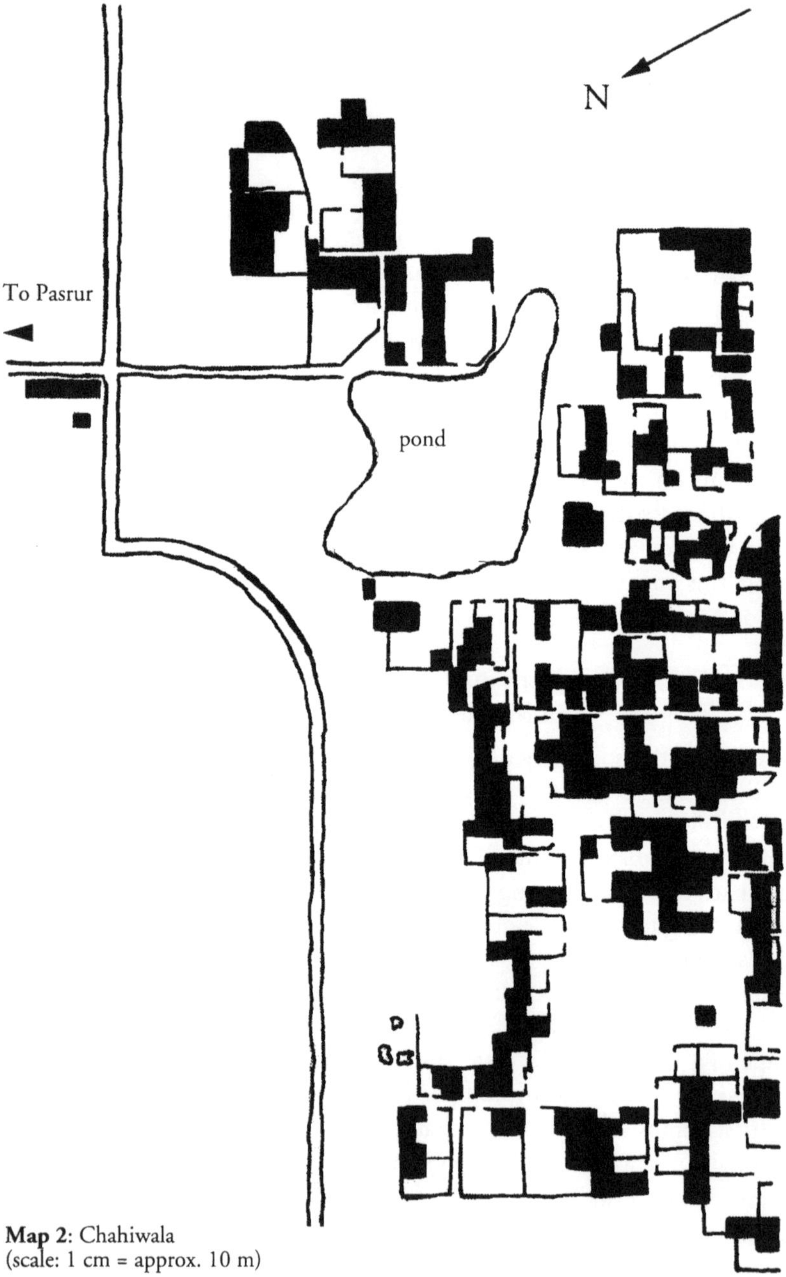

Map 2: Chahiwala
(scale: 1 cm = approx. 10 m)

pond

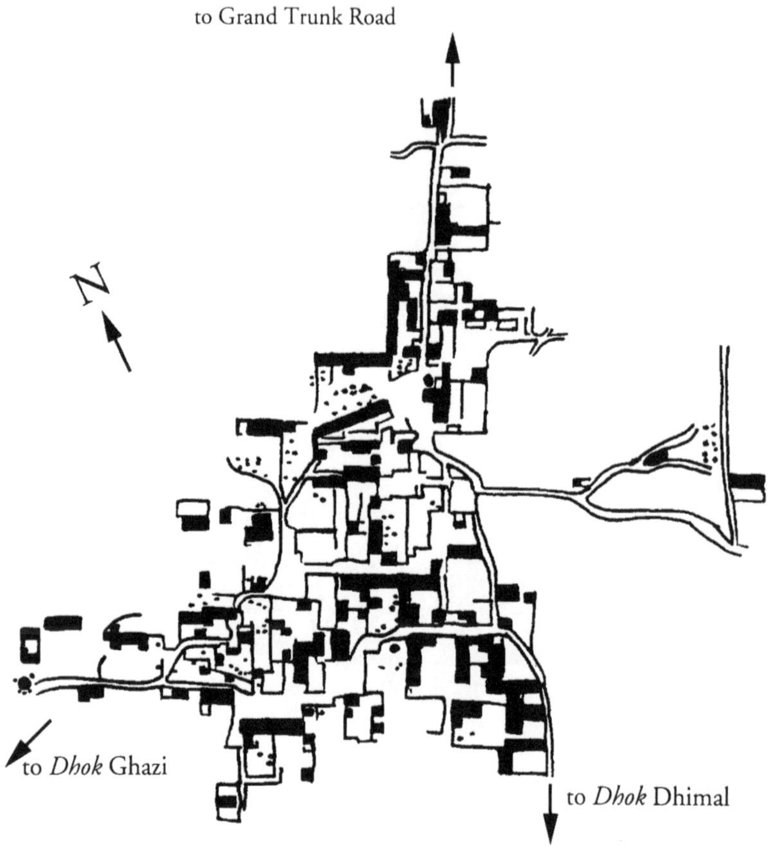

Map 3: Baranpur (central part)

the Moghul emperors. Muslims, although constituting the political ruling elite, always remained a cultural minority.

A ranked status among Muslims of the subcontinent certainly exists, as anthropological literature has shown.[1] The socio-economic status of the individual is a very important factor which the villagers take into account in their relationships. People are very status-minded because fundamental values of honour and prestige are related to each position. Competition among individuals occurs across the social divisions and within a framework of commonly shared values where honour (*izzat*) and prestige (*nak*) occupy a central position. However, is such a social

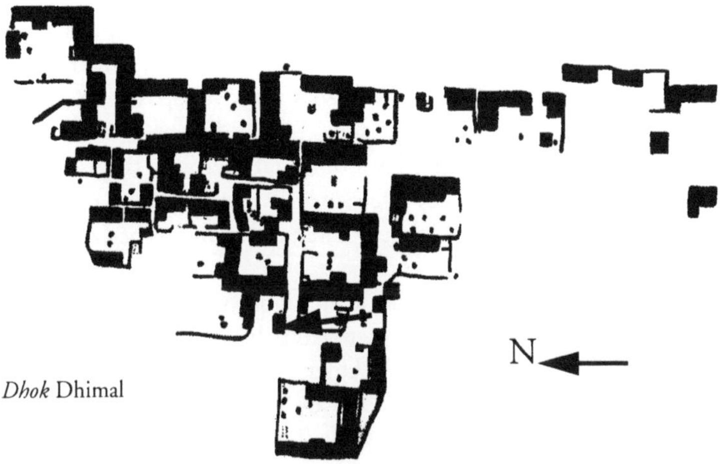

Map 4: *Dhok* Dhimal

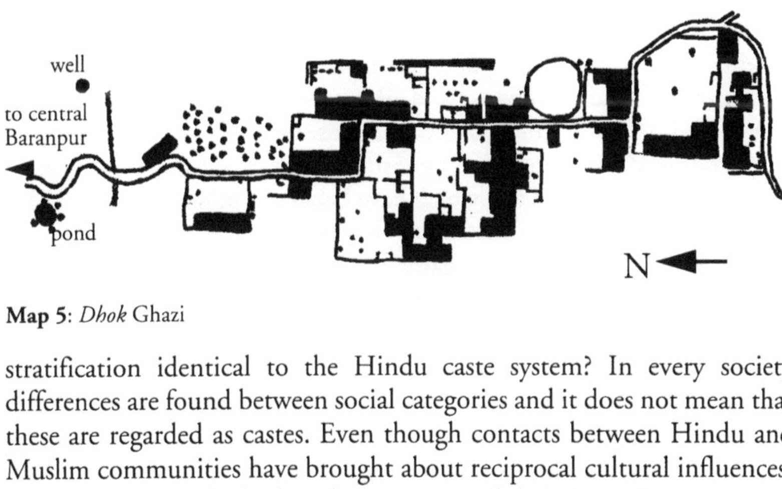

Map 5: *Dhok* Ghazi

stratification identical to the Hindu caste system? In every society differences are found between social categories and it does not mean that these are regarded as castes. Even though contacts between Hindu and Muslim communities have brought about reciprocal cultural influences, the basic criteria which identify the castes and their interrelations are not present amongst Muslims. In the Muslim social order, there is no emphasis on ritual purity, nor are there any restrictions on commensality between different social groups, or a hierarchy based on religious criteria.

For example, the Syeds, the Shaikhs and the Sharifs are honorifically considered to occupy the highest position on the social scale, similar to the Hindu Brahmans, because of their ancestors' closeness to the prophet

Mohammed and his tribe. However, this does not mean that they are accorded special privileges.

The structural grading in the Punjabi village is multi-dimensional. It is based on different criteria which refer to ethnic, kin, religious and occupational groups. These may or may not overlap, but in all cases they are not mutually exclusive.

In everyday life, the first level of social divisions through which the villagers identify themselves refers to a distinction based on occupation, namely in the division of labour. They differentiate between the *quoms* of landowners (*zamindars*) and the *quoms* of craftsmen (*kammis*),[2] with the former category being accorded a higher status. The word *quom* has several meanings. It can be translated as tribe, sect, nation or caste. In the work of F. Barth (1960) and Z. Eglar (1960), the term 'caste' has been retained because *quom* is the level of social organization which most resembles the Hindu ranking system. The term 'caste-like' has also been suggested as a more satisfactory concept for the analysis of this stratification. Here, the term 'class' is used in the actual context.

To own land is still the most honourable and respectful position in the villages. This distinction does not mean that all the members of the *zamindar quom* are landowners and all the members of the *kammi quom* are engaged in their traditional occupations, but there is little room for social mobility between these two status groups. Households which traditionally owned land but which have become landless continue to be considered as members of the *zamindar quom*. Conversely, *kammis* who have purchased land are still regarded as craftsmen even if their landed property surpasses the holdings of many *zamindars*.

Within each of these two main economic divisions, the villagers distinguish between several units (*zats*). The *quom* of landowners is subdivided into several patrilineal descent groups which each refer to a common ancestor.[3] At this level the stratification relates to identification markers issued from historical fame and religious leadership – real or mythical – attributed to the respective forefathers. The extended descent group can be further divided into unilineal descent groups (called *aals*).

The division among craftsmen is based on hereditary professions. Each activity occupies a different ranked position in popular perception. Craftsmen with an occupation directly related to agriculture, such as carpenters and blacksmiths, are more respectable than those associated with domestic service provided for the cultivators. However, the occupational *zat* by which the *kammis* are called does not necessarily correspond to their own perception of their identity. Economic changes through generations might have led to new and less prestigious professions which are today labels of identification but their members' identity as a social body is still attached to the common activity of their ancestors. This explains why some *kammis* have a double name.

At the opposite end of the scale one finds cases where the name of a new occupation is used as an identification label but it does not mean that this self-proclaimed change of social identity is recognized by the other craftsmen – let alone the landowners – because it is confusing to have lineages which bear the same name whilst descending from unrelated forefathers. It also increases the competition within a very fragile economic equilibrium between craftsmen.

Endogamy between these different occupational *kammi zats* is as strict as among the landowners. It strengthens the group solidarity and confirms the *zat* identity.

Although vocational mobility was limited in the traditional Punjabi society due to the absence of alternative livelihoods, it was nevertheless possible. Despite the fact that fatalism influences the villagers' self-perception, a desire to advance to a higher social position is a permanent driving force behind the people's behaviour. This dynamism exists because the individual's place in society is not rigidly and irreversibly determined at birth by a cosmological order, as is the case among Hindus. A change of social status is possible, if not in the village at least by moving away to some place where an individual's former socio-economic position is unknown.

In fact, the landowners reluctantly accept a transformation of the traditional social order. Within the village, a change of occupation does not lead to a change of *quom* and *zat* since social and economic status do not automatically coincide. Even though the two *quoms* have social interactions, the difference of status is always present in the people's manner of communication. However, the social scene is not identical in the two villages. The people's values are generally much more conservative and traditional in Chahiwala than in Baranpur. The attitude of the landowners towards craftsmen is more unfair in Chahiwala: they treat them as arrogantly as if they were servants. This conservatism could be explained by the proximity of Chahiwala to India – which certainly accounts for the very rigid social mobility. Also Chahiwala's economy has been self-centred, while the villagers of Baranpur on the other hand were recruited in the army and the police at a very early stage during British rule and therefore had the possibility of transforming their worldview.

The labour relations between landowners and craftsmen are institutionalized in the *seypi* system, which bears many similarities to the *jajmani* system in India. The *seypi* system is a contract between cultivators, either landowners or tenants, and villagers whose traditional occupation is to offer services. It is built upon an intricate network of reciprocal patron–client ties, where several cultivators' households are in a relationship with several households of craftsmen. The cultivators use the services of the village craftsmen for the manufacture and maintenance of agricultural equipment. Today only the carpenters and blacksmiths remain in the two villages. They are remunerated in kind after each harvest according to a fixed amount which is not indexed to the actual quantity of yield. Craftsmen from other professional *zat*s – like the barber, the water-carrier, the shoemaker and the bard – endeavour to cover all the cultivators' needs according to their hereditary specialization. Besides crops, they also receive small amounts of money (*laag*), second-hand clothes and cooked food. The *seypi* interrelations between craftsmen are not remunerated in cash or kind but consist of an exchange of services. In other words, the *seypi* system is the local form of barter economy.

This social division between landowners and craftsmen is economic. The relationship between the two groups is closer to a division between two social classes than between two caste-like groups. No notion of ritual pollution and commensality influences the daily interactions, and men from both groups are able to mix socially. Any similarity with the Hindu castes is structural, not cultural. The ideology sustaining the *seypi* system is to secure an occupational monopoly for each *zat*. Another aspect of this ideology is the landowners' moral obligation to ensure a means of subsistence to the landless villagers. They cannot therefore break the *seypi* relationship. This system is hereditary and the employment relationship is divided up like property between heirs within the same *zat*. It means that the subsistence level is reduced from generation to generation if the agrarian transformation entails a reduction in cultivators. The craftsmen may then come out of the *seypi* relationship and find new sources of income. However, in most cases the craftsmen have no economic alternatives within the village and must therefore be unconditionally at the service of the landowners. One cannot talk of an economic partnership with equal rights between the *quom* of landowners and the *quom* of village craftsmen but rather of a social class dominating another through power related to landed property.

Now when using the concept 'social class', as has been developed by Karl Marx, a distinction has been made between 'class-in-itself' and 'class-for-itself', with the former being an economic category and the second referring to a group of people who are politically conscious of their position in the society. In the context of the two villages, 'class-in-itself' is particularly appropriate. The class of landowners and the class of craftsmen are two groups with specific socio-economic status, but their members do not show a class solidarity in their actions but a solidarity towards their patrilineage (*biraderi*) or its sub-division (*patti*).[4] This is especially the case for the landowners who are engaged in conflicts with several *biraderi*s for the control of the village or between *patti*s of the same *biraderi* for the control of the latter. The *patti* was originally an administrative division created by the British rulers for the collection of land revenue in the villages. Due to the individual and collective responsibility of this payment, there developed feelings of solidarity between members of the same descent group. As H. Alavi has underlined (1972: 4), the *patti* therefore corresponds to a segment of the ancestral land.

The *quom* of landowners and the *quom* of craftsmen are heterogeneous economic groups with a ranked status between each constituent unit. The landowners differentiate between these units on the basis of the size of the cultivated area and on the type of land tenure, with the landlord leasing out his land at the highest position of the social scale, followed by the self-cultivator, the owner-cum-tenant, and the tenant.[5] The grade of power in the decision-making process is related to the quantity of land which is used and to its form of control.

No clear boundaries separate the different categories of peasants in the villages. They overlap each other because most landowner households have difficulties in making ends meet due to the reduced size of their holdings.

In addition to the awareness of belonging to different social classes, the kinship network is the other immediate frame of reference for each individual. The kinship relationships are ordered by the institution of *biraderi* in the Punjabi villages. It is constituted of all those who consider themselves 'brothers' with people of the same generation and who claim to have a common male ancestor. Since the kinship system is of a classificatory type, the Punjabis also assimilate non-kin in their *biraderi*. The nature of *biraderi* ties also depends on the rigidity of the endogamous practices. Endogamy is in turn determined by the economic resources at the disposal of different households. Rich and poor *biraderi*s do not exist, but within each is found a continuum of households at different levels on the economic scale, with the better-off households in more favourable positions, for example regarding marriage propositions, which ideally should occur between patrilineal cousins (father's brother's daughter). For several reasons, exchanging women folk within the *biraderi* increases the status of households. The villagers believe in the notion of blood purity specific to each *biraderi*. Siblings external to the descent group might alter its positive pecularities. *Biraderi* endogamy also facilitates the resolution of eventual conflicts between two families. It is finally a proof that the traditional authority is respected by the young generation since marriages are arranged by elders. The practice of all these traditions gives prestige, but the poor villagers with less honour to lose have a more lenient form of endogamy, especially if economic or social profit is to be achieved.

In case of exogamous marriage for the sake of establishing alliances, the bride becomes a member of her husband's *biraderi* and their children belong to the father's lineage. Consequently, all the members of a household belong to the same *biraderi* and in the village a *biraderi* is constituted by related households. If *biraderi* exogamy occurs, marriages must nevertheless always be celebrated within the *zat*.

Concerning the craftsmen, Saghir Ahmad (1977) writes that they do not refer to patrilineal kin groups as a self-definition of their identity but only to their professional occupation. Such is not the case in these two villages. It is true that when a *kammi* is asked about the name of his social group, he answers by mentioning a profession. However, since it is the traditional profession of his ancestors, this answer can be interpeted as a reference to his *biraderi*. The apparent weakness of the patrilineage among the class of craftsmen is only due to the spreading of relatives to many villages. Even if these villagers do not own land and are therefore not concerned with a property which is attached to an emotional value because it originated from a common ancestor, they are also hinting at their *biraderi*. They demonstrate the same importance and respect for their forefathers as the landowners do.

The boundaries of *biraderi* are loose and vary according to whom an individual recognizes as its members. A ritual of prestations and counter-prestations called *vartan bhanji* (literally 'giving sweets') permanently expresses the categories of different *biraderi* relatives and reaffirms the cohesion of the *biraderi*. *Vartan bhanji* refers to the reciprocal exchange of gifts occurring at life-cycle ceremonies celebrated by all members of the *biraderi*, such as childbirth, circumcision, marriage or funerals, and to the reciprocal exchange of a whole range of services, favours and good deeds in everyday life.

The frequency and degree of involvement in the *vartan bhanji* distinguish the different categories of a *biraderi*. First there is the descent group as a whole or *biraderi* of recognition (H. A. Alavi 1972 and 1973) which includes all the people who claim blood ties with common forefathers irrespective of the number of generations but who do not participate in the life-cycle ceremonies.

One also finds the '*biraderi* of participation' (H. A. Alavi 1972 and 1973), which refers to the close relationships between people and households. These ties might be between individuals who are kinsmen and/or just friends, and who live within or outside the village. Members of the *biraderi* of participation are obliged to take part in ritual exchange. These ties are called *pakki vartan* (strong and permanent ties) and are the opposite of those unhereditary relationships which the host wants to maintain (*kachi vartan*) by inviting for example friends, neighbours, or members of other *biraderis*. No obligation exists between the host and this latter category of guest, and both parties can resume the relationships at any time.

All the gifts (*neondra*) are recorded in a register called *behi*, which almost every household possesses. In this book the host enters the type of items, their value and the donor's name with the giver, the receiver and the guests as witnesses. When the occasion arises, a household consults its register so as to verify its position in the constant mechanism of gift-giving and gift-receiving.

The *vartan bhanji* ritual has two purposes. It maintains and confirms the social relationships between members of the *biraderi*. The *biraderi* also provides assistance in all spheres of life to its members. The gift-giving is based on the principle of unequal reciprocal exchange. The donor must always return more than his host gave him at a previous ceremony so as to pay back a debt and to create a new obligation on the part of the receiver. For example, if A gives a pair of suits and Rs 20 at the marriage of B's daughter, B should give back at least a pair of suits of the same quality or preferably of better quality and Rs 40 when the marriage of A's daughter occurs.

This obligation of returning gifts of a higher magnitude at each new occasion allows the relationships between the households of *biraderi* to continue. However, a wealthy household does not try to challenge a poorer one by giving goods which the latter cannot reciprocate. If this occurs, the donor wants to assist the receiver economically and at the same time to increase his prestige through, on the one hand, helping the poor, and on the other hand through displaying his wealth.

It is very difficult to stop this system of reciprocal relations. Disputes and hostility between two families do not prevent the obligation of returning the advanced amount. Pressure is exerted by the other members of the *biraderi* if one of the two parties wants to discontinue the *biraderi* relationship by offering an amount equal to the old debt. This family, regardless of its political importance in the village, has to accept the decision of the *biraderi* or to part company with it and start a new cycle of *vartan bhanji* with other relatives.

In reality, the life of a *biraderi* is often hit by factions and is sometimes split. However, the villagers mainly remain loyal to their patrilineage because of its integral functions. The individual and the group gain assistance and support – both material and psychological – from their *biraderi*. Through a definition of rights and duties, the *biraderi* offers a basis for social security and defines one's identity. Therefore, a newly established household is obliged to enter into the reciprocation cycle between *biraderi* households. Non-engagement in the *vartan bhanji* ritual is tantamount to social ostracism – a situation which would be very difficult to cope with since there do not yet exist any other social relationships which could function as alternative primordial loyalties to the kin ties.

As H. A. Alavi (1973) writes, the patrilineage is in fact a *primordial loyalty* before any kind of class solidarity. A look at political elections at village level illustrates the role of the *biraderi* as an institution. The choice of a candidate is not made on the basis of socio-economic and ideological criteria but is related to feuds between factions of landowners. Moreover, the choice is not individual but is imposed by the leaders of the lineage who function as a corporate group. The leaders of the *biraderi* tell the men whom they should vote for, and they in turn tell the women folk of their households.

Members of the class of craftsmen are not able to express their own opinions in the case of feuds. They are bound by the *seypi* relations to some specific landowners via their kinship ties and are expected to give them their allegiance. They are compelled to take up a position against members of their own lineage just because their respective landowners are fighting with each other. In case of disputes between patron and client, the landowners have more power, more education and tend to have greater economic means for meeting judicial costs, and are therefore generally the winners in such cases.

History of the Villages

Both villages are very old and the narration of their history consists of real events combined with mythological elements where ancestors are always glorified as exceptional men because of their courage, honesty, religious fervour and honour. Since all informants belong to the Muslim community, one can expect a bias in their interpretation of the pre-independence history. However, their narrative of the relationships between the different religious communities corresponds to other studies of Punjab's history (Sir M. Darling 1947; S. S. Thorburn n.d.).

The social life of each village was based upon the co-habitation of several religious communities and the present social organization of space is directly derived from the first dwellers' pattern of settlement.

Chahiwala was a village of Muslim cultivators and artisans with Sikh and Hindu minorities. The latter were engaged in trade and usury. Christian families occupied the bottom rung of the social ladder. The composition of the population was the opposite in Baranpur with a majority of Hindus and Sikhs and a minority of Muslims engaged in agriculture and craftsmanship. No Christians lived there.

The Economic Situation before Partition

Chahiwala

This history of Chahiwala is based on a compilation of tales from several elders who belong to various *zat*s of landowners and of craftsmen:

> When this area was covered with jungle, a man called Chahi came and started to live here. Later other people joined him. They called the place Chahiwala in honour of the first dweller. A fort was constructed by a Moghul emperor on a hill which is now located in the centre of the village.
>
> This area of Punjab was densely populated by Sikhs although the country was under Moghul rule. Sikhs and Muslims have always fought

> against each other. The Moghuls were considered by the Sikhs as the foreign rulers to be expelled.
>
> The village was inhabited by Muslims of the Blagan *aal*, a sub-lineage of the Virck *zat*. Due to their small number, they were not able to resist the Sikhs' domination. These considered the Muslims as their servants. For instance, when a Sikh was coming, carrying a load on his back, he just had to touch the shoulder of a Muslim villager to make him understand that it was his duty to bear the load.
>
> During the tumultuous years at the end of the Moghul era, the fort and the adjacent village were destroyed. One of the survivors Matto asked for the help of the Virck people in order to resist the constant raids of the Sikhs. Three brothers, named Malik, Kala and Dhedo, responded to his demand and came from the village Virkaet 48 in the Sheirkhupura district. It is not far from here. As a reward, they received three-quarters of the land. From that day, the village has been divided into four parts (*pattis*). They are called *patti* Matto, *patti* Malik, *patti* Kala, and *patti* Dhedo, according to the common ancestors' names.
>
> The Vircks became dominant and strong in the village and the Blagans had to bow to their will and decisions. Although the Blagans could have become independent through the passage of time, the lack of strength of their men has meant that they still follow the Vircks today. During the reconstruction of the village, people arrived from different villages where their economic situation was difficult. They settled in Chahiwala due to their search for work.
>
> The first to come were the people of the Fakir *zat*. They received some plots of land from the landowners for their livelihood. In return, it was their duty to keep the fire burning at the meeting place (*dara*) of each *patti*, and to prepare the landowners' water-pipe at least once a day.

Thus, Muslims were the founders of Chahiwala. However, Hindus were invited to settle among them because the Muslim community needed their economic activities as shopkeepers and moneylenders.

In those days, the agriculture mostly depended on rainfall. Ponds on the four sides of the village gradually appeared as a result of the villagers' digging up the earth to build their houses. This allowed a very primitive form of irrigation. The cultivators linked these ponds to their fields with small ditches and bailed out the water with shovels. Tiny paddy- and fodder-fields lay close to the wells. Eighteen wells were installed before Partition. They had a depth of 42–47 ft and the surface of the water laid at 7–10 ft.

The landowners co-operated. For instance, if someone did not have bullocks for ploughing, he could borrow them from another landowner for an amount of wheat to be paid after the harvest. This payment was not fixed but was settled at the time of the loan. The borrower had to reimburse by a certain time and if he was unable to pay, he had to borrow wheat from the Hindu merchant.

For some years the drought hindered all kinds of cultivation. People could not find work outside the village. The economic conditions were then very harsh. Some families left the village for other areas of Punjab where the British had begun the construction of a complex system of irrigation. The remaining villagers had very little to eat: boiled greens made of the leaves of rape and gram (*saag*) with salt during the winter; turnip, radish and carrot during the summer. They owned only few clothes made of hand-woven white cotton (*khaddar*) to protect their body from the cool winter season. People were also too poor to pay for transportation means like horse-carts (*tanga*) and used to walk to Pasrur and Gujranwala.

During this time the area was known for its buffalo business. Some villagers started this trade to obtain an extra income which could supplement the low production of the agricultural activities. The initiator was a Brahman who was later joined by members of the Fakir *zat* and by Muslim landowners.

When the Muslim landowners of Chahiwala were unable to cultivate sufficiently they could not cover their families' basic needs. They had to depend economically on the Hindu merchants and moneylenders who belonged to the Khatri and Brahman castes, respectively. Twenty-five Hindu families lived in the village where there were at least ten shops. Hindus and Sikhs were also store-dealers and the Muslim cultivators gave them their crops for storage. After three or four months, the Muslim cultivators had nothing left to eat and had to borrow from the Hindus on a system of compound interest, not only food and seeds but also money both for daily consumption and for social ceremonies.

For 1 *maund* of wheat lent, the shopkeepers took 1 *maund* 20 kg in return after a six-month period. For Rs 1 borrowed, the moneylenders demanded Rs 1.20 after every month. If the debt was not reimbursed at the time of harvest, the creditor took all the debtor's yearly agricultural production. Only the interest was considered to be reimbursed through this coercive payment. The amount of the debt was not reduced.

The moneylender could also ask the debtor to sell his cattle or other valuables, like his wife's wedding jewels.

An old landowner, Fazal Din, gave a typical example of the situation by telling a story about his friend Amin.

> Amin borrowed Rs 1,200 from a Hindu called Lal Jat for marrying his son. He promised to pay him back after one or two years but was not able to do so. Lal Jat took Amin's wheat every year for 12 years and this was only to pay the interest. It did not decrease the amount of the borrowed money.
>
> After 12 years, Lal Jat wanted to get back all his money. Muslim and Hindu leaders met and discussed the matter. Amin said that he would give everything away to make the repayment, but he hid one pregnant buffalo in another village. I advised him that it was better to also give the buffalo if he wanted to be all clean. He did so and afterwards Amin had nothing left in his house and had to borrow again from Hindus.

The Hindu usurers never terminated these relationships with their debtors even if they paid them back very irregularly. It was much too profitable a business to give up. They also took land as a form of reimbursement and the former landowner tilled it as a landless tenant. After the harvest, the crops were divided into five equal shares, three for the Hindu creditor and two for the Muslim debtor.

This transfer of property was called to take land 'on *guerao*' and was not recorded in the land registrar's (*patwari*) book. The Muslim landowner was still the official owner of the landholding. Lacking economic power, the Muslim community could not protest against these practices and had to bear the humiliating behaviour of the usurers.

Hanif said:

> A strong landowner could borrow wheat without difficulty. However, when it was a poor landowner, the creditor first asked to have his fodder cut. It was a very difficult task in those days. It took three–four hours because the grass was cut horizontally and vertically since they did not have many fodder-cutters. When it was done, he told the poor man to come back the next day to get his wheat.

The debts were transferred from one generation to the other.

Faced with these economic problems, the poor villagers could have taken jobs in towns and cities. But the men of this area were not recruited for the police or the army by the colonial administration. There was no tradition for this kind of work as a source of income.

Even if the Christian community does not constitute a *zat* by definition, it is perceived as such by its members and by the other villagers. Christians appeared in the village at the beginning of the twentieth century when very active missionaries converted many untouchables in the area. Proselytism was practised through the opening of schools and the distribution of free food and clothes. Untouchables, who belonged to the Salotri and Tchure castes, were more receptive to the missionaries' message than the Muslims because they saw in the Christian rhetoric a possibility to improve their social status.

As a result 20 Christian families lived in the village before Partition. However, their economic position remained worse than that of the Muslim community. They were landless and worked on a *seypi* basis as agricultural labourers for the Hindu and Sikh landowners. They built the irrigation ditches in the fields and cut the crops. After each harvest they were paid 1 *maund* of wheat for every 12 *maunds* cut. They guided the bullocks which powered the mechanism of the Persian wheels. They tended the cattle and made dung-cakes. They started these *seypi* relations after they had become Christians. They were free to choose the landowners they worked for and were not compelled to continue this work relation from one year to the next. All the scavenger tasks of the village were also part of their duties.

Baranpur

All the villagers are unanimous in their opinion that Baranpur was a dynamic town before Partition. They speak of this period as a golden age when Baranpur looked more like a town than a village, with paved streets, two-storey buildings made of brick and an active market-place. There were 25–30 shops offering all kinds of goods: 4–5 jewellers' shops, 3 shops for roasting wheat and barley, 7–8 shops selling clothes and 7–8 general merchant stores where petty hawkers from other villages came to buy their goods. The importance of this little town explains the existence of a railway station on the Peshawar–Lahore line.

At the beginning of this century, the total number of inhabitants reached about 1,000. The majority of the population was composed of Hindus and Sikhs. These two communities were settled mainly in the centre of Baranpur, while the Muslim community lived in two adjacent hamlets (*dhok*), *dhok* Dihmal and *dhok* Ghazi.

Each community was far from being an economically homogeneous entity, since the Hindus and the Sikhs comprised both poor and wealthy people. The Muslim population on the other hand was only made up of poor households.

It was not easy to obtain precise information about the Hindus and Sikhs from the elder Muslim villagers. Many of them consider Hindus and Sikhs to be members of the same *zat*s because they are non-Muslim, especially after they started to intermarry. Confusion might thus alter their memory. Luckily, some genealogical charts contained in the 'Records of Rights' (*Misle Haqiet*) provide supplementary details about the socio-economic life of the village for the last hundred years.

The merchants of the marketplace were mostly Hindus. There were two types of dealers. The first category, known as the bankers (*sahookar*s), were shopkeepers who paid a tax to the government. When they sold goods on credit, they entered in their account books the value of the commodity as well as the amount of interest. These figures were given an official stamp and in the case of non-payment, they could make a claim in the court.

The other category of merchant validated their sales only with the thumbprint of the debtor. Whichever category or faith the merchants belonged to, they practised the same system of compound interest as in Chahiwala, which ruined the customers financially. Many people were short of the basic food products such as wheat flour and were forced to buy them on credit. The rates of interest were even higher here than in Chahiwala. For Rs 10 of purchased items, Rs 15 had to be paid back within a year. Interest on credited wheat had to be repaid every six months. For 1 *maund* of credited wheat, 1 *maund* 10 *seer*s had to be repaid within six months, or else the debt was doubled.

When the debtor was landless and without cattle, the debts continued to increase month after month. If he owned land and cattle, he very often had to sell these commodities to pay back his creditor. The creditor himself fixed the sale price and when a buyer could not be found, the assets were transferred into the creditor's name.

The Hindu merchants and usurers were also landowners (see Table 2.1).

Within 90 years, the number of landowners increased five-fold while the cultivable area remained the same. It is interesting to note that the

Table 2.1: Breakdown of Baranpur landowners according to religion before Partition (no. of households)

Year	Hindu	Sikh	Muslim	Total
1860	32 (43%)	34 (46%)	8 (11%)	74
1886	83 (44%)	72 (38%)	35 (18%)	190
1905	67 (30%)	121 (54%)	37 (16%)	225
1947*	131 (35%)	165 (45%)	72 (20%)	368

* These figures are mentioned in the 'Record of Rights' of 1956–57 but they were recorded just before Partition.

largest increase has occurred among members of the Muslim community who did not enjoy the same opportunities for finding employment outside the village as the Hindus, whose number of landowner households decreased by 8 per cent, and the Sikhs who retained almost the same percentage of landowner households throughout the first half of the century. The Muslim community's dependence on land cultivation meant that it was not in a position to improve its economic situation.

Moreover, the increase in the number of landowners meant a decrease in the size of landholdings from generation to generation, during which time it was impossible to improve production due to the absence of means of irrigation. Before the arrival of modern techniques of cultivation, agricultural production was very limited. Many elderly villagers remember their fathers talking about years with no crops because of droughts. At one point at the end of the last century, the situation was so critical that the price of flour was called *daya seer kal*, the Punjabi words for 2.5 and famine. Two-and-a-half *seers* of wheat flour cost Rs 1. To compare, one could buy 25–28 *seers* for the same price just before Partition. Even though a severe drought has not occurred again during this century, many villagers have experienced great poverty and hunger.

The activities of the Hindus in the marketplace prevented them from tilling their land themselves. Their high incomes as merchants and usurers enabled them to have tenants and pay them with half of the yield. It explains why, already in 1905, all the Hindu landowners rented their land out to tenants (see Table 2.2). Seasonal labourers were hired. They were remunerated one bundle of wheat for every 25 bundles cut, (i.e. 1/25th part of the yield against 1/5th today).

Table 2.2: Breakdown of Baranpur tenants according to religion before Partition (no. of households)

Year	Hindu	Sikh	Muslim	Total
1860	3 (43%)	–	4 (57%)	7
1886	39 (66%)	1 (2%)	19 (32%)	59
1905	74 (55%)	–	60 (45%)	134
1947	n.d.	n.d.	n.d.	n.d.

At the opposite end of the scale, almost all the landowners from the Sikh and Muslim communities were self-cultivators. They needed all the production from their fields for their personal consumption because they did not have lucrative extra jobs besides agriculture. It was very difficult for the peasants to find job opportunities outside the village. Offers were very limited, and consequently there was great competition for land to cultivate on a tenancy basis, since this was usually the only way to improve the family's food rations.

The village's economic situation certainly deteriorated between 1886 and 1905. While the numbers of renting-out landowners and of tenants were identical in 1886, the situation was transformed in 1905, when there were twice as many tenants as renting-out landowners. This is an indication both of the competition among the poorest cultivators for access to small supplementary acreages of land to cultivate and of the strong socio-economic position of the more wealthy landowners.

All the members of the Hindu community were far from being rich merchants. Information concerning the untouchables of the village was not available but Table 2.2 indicates that 74 members of Hindu households worked as tenants. A few supplementary kilograms of crops were very much appreciated. Hunger affected the poorest households of the three communities equally.

Many villagers were so weak that they could not resist the two plague epidemics which hit the area, first in 1900 and then about 10 to 12 years later. An old woman, called Farman Bi, lived through the second epidemic. She remembers:

> The roofs were *katcha*.[6] Many rats lived there. One day, they began to drop dead on the floor. Because of them, many people got ill. They were ill for between five and seven days and died. They had abscesses under the armpits, in the neck and in the groin. Many families moved out from their houses and lived under tents in the open fields. The men working as soldiers provided the tents. Otherwise, people built shelters with blankets. There was no treatment against this illness, and everyone who became ill died. Every dead person was washed and buried in the regular way. Nobody was afraid to become ill through the contact with the dead because they were close relatives. The Hindus burnt the bodies of their dead by the water stream between Baranpur and *dhok* Dhimal. This plague started suddenly and was over within one month. The families returned to their houses. They cleaned them. They made smoke in the rooms. They spread phenol to kill the remaining insects. They read the Qur'an. They distributed food to the poor and the Qur'an readers. The plague was a punishment of God because it was a sudden disease. We thought that we should pray to God, that He might forgive us for our bad deeds.

The state of poverty was such that many needy Hindus converted to Sikhism at the beginning of this century because the British rulers preferred to recruit soldiers from amongst the Sikh community. The British considered it to be a martial race, and moreover it had not been deeply involved in the 1857 uprising.

The records show that the number of Hindu landowners decreased by 14 per cent between 1886 and 1905, while the number of Sikh landowners increased by 16 per cent (see Table 2.1). The genealogical chart of some landowning families shows this change of faith too (see Appendix 2). They added the term Singh to their previous name. In this way, a Hindu called Pola became Pola Singh.

Another reason given by the villagers for this shift to Sikhism was the impossibility for the Hindus of marrying their daughters in the village because of the exogamous rules within the *biraderi*. They had to travel quite far away to find suitable partners for their children. It is also easier for Hindus to change their religion than it is for believers of other faiths because of the essence of polytheism in Hinduism. Therefore, the conversion to Sikhism was a means of resolving both the economic difficulties and the problems of marriage within the Hindu community.

Many Sikhs lived in Baranpur before Partition. Until the beginning of the century, there were almost as many Sikh landowners as Hindu landowners, but the majority of the Sikh landowners were self-cultivators, with very few tenants. In fact, some Sikhs were literate and could supplement their agricultural production by working as clerks in different government departments, such as the railway department in Rawalpindi or the local court in Gujar Khan. Another job possibility outside the village was the army.

The pay of a soldier (Rs 11 per month and a retirement pension amounting to a quarter or a fifth of this pay) was not sufficient to purchase items which could have greatly improved the standard of living of one's family, but it nevertheless covered the basic needs. Moreover, the army men received free food, accommodation, clothes and medicine. These advantages were a great economic help for the families.

The villagers were usually sent to three types of army corps: the artillery, the cavalry and the infantry. They were engaged in service and held posts like stable-boy, washerman, barber, cook, etc. They travelled to countries such as Burma, Malaysia, Singapore and Iraq with their British regiments.

The Muslim families mainly lived in *dhok* Ghazi and *dhok* Dihmal and occupied the bottom rung of the socio-economic ladder. Some of them were petty landowners but the majority were owner-cum-tenants. There were 60 tenant households against 37 landowner households in 1905. This means that 38 per cent of the tenants were landless compared with the 9 per cent of the Hindu community. To be both landless and Muslim was an unfortunate combination. In fact, religion was undoubtedly significant when a landowner chose a tenant. In 1905 the majority of landowners renting out their land were Hindu (94 per cent), and the percentage of tenants was higher among the Hindus than among the Muslims (55 per cent and 45 per cent respectively). The number of Muslim tenants also increased most rapidly, augmenting threefold between 1886 and 1905 as opposed to 1.9 times for Hindu tenants.

Income from agriculture was very low and the Muslims carried out all kinds of tasks for the Hindus and Sikhs, mostly construction and manual work.

It was also amongst the Muslim community that one found the majority of craftsmen of the village. These accomplished various tasks required by the landowners on the basis of *seypi* relations. They worked as blacksmiths, carpenters, weavers, tailors, printers, dyers, barbers and shoemakers. Some of these tasks were defined by the rules of defilement of the Hindus. For example, Hindus refused water brought by a Muslim water-carrier, and only used the services of Hindu water-carriers. The water-carriers only worked on the occasion of weeding, when the demand for water was high. In everyday life, water was fetched by the women of each community. The village had six wells which the Muslims were allowed to use for washing their clothes or for watering their cattle but not for drinking.

Other craftsmen tended to be found amongst the Hindus and Sikhs because of the obligation of avoiding pollution and the impossibility of Muslims carrying out the required services.

The economic situation of Muslim craftsmen was difficult because the *seypi* payment depended on the yield of the fields. Also illiteracy prevented these villagers from finding work in an office. Moreover, they were not enrolled in the army because the British rulers were very suspicious of the Muslims after the 1857 outbreak, since they were considered to have had the greatest involvement in the uprising.

The Organization of the Social Space

Relationships between the three communities were generally good, especially between the Hindus and Sikhs. The villagers had social contact through their economic relationships in the marketplace, through the *seypi* tasks, and at harvest time when the Hindu and Sikh landowners came to supervise their tenants.

Social ceremonies, like funerals, were occasions for meeting too. Hindus and Sikhs both male and female came to the Muslim houses and vice versa. But Muslims did not attend ceremonies of cremation. Similarly, Hindus and Sikhs did not participate in the funeral prayers of the Muslims.

Nevertheless, the main cause of conflict was religion. This occurred mainly because of the liturgical differences between the three cults. For example, the Muslims had to hide themselves or to go to a Muslim village when they slaughtered a cow, and they blamed the Hindus and Sikhs for not slaughtering animals in the appropriate religious way. The Hindus were irritated by the five daily calls to prayer from the *mullah*.

In Baranpur the primary school for boys, which was built in 1825, was multi-denominational. The teachers were both Hindu and Muslim. No Christian missionaries came to the village, however, since the Hindus and Sikhs forbade them to evangelize. Each faith provided religious education to their youth. As Chaudry Akhbar from Chahiwala said:

> We shared each other's happiness and difficulties. But at the creation of Pakistan, all the relationships between the communities finished. We had lived together economically and socially for many years and we became mortal enemies. Our behaviour towards each other was disgusting and horrible.

The Colonial Rulers

After the annexation of the Punjab to the British Empire in 1849, both villages were submitted to the same colonial rule until Partition in 1947.

The presence of the British was directly felt in the villages for the first time after 1855, when the Settlement Scheme was introduced along with a series of important state measures which ensured the levy of land taxes. All the residential and agricultural areas were measured and land records started to be registered. For this purpose, the colonial administration created several categories of functionaries, like the village registrar (*patwari*), the revenue officer (*gardawar*), the revenue collector at the village level (*lambardar*) with one for each *patti*. The rate of the land revenue was fixed by law. It was deposited by the *lambardar* at the *patwari*'s office at the time of harvest of the winter and summer crops. They received 5 and 11 per cent of the land revenue respectively.

Native officials of the pre-annexation time were maintained because of their efficacy and importance. So too were the revenue collectors (*tehsildars*) who were confirmed in their police and judicial authorities, and the village watchman (*chowkidar*), who was also in charge of maintaining the birth and death records. Other local officials made up the links between the government and the population. These were the police informer (*sufaid posh*), who was responsible for all intelligence information about the social and political situation in the village, and the information officer (*zaildar*), whose duty was to inform the villagers about the policy of the British rulers.

In 1868 all the steps which had been initiated in 1855, gained a legal authority with the introduction of the first Tenancy Act in the Punjab. Rules and conditions of tenancy were recognized and secured. Two categories of tenant were recognized:

- *the occupancy tenant* refers to the cultivator of the same plot of land for 12 years or more, who could become owner of this land. The duration of this tenancy was not fixed.
- *the non-occupancy tenant* refers to a peasant who has cultivated the same plot of land for less than 12 years. In this case, the landowner could break the tenancy contract at any time, although not in the middle of an agricultural season.

It was the tenant's duty to sow the seeds and to cut the crops. He did not ask for the help of casual labourers for the harvest in order to keep the maximum quantity of crops for himself.

Payment of the tenancy rent was fixed. Half of the production was given to the tenant where the landowner himself provided the water. This payment occurred after the two parties had equally remunerated the craftsmen. Otherwise, one-third was kept by the tenant, one-third was given to the man supplying the water, and the final third went to the landowner. The tenants had the right to plant trees, but only the occupancy tenants could keep the income earned through these.

In Chahiwala until 1931, the tenant could not receive husk, wheat-sticks and maize-sticks from the fields which he tilled.

After World War I, the British rulers implemented the *taccavi* loan system. Its aim was to improve the villagers' economic situation by increasing their consumption and raising their cultivation. If someone wanted to obtain a *taccavi* loan to buy consumer goods (for example rice, wheat, or spices), he did not have to pay interest. On the other hand, if a landowner obtained a *taccavi* loan to purchase bullocks for his cultivation or to dig a well, interest was levied and some of his land was mortgaged as a guarantee.

Until the end of World War II, the yearly tax on land revenue was 75 *paisas*–1 Rs per acre, and on the trade of buffalo, Rs 5–7 per buffalo. The Muslims were often unable to pay the government taxes, especially when they had to be given in cash instead of grain, as was the practice when the area was under Sikh rule. Muslim cultivators were therefore obliged to borrow money from the Hindus since they did not produce enough to sell part of their harvest on the open market. For others, this economic burden forced them to emigrate to the irrigated areas in the south of Punjab (for example the area of Bahawalpur), where they worked as casual labourers.

During the two world wars, the criteria for army recruitment were not as stringent as they used to be during peace time because the British needed troops from the colonies. Different attractive incentives were offered. For instance a Rs 50 reward was paid to any man enrolling during World War I. Promises of political independence were elements of the propaganda rhetoric during World War II which was spread by the local representatives of the colonial administration. The villagers were told about the causes of the war and the necessity to defend democracy. There were rumours that the British enrolled men by force, but this did not happen in the two villages.

More villagers than usual became soldiers, not because of ideological identification with the British propaganda but for economic reasons. War made it easier to gain access to the sorely needed income which a soldier's pay represented. When the hostilities ended, many villagers were demobilized without a pension since they did not fulfil the criteria to receive one. They returned to their previous occupations.

The two world wars had different impacts in the two villages. In the Baranpur area many more men joined the army than in the Chahiwala area. This was mainly because of the the more limited agricultural production in the rainfed area. This difference could partly explain the violent clashes which took place in Baranpur in 1947. Demobilization sent men back home with an increased understanding of their political rights.

The burden of war was also economic, since higher taxes were levied during these crises for the war loan and the price of consumption goods greatly increased.

The Time of Partition

In Chahiwala no clashes occurred between Hindus, Sikhs and Muslims at Partition. The Hindus left the village, not because they were violently expelled by the Muslims but because they were afraid of the whole situation. They thought that it was only a temporary crisis and that they would be able to return later. In order to decide whether they should leave or not, the Hindus threw a plate of oil with a lit wick into a well. If it continued to burn, they believed that they should remain in the village. But at every attempt, the flame went out. So the Hindus understood that they had to depart from the village. A camp for Hindu refugees was established near Pasrur. They were psychologically very depressed and demanded the help of the Muslim landowners. They took their movable belongings with them, including their cattle. They hid money and gold in their shoes. However, they did not ask for the payment of the debts and asked their Muslim friends in the village to keep their granaries of wheat.

Some Muslim villagers who worked as shopkeepers for the Hindus took over their shops and others took their property.

Conversely, the period of Partition was more violent in Baranpur. Just before the wheat harvest of 1947, the town was deserted by all its inhabitants because of the regular raids organized by Muslim groups from other villages against the Hindus and Sikhs. The latter left the village for Gujar Khan with all the goods they could carry, while the Muslim inhabitants fled to the village of Moolta Moora where many Muslim landowners lived: they felt safer there. However, the Muslim cultivators, who were tenants of the Hindus and Sikhs, harvested the fields and gave the share of the production to the landowners. There was no hatred between people of the same town or village.

Baranpur was destroyed and burnt like other places in the area where Hindus and Sikhs had lived. These actions were in retaliation against the destruction of Muslim properties in India. After three months, the Muslim community returned and found their houses had not been burnt. The damage was restricted to the Hindu and Sikh properties.

From Partition until Today

Many Muslim refugees coming from India passed through Chahiwala just after Partition. They stayed one or two nights and snatched whatever they could carry from the Hindu houses. Later, 18 families were sent by the Pakistani government as a part of its resettlement policy. They were given land and shops by the authorities but they did not like to be in the village because it was economically difficult to manage. Their traditional profession was fishing and they belonged to the Mahergir *zat*. After two years, all of them had left and some of the villagers appropriated their possessions.

Slowly, with the Hindu usurers' departure, the Muslim community became better off. There were no longer professional moneylenders. When someone needed money, they could borrow without interest from friends and relatives. People generally felt more free, united and hopeful about the future. They did not have to worry about belonging to a religious minority as they did in British India.

A second reason for the improvement of the economic situation was the good production of wheat and fodder for several years in a row during the late 1940s and the beginning of the 1950s due to adequate rainfalls.

A third reason was the digging of the Upper Marala–Ravi link in 1954. Although it was not designed to provide water to this area, the surface of the underground water rose, and it became easier to sink tubewells. The villagers began to send their children to school now that they could afford it. They started to eat rice more often and to buy china which they displayed on the shelves of the sitting-room of the house. The living standard of the village improved further with the electricity connection in 1978.

The situation changed more radically in Baranpur. At the beginning of 1948, 15 families came from India to what was left of the town. They received some of the land vacated by the Hindus and Sikhs. However, before long they left again because of the hostile attitude of the native population towards them. The fields they vacated then started to be tilled by the native Muslims who had returned to Baranpur.

In 1953, a massive flow of refugees arrived in the village as a consequence of the government's refugee rehabilitation policy. They came mostly from Kashmir where they were cultivators. They first stayed in refugee camps for six years and were then transferred to different villages.

One refugee, called Pinda Khan, wrote a diary during these tumultuous days. His son showed it to me. It says:

> The enemy took over the area of Rajouri and Punch [in Kashmir] in October 1948. In the middle of the night, our family fled from Pumbergali and from there, with all the children, we reached Sehra Tata Pani. We remained there for one night. Suddenly, firing started in the area and some refugees were killed. We escaped to the village of Plag near Mirpur. There, we found trucks sent by the Pakistani government. They transported us to different refugee camps (*chak* Jahmal, Wah Camp and Baranpur).

> For one year the refugees could travel without paying fares and at the beginning they received free food with a system of ration cards. It was easy and peaceful to live on this food supplied by the government.
>
> In 1953, the government decided to give residential and agricultural land to the refugees because they did not feel healthy in the refugee camps. When the government announced this programme, all the refugees were very happy and they shouted *Pakistan Zindabad* (long live Pakistan). It was the government's policy to give 20 *kanals* of land to each member of a family. By this procedure, the Pakistanis started to rehabilitate the refugees. We are happy to live in good conditions thanks to the grace of God and to the efforts and kindness of the Pakistani government.

When the refugees arrived in Baranpur, the Hindu and Sikh houses were still in ruins. The native Muslims had not occupied them and the refugees began to rebuild them.

The native villagers had to hand over to the refugees the land of the Hindus and Sikhs which they had been cultivating. This did not occur without dispute and bitterness, even though the native people knew that it was not their property and that they would have to give it back one day. The refugees had to enlist the help of the *tehsildar* and other officials of the Revenue Committee in order to have their rights respected. The size of distributed land depended on the number of members in a family. The rate was 20 *kanals* or 2.5 acres per person with a maximum of 100 *kanals* or 12.5 acres for a family of five persons or more. The ration cards, which were issued in the refugee camps, were used as a means of combatting fraud. The land was given to the refugees as a provisory allotment and therefore it could not be sold. After some years, when they had paid fees to the government, the refugees became permanent owners and were then allowed to sell their holding, which many did.

At the first harvest after their arrival, the refugees kept half of the production, while the other half went to the native Muslims who had cultivated the fields. It took several years before the refugees could begin to cultivate the land themselves, since they arrived without agricultural implements or working animals. During this period most of them rented out their new property to the peasants who were already cultivating it. The production was divided into two equal shares. Some of the refugees obtained *taccavi* loans from the government to buy agricultural tools. The maximum loans were of Rs 1,000 without interest for the first three years, and with a 5 per cent yearly interest thereafter. In the early 1950s, a family could purchase two bullocks, one plough, one yoke and one levelling beam for Rs 200.

The early years of cultivation only yielded wheat for a five-to-six month period. However, many refugees did not take advantage of a government loan because they were afraid of not being able to pay it back within the due time. Instead they preferred to work as unskilled labourers, mostly on construction sites in Rawalpindi or Gujar Khan. It was difficult but not impossible to get a job. Every day, people walked the 5 miles between Baranpur and Gujar Khan and asked around for work. The average daily wage was 8 *ana*s, and Rs 1.4 *ana*s for the best workers.

All in all, 304 refugees from 17 different *zat*s received land in the 1950s. The number of Hindu and Sikh landowners who fled from the village was 296. The native Muslim population could not therefore increase the size of their landholdings.

Until the 1970s, money was not used in the daily economy. People were short of cash and therefore exchanged goods. Wheat was the commodity used as a standard. Before World War II, 1 rupee was equal to 30 *seer*s of wheat, which is equivalent to 27 kg. If a man had a sufficient amount of wheat, he could sell it at the market or exchange it. A barter economy ran parallel with a cash economy. The most important condition was to possess wheat. This system was practised by those households which were making a living only from cultivation and which consumed the greatest part of their meagre production. In other words, these were households where no one was in the army or had a job outside the village. Nowadays, nobody is willing to exchange goods because of the high price of wheat on the market. It is more advantageous to sell it. The bartering of goods ceased during the 1970s when people began to go abroad and to have access to more cash.

The Demographic Situation in the Two Villages

The ten-yearly censuses since 1886 and my own calculation for 1982 show that the population has increased regularly in Chahiwala during the century, from 947 persons in 176 households (mean size of household: 5.3 persons) to 1,392 persons in 216 households (mean size of household: 6.7 persons). Nowhere in Chahiwala are there any signs which indicate that the number of households was larger in the past or that damage occurred at the time of Partition which led to the inhabitants' departure. Discussions with elders offer the same conclusion.

In Baranpur, however, the dramatic events at the time of Partition resulted in a drastic fall in population: from 2,944 in 1947 to 280 persons in 1951. However this reduction was only temporary. Even though economic transformations led to an increased flow of rural–urban migration, these departures have not modified the pressure upon the land and the need for non-farming sources of income because the population of Baranpur has continued to increase since the 1950s. It has more than doubled since the 1961 census and the average number of members in the household has increased by 45 per cent. In 1982, the population consisted of 910 persons distributed over 135 households (mean size of household: 6.7 persons). The same tendency has occurred in Chahiwala with a 46-per-cent growth of the total population. This demographic expansion has worsened the villagers' economic situation.

Table 2.3: Distribution of craftsmen in Chahiwala village (1981)

Occupation	No. of households
1) Blacksmith–carpenter	20
2) Bard and holder of the landowner's genealogy (*Merassi*)*	6
3) Weaver (*Goundal*)	4
4) Weaver (*Bhatti*)	5
5) Caretaker (*Ghuman Fakir*)	8
6) Caretaker (*Joya Fakir*)	15
7) Barber	7
8) Shoemaker	7
9) Christian people (various activities)	8
10) Kashmiri people (various activities but especially shopkeepers)	7
11) Water-carrier	10

* The term in brackets refers to the name of the *zat*.

Chahiwala consists of 216 households. There are 97 households of craftsmen categorized by occupation (see Table 2.3). The blacksmiths, the carpenters and the Christians are involved in agricultural activities. The class of landowners consists of 119 households divided into six *zats* (see Table 2.4).

Table 2.4: Distribution of the landowners' *zat* in Chahiwala village (1981)

Zat names	No. of households
1) *Jat Virck*	108
2) *Jat Bajwa*	2
3) *Jat Kharl*	3
4) *Jat Guria*	1
5) *Jat Blagan*	4
6) *Jat Ghoki*	1

In Baranpur there are 21 households of the class of craftsmen distributed among 6 *zats*:[7] *Awan* (7) (shoemaker), *Awan Qutab Shahi* (5) (various occupations), *Khokar Qutab Shahi* (2) (weaver), *Gondal* (1) (barber), *Monghal* (3) (tailor and blacksmith), *Rajput Janjua* (3) (weaver). Except for the barber, all these households are native villagers.

There are 114 households of landowner class; these belong to 17 different *zats*, either native to the village or displaced from India at Partition:

- refugees included the *Syed* (1), *Rajput Bhatti* (5), *Rajput Munhal* (46), *Rajput Kalotri* (5) and *Rajput Minhas* (1);
- migrants from another area in Pakistan comprised the *Rajput Hernial* (1) *Rajput Kalotri* (1) and *Mughal* (3);
- native to the village were *Rajput Dihmal* (23), *Rajput Nangial* (7), *Rajput Dar* (3), *Monghal* (3), *Mughal Kashmiri* (3), *Mughal Pathan* (2), *Mughal Bhutt* (1), *Mughal Meer* (1), *Sheikh Mughal* (1) and *Sheikh* (2).

The differences in the economic situation between the two villages are reflected in the ratio of landowners/craftsmen. In Chahiwala the population is almost equally distributed between the two social classes (55 and

45 per cent respectively). In Baranpur, the still very mediocre agricultural conditions have led to a transformation of the social composition to one with 85 per cent landowner households and 15 per cent craftsmen's households, since many of the latter have migrated to towns. In other words, life in Chahiwala still follows an old pattern whereby the landowners socially and economically control the landless people's lives, often through coercive means. In each village one *biraderi* of landowners is largely dominant (the *Jat Virck* in Chahiwala and the *Rajput Munhal* in Baranpur). This is obviously important for an understanding of the political life in the villages. Even if there are factions within the *biraderis*, to know that one's own *biraderi* is the most dominant gives a feeling of superiority and strength to its members.

In Chahiwala, the actual settlement of the population confirms the spatial distribution of the different religious creeds before Partition. In Baranpur, craftsmen are still found in the two hamlets at the periphery of the village and are native to the area. The refugee population is made of landowners and is settled in centre of the village. These people have occupied the place vacated by the departure of the Hindus and Sikhs. Demographically, the native landowners of the *zat Rajput Dihmal* have been surpassed by the arrival of a very heterogeneous flow of refugees from India, which today explains the presence of a great number of different landowner *zats* without kinship relations to each other.

This geographical distribution of the inhabitants is the first source of conflict between the three parts of the village, with the two hamlets (*dhok* Dihmal and *dhok* Ghazi) inhabited by native Muslims on the one side, and the centre of Baranpur inhabited by the refugees on the other side. This community is perceived by the native population as united besides being numerically stronger, and they are still called refugees (*mohajar*) decades after their arrival in the village. They have never been really accepted by the native villagers, who think that they still might return to India.

The second source of conflict, which is directly related to the first one, is the allocation of land made to the refugee landowners in the 1950s. The native landowners have never been satisfied with this policy, and consider that the refugees have taken their land. The loose type of affiliation to the land, which the refugees are believed to have, strengthens the native population's feeling that the refugees do not consider this place as their home. They are criticized for selling their land when they are in need of money. The native families buy their fields and think that it is shameful to market one's property because 'Land is just like a mother. It gives everything.'

Another example of the absence of strong village affiliation by the refugee population is their lack of interest in communal matters. A project to build paved streets in the village was proposed on a self-help basis. In this type of project, if the village community is able to finance 30 per cent of the costs, the government provides the remaining 70 per cent. Only Rs 1,400 of the required Rs 3,000 were collected from among the refugee families of Baranpur while Rs 5,000 were supplied by the native population of the two hamlets. This rivalry between the two communities leads to infrequent social interaction. It is hardly surprising then that they do not intermarry.

Table 2.5: Breakdown of the Chahiwala population in 1982

Class	**Adults**			**Children under 15**			**Total**		
	M	**F**	**Total**	**M**	**F**	**Total**	**M**	**F**	**Total**
Craftsmen	142	146	288	149	141	290	291	287	578
Landowners	236	197	433	185	196	381	421	393	814
Total	378	343	721	334	337	671	712	680	1392

Children under 15 make up 48.2 per cent of the total population. This is an important figure since the present generation of landowners will not be able to pass on to the next generation landholdings of a sufficient size to make a living. The landowners' rural–urban migration will increase and consequently the craftsmen's economic resources will diminish. The landless people will continue to leave the village as they have done over the past two decades.

Another important observation is the high difference in the sex ratio among the landowners, namely 54.5 per cent of men versus 45.5 per cent of women. This factor should be taken into account when one tries to understand the number of disputes about women which occur in the village.

These figures highlight two other facts in the village. First, they indicate an higher death rate among adult women since the discrepancy in the sex ratio is not as high among the population under 15. Second, they illustrate the marriage customs. When a family has daughters and sons in succession, the former have to be married first for the sake of protecting the family's honour. As the form of residence is virilocal, the daughter leaves her parents' village after marriage. Moreover, due to the dowry system, the family has to face very high expenses and the sons must then wait for their turn after all their sisters have been married. Consequently, the arrival of new brides from other villages is postponed. This is another reason for the lower number of adult women.

Table 2.6: Breakdown of the Baranpur population in 1982

Class	Adults			Children under 15			Total		
	M	F	Total	M	F	Total	M	F	Total
Craftsmen	43	44	87	27	24	51	70	68	138
Landowners	226	187	413	202	157	359	428	344	772
Total	269	231	500	229	181	410	498	412	910

By comparing Tables 2.5 and 2.6, one can see that proportionately the population shows similarities in both villages, except for the number of craftsmen, as previously mentioned. The sex ratio for the whole village and for the landowners is identical (1.20). The discrepancy in favour of the male population does not solely explain the feuds of Chahiwala. If a lack of women was the main cause of disputes, they would also occur in Baranpur. Supplementary reasons therefore have to be found.

The child population is also very high in Baranpur (45 per cent of the total population). This should not be a surprise since no birth control policy is seriously implemented in the rural area of Pakistan.

Civic Facilities in the Villages

Chahiwala and Baranpur lack an adequate infrastructure to make the people's lives less constraining. Both villages have a boys' school but the buildings are in such a bad condition that heavy rain seeps through the roof, and thus, the pupils sit outside on the ground under the trees most of the year.

The building of a new girls' school has never been finished in Chahiwala due to disagreement between factions in the village. Consequently, it is

Figure 3: Boys' school in Chahiwala

difficult to find a female school-teacher who is prepared to work permanently in the open air with no proper walls around the school-yard as a symbolic protection from foreign men. Like any other traditional Pakistani woman, the school-teacher observes the rules of gender apartheid (*purdah*), especially since she would be a stranger to the village community, as no women of the village are sufficiently educated to take up the job.

The situation is similar in Baranpur, where the villagers took the initiative first to collect Rs 2 from each female pupil, and since this was not sufficient, subsequently to ask for Rs 5 from each household to build a wall around the yard of the girls' school.

Figure 4: Girls' school in Chahiwala

Parents think that it is a good example for their daughters to see that female teachers coming from the city observe *purdah* because it is commonly believed that education can have a negative effect upon a woman's moral character. In fact, female education is not considered a priority by the majority of the villagers. In their value system the girls' activities in their adult life will be limited to domestic tasks and the rearing of children. When villagers send their daughters to school it is only so that they can write letters to them if they have problems with their husbands and in-laws. They do not want them to acquire some kind of professional qualification in order to earn an income.

Parents' aspirations for male children are more ambitious. They are aware that the village economy cannot support so many labourers in the future and that their sons will have to find jobs in cities and/or foreign countries. To deal with this new situation parents are very strict in the schooling of their sons and complain about the absence of sufficient facilities for technical education. When agriculture becomes an unsatisfactory source of income, attitudes towards vocational training are no longer shaped by the traditional discriminatory beliefs in the lower status of manual work. Parents are therefore ready to spend the Rs 100 on their sons for the yearly expense of books and school uniforms.

Modern medical facilities are non-existent in both villages. In the case of illness, people go to traditional healers and/or Western-educated doctors in the nearby towns. However, there are midwives and a traditional women's doctor (*hakim*) in Chahiwala. Nawal Bibi learned this skill from her mother and brother but did not practise it. It was her husband's death, when she was only 25 years old, that compelled her to start this profession as it was the only way she could make a living. She also teaches the Qur'an. Another widow and a crippled woman also teach the Qur'an in their houses and complement the Qur'anic lessons provided by the *mullah* in the mosque. These women complain about the parents' lack of respect towards them as Qur'anic teachers, and about their ignorance concerning the importance of a religious education. Their pupils represent only a fraction of the total number of children in the villages. They also complain about their remuneration, which is their only source of income. They are paid only after the reaping of crops and the amount is not fixed.

A UNICEF inquiry into the health and hygienic situation, which was conducted in Baranpur at the beginning of 1982, indicates that the water supply comprises seven handpumps (although I counted 10), four wells and four ponds. All the drains are open and uncemented. Rubbish is thrown in the fields and some of the village streets are polluted by human faeces.

The villagers were asked their opinion on basic necessities which are missing in the village. In their answers, they gave priority in a decreasing order of importance to the construction of latrines, the installation of handpumps in houses, the amelioration of the school facilities, and the creation of cottage-industry jobs for women.

The situation is a little better in Chahiwala with 77 per cent and 48 per cent of landowner's and craftsmen's households respectively having handpumps in the yard. Electricity has been installed in 16 per cent of the landowners' households, and 9 per cent of the craftsmens' households.

To summarize this general introduction of the two villages, it can be said that poverty, indebtedness, malnutrition and even starvation during periods of drought characterized most villagers' lives until Partition. Even though their living standards have greatly improved since independence,

Figure 5: The Qur'anic school in Chahiwala

economic conditions for a majority of households are still unsatisfactory. Basic facilities like running water, latrines, sewage systems, drains, medical assistance for people and animals, adequate schooling opportunities for both genders, and link roads are absent in the two villages. Baranpur has even more acute needs since no electricity supply has yet been installed and very few houses are equipped with a handpump in the yard.

These unsatisfactory living conditions are the main cause of international labour migration. The villagers' constant worry is how to improve the subsistence of their families. In order to build up a picture of their ability to cover their basic needs, we shall next discuss the economy in both villages at the beginning of the 1980s.

Notes

1 McKim Marriott (1960); Gerald Berreman (1963); Fredrik Barth (1959 and 1960); Saghir Ahmad (1970 and 1977); Akbar S. Ahmed (1976 and 1980); Mattisan Mines (1972); Muhammad Rafique Raza (1969); Hamza A. Alavi (1972); Tariq Mahmood (1981).

2 The landowners call the people who do not belong to the landowners' *quoms* their *kammis* (village servants). To avoid this pejorative connotation, *kammi* has been translated throughout the book into the term 'craftsman'. It refers to the various types of tradespeople who provide their traditional skills to the other

villagers, whether agricultural or not.

3 With the geographically wide dispersion of the members of the patrilineal descent groups, villagers also commonly refer to their *zat*s as their *biraderi*s (H. Alavi, 1972, p. 25).

4 A *patti* is both a social division and the spatial expression of a landowner's sub-lineage, which are associated with the necessary *zat*s of craftsmen.

5 As is discussed in the next chapter, a distinction is made between three types of landowners:

- *self-cultivator* refers to a landowner who cultivates only the land he owns;
- *owner-cum-tenant* refers to a landowner who cultivates partly his own land, and partly the land rented from other landowners;
- *renting-out landowner* refers to a landowner who rents out part or all of his land.

6 A *katcha* roof is a roof made of several layers of wood, straw and dry clay.

7 The figures in parentheses indicate the number of households for each *zat*.

3 TRADITIONAL SOURCES OF INCOME IN THE VILLAGES

The necessity of improving the economy of the household is the sole motivation for obtaining a work-contract in a Middle Eastern or European country. A man's departure from the village has nothing to do with the desire to live in a new socio-cultural environment or with political disagreement with the Pakistani rulers, or with the intention of acquiring a professional skill. People are very emotionally attached to their village, which is the land of their ancestors, regardless of how many generations have lived there.

The overall assumption guiding this study is of a direct relationship between the level of the subsistence economy and the size of the international labour migration: in other words, the higher the agricultural output, the less necessary is the villagers' departure to a foreign country. Consequently the migration ratio should be lower in the village with irrigated agriculture, where the tillage of land gives higher yields and fairer payment to the landless craftsmen than in the village with rainfed agriculture.

In order to verify this hypothesis, the sources of income available in a village will be analysed. The villagers have traditionally been occupied in three types of activities, namely agriculture, cattle rearing and craft industries. The two first types will be examined in this chapter to determine the economic situation of the cultivators' households and their ability to ensure their social, economic and ideological reproduction.

Types of Land

In Chahiwala, the soil is generally fertile but rather sandy in some places. The average rainfall is moderate (up to 1,000 mm yearly), reliable and relatively well distributed through the year. The highest rainfall occurs between July and September, and the dry months are May, June, October and November. Rainfed cultivation is therefore possible for the summer and winter crops.

Until the end of the 1960s, 72.5 per cent of the cultivated land was occupied by rainfed agriculture (*barani* land). However, the groundwater has enabled cultivation through well-irrigation for many generations, although in a smaller area. In 1972, 27.5 per cent of the fields were irrigated through wells. This category of land is called *chahi* land from the Urdu *chah*, meaning well.

An important change occurred during the 1970s with the sinking of many tubewells which replaced the old Persian wheels. Although some tubewells were already found in the village in the 1960s, their number greatly increased over the following 15 years because of the raising of the groundwater due to the construction of a canal. More and more fields were irrigated through this technique.

The land irrigated by tubewell is called *nal chahi* land (from the Urdu *nal*, meaning pipe or tube). In 1979 this land represented 36.7 per cent of the total cultivated area. This new watering technique has increased the amount of irrigated land to more than 66 per cent of the cultivated area, although on the down side waterlogging and salinity have begun to appear in some of the fields. In the last 70 years the uncultivable area has doubled and now makes up 12.3 per cent of the total land of the village.

The average acreage of field has hardly changed since the beginning of the century. In 1918 the average field was 0.3 acre. By 1979 it had only increased to 0.45 acre. Because of the absence of new available land to cultivate and population pressures, the farmers could not improve their productivity until the arrival of the Green Revolution, which allowed for an agriculture based on a land-saving technology.

The distance between the cultivated plot and the village is another distinction the villagers make when they talk about categories of holdings.

Figure 6: Traditional form of ploughing (Chahiwala)

Fields situated near the village are called *nai.* To this term is added the type of irrigation used which gives a more precise taxonomy:

- *nai chahi* fields, i.e. fields near the village and irrigated by a well;
- *nai nal chahi* fields, i.e. fields near the village and irrigated by a tubewell.

The price of land depends on a combination of the localization of the fields with the form of watering. It is an advantage to own an irrigated field near the village estimated at Rs 30,000 per acre, since the cultivator saves time going back and forth. Moreover, the quality of the land is very good there. Similarly, plots situated near the main road are in great demand (Rs 20,000 per acre). It is very convenient to transport the produce to the town if one has direct access to the fields with a trolley or an ox-cart.

The low price of land situated near the canal is not surprising (Rs 18,000 per acre) since irrigation in these fields is not provided by the canal but by tubewells. In addition, the quality of soil is not very good here because of its sandy texture.

In Baranpur too, the cultivated acreage has not increased in proportion to the number of cultivators. In 1860, 386 acres were tilled and divided into 1,182 plots. In 1981, the corresponding figures were 517acres and

1,564 plots. It means that the average crop holding per able-bodied cultivator has remained at 0.32 acre for the last 120 years. The density of the population has led to this heavy pressure on land. It is likely that the peasants have now cultivated the total fertile area since its size has only increased by 6 acres since 1860. Generally, the agricultural conditions are much less favourable in Baranpur than in Chahiwala. Beside their dependency on rainfall – only 3 acres (0.5 per cent) are irrigated by hydraulic means – the cultivators of Baranpur also face the handicap of having only 70.4 per cent of arable land compared with the 87.7 per cent in Chahiwala. No new track can be cultivated because of the rocky and infertile nature of the soil. Sometimes a landowner levels his eroded land with a bulldozer to increase the cultivated area but heavy rains wash away the reclaimed fields and bring the terrain back to the preceding topography.

The cultivated land is divided into four categories which have differing market values:

- *lapara* fields; i.e. fields near the village (Rs 32,000– 40,000 per acre);
- *lass* fields, i.e. fields in the bottom of hollows where the rain remains (Rs 24,000–26,000 per acre);
- *maira* fields, i.e. fields at a distance from the village (Rs 20,000–24,000 per acre);
- *rakkar* fields or low quality land (Rs 12,000–16,000 per acre).

The length of fallow is another means of distinguishing between the types of land:

- *banjar qadim* land (old fallow land), i.e. land which has been untilled for four successive years (Rs 12,000–16,000 per acre);
- *banjar jadid* land (new fallow land), i.e. land which has not been brought under cultivation for the past two years (Rs 8,000–10,000 per acre).

Finally, there is also land which is impossible to cultivate (*ghair mumkin*). It is under government control and cannot be sold.

The price of residential land ranges between Rs 40,000 and Rs 80,000 per acre.

Although agricultural conditions are more difficult in Baranpur than in Chahiwala, land prices in Baranpur are more inflated because of the greater scarcity of holdings. In both villages, prices have soared and are totally disproportionate to the peasants' average income. This is one of the most common causes of feuds between people.

Agricultural Technology

The same agricultural technique has been practised in both villages for generations. Changes occurred for the villagers of Chahiwala with an improvement in the watering facilities, leading to a more effective implementation of the Green Revolution than in Baranpur.

Traditional Farm Implements

Every cultivator possesses a minimum quantity of tools for the maintenance of his holding. Their number varies with the size of the farm and the intensity of cultivation. Some of the tools are owned individually, while others are possessed jointly, for instance by a father and his son or by several brothers. The patterns of ownership depend on the frequency of their use and their cost.

A plough, a yoke and a flat plank constitute the basic equipment of the household and define a man's status as a cultivator. The rate of payment of the craftsmen for agricultural tasks is based on the number of ploughs possessed by the cultivator and increases proportionately with it.

Tools are individually owned when they are used daily, such as a sickle for cutting fodder and a trowel for uprooting dried grass to give to the cattle. Commonly owned implements are also either used daily, like a fodder-cutter, or seasonally like a cane-crusher. Many landowners do not own a hand-operated fodder-cutter because of its high cost. They either bring their fodder to the owner of a fodder-cutter, or they cut it with a sickle. A landowner does not use his fodder-cutter for more than a couple of hours a week. This is enough to chop sufficient fodder for the cattle since no one in the village possesses a large herd. His fodder-cutter is then available for those with whom he is on good terms. Finally, tools that are not needed daily are commonly shared by landowners.

In both villages, most of the tools can be purchased in the nearby market towns of Pasrur or Gujar Khan. However, one has to go to a larger city like Sialkot or Rawalpindi for a specific need, for example the sharpening of the fodder-cutter blades.

It is also the duty of the village carpenters and blacksmiths to manufacture and repair tools under the *seypi* relations. As a rule, the peasants prefer the tools manufactured in the village to the ones purchased at the market because they are a little bit cheaper, and are also more solid. However, they are not always available at the village craftsmen's workshop, and an order might not be met in time.

Characteristics of the Main Implements

Until tubewells are available in Chahiwala, the basic agricultural equipment is identical in both villages: the plough (*hal*), yoke (*panjali*), flat plank (*sohaga*) and harrow.

The light model of plough is used, which does not furrow deeply. The heavier type requires stronger animals which the cultivators cannot afford. Wood with different levels of resistance is used according to the specific function of each part of the plough. The plough-beam is built with any kind of ordinary wood like *acacia arabica* (*kirkar*). The central part of the plough-beam is made of a very strong wood, *dalbergia sissoo* (*shisham*) or *melia acedarach* (*dhrek*), while the bottom of the plough is made of acacia wood. There is no guarantee for how long a plough will last. It can last up to four years, but a piece could suddenly break. Its total cost at the marketplace is Rs 300. The carpenter assembles its main parts and receives Rs 15 for this work.

There are two models of yoke (*panjali*). One type is used for ploughing and the other for circular track work like the grinding of crops or using the fodder-cutter. This latter model is shorter in order to reduce the distance walked by the bullock, which is yoked on the right side. The yoke consists of several pieces. The upper part resting on the neck of the bullock (*jula*) is the main component. It is made of *melia acedarach* wood, which is both soft and strong. It can break at any time, but lasts, on the average, four to five years like the plough. It costs Rs 50 at the marketplace. The yoke-pins (*arlies*) and the lower part of the yoke placed, against the chest of the bullock (*phat*) are made of acacia wood or any other kind of wood found around the village.

The flat plank (*sohaga*) is made of heavy timber and is powered by a pair of bullocks. It breaks the clods of earth after ploughing and levels the fields after sowing so as to retain the moisture in the soil. The flat plank is made of *dalbergia sisoo*, or *melia acedarach wood*. It costs Rs 150–200 at the marketplace, and when it is made by the carpenter the payment is included in the *seypi* relationships. It lasts from five to seven years.

The harrow, which has a V-shape for traction by bullocks, costs Rs 300 and lasts up to two years.

The cultivators also use several other implements daily: the sickle, a ladder and twine (*rassa*). The sickle is used for cutting grass or a larger size is used for harvesting wheat and rice. After two to three days of wheat cutting, the blade has to be sharpened by the blacksmith. During the rice harvest, this is necessary every four to six days. The handle is made of acacia wood. When it breaks, the carpenter repairs it or the peasant purchases a new one at the marketplace. A sickle costs Rs 10–60 and lasts two years. The cultivators do not use tools for threshing the crops. The sheaves of wheat and rice are either beaten with drums or wooden beams, or trampled by bullocks.

There is a ladder in every house. It is made of trees found around the village and is available at the carpenter's workshop. Its price is Rs 100 at the marketplace and it lasts two years.

Twine (*rassa*) is used for many purposes, such as tying up the cattle or constructing woven beds (*charpai*). In Chahiwala, it is made of a variety of fibres called *shorea robusta* (*san sutri*), which grow in the fields nearby. The stalk is immersed in water for 12 days, which makes it easier to unravel the fragile peel. The fibrous heart of the plant is then rolled up on itself to obtain a twine. This operation is repeated as many times as desired. The price at the marketplace is Rs 15 per kg for a thin twine and Rs 45 for a thick one.

In connection with the tending of cattle, several implements are used: sticks, stakes (*kila*), baskets, a piece of material, a fodder-cutter, blinkers and a cattle trough.

Sticks are used for guiding the cattle into the fields and for protection against dogs, snakes or enemies. The villagers make them from acacia or from branches of trees found around the village. They can also buy them at the marketplace for Rs 5 and they are made of *olea cuspidata* (*kao*).

Stakes (*kila*) are driven into the ground and the animals are tied up to them. They are made of acacia or *dichopsis polyantha* (*tali*) and are obtained from the carpenter under the *seypi* relationship or sometimes from the marketplace for Rs 2. They last two to three months.

Baskets are used for carrying the fodder. They are made from the stalks of various plants, such as the *tamarix dioyca* (*pilchi*), or the *morus alba* (*tut*). Every cultivator owns one and it lasts six months.

A piece of material is also used for carrying fodder. Each household purchases a new one for Rs 50 at the marketplace every six months. A fodder-cutter is only available in large cities. It costs Rs 800 and lasts ten years. Blinkers cost Rs 100 and last four years and a cattle trough costs Rs 300 and lasts four years.

Due to the irrigated agriculture, the peasants of Chahiwala also use tools which are not found in Baranpur: ridge-makers and cane-crushers. A ridge-maker costs Rs 20 at the marketplace and is paid for through *seypi* remunerations when it is obtained from the carpenter. A good ridge-maker may last five years. The peasants of Chahiwala purchase a cane-crusher for Rs 5,000 in Faisalabad, a city which is a three-hour bus ride away. This tool lasts 10 years.

Access to Water

Quantity, adequate timing and regularity of water available for irrigation are the key-words for improved agricultural output. These are the main differences between the two villages. Positive changes in agricultural conditions in Chahiwala are however, relatively recent.

In fact, the area of Chahiwala used to be famous for its shortage of water. I once heard a story about a woman coming from another village where water was plentiful. She married a man of Chahiwala and moved in with him. When she noticed the lack of water, she became sad and upset. During one of her visits to her parents' village, her family asked her opinion about Chahiwala. She expressed her feelings in a song:

> There is plenty of food to eat in Chahiwala
> But there is shortage of water
> I pay many thanks to God
> When I leave Chahiwala.

However, there was not always as much food as expressed in this song. Most of the agriculture was rainfed. Wheat, chick peas (*gram*) and maize were produced in the winter season. As previously mentioned, production was so low that the peasants had to buy food on credit from the Hindu shopkeepers under a system of compound interest and this led to a vicious circle of dependency.

Only a few fields were irrigated through the method of rain harvesting. Water was collected in ponds and spread in ditches in the fields by cultivators pushing it with shovels. Another traditional form of irrigation – the Persian wheel powered by blindfolded bullocks – was also practised. The Book for the Registered Rights (*Misli Haqiqt Bandobast*) of 1972 indicates that there were 26 wells for irrigation of the fields; 18 of them were not in use at the end of the 1960s. Their depth was between

12–14 m and the water was 2–3 m deep. The quality of the water was called 'thick water'. Only the tracks of land located near the sources of irrigation could yield a small quantity of rice. The land lying farther away from the wells was not cultivated and was used as grazing areas for cattle. Water remained in the irrigation ditches for about a month. Nobody owned it and it was therefore not a commodity which could be sold to other cultivators.

The conditions of cultivation changed radically when the Marala–Ravi link was established in 1954. It is one of the link canals built after independence when the river system of the Indus Basin was divided between India and Pakistan. The Marala–Ravi link connects the rivers Chenab and Ravi and supplies additional water to the Balloki–Sulaimante link which joins the rivers Ravi and Sutlej. Although this canal does not provide irrigation water to the area, it has affected cultivation by bringing the water-table closer to the surface and consequently making the installation of tubewells easier and cheaper. Water flows in the canal only during the three monsoon months (from July to September). The villagers are allowed to take their cattle to drink and to bathe in the canal during this period but it is forbidden to divert some of the water for the irrigation of the fields. Surveyors of the Irrigation Department patrol the banks of the canal, especially at night, to make sure that people do not cut the trees which are planted there, or do not water their plots.

Facilities of irrigation increased again when the village was connected to the electricity network in 1978, since it allowed the installation of electric motors.

According to my census, there were 38 tubewells in Chahiwala in 1981: 32 were powered by diesel engines and 6 by electric motors. The price of a tubewell depends on the length and diameter of the pipe, on the power of the engine, and on the nature of the soil. In Chahiwala, the pipe is on average 12–15 m long with a 15 cm diameter. The engine has a power equivalent to 18 hp. Tubewells cost from Rs 5,500 to 28,000, with most costing between Rs 10,000 and 15,000, which is an amount very few villagers can afford.

The half-yearly costs of operating the diesel and electrically powered tubewells are Rs 4,000 and Rs 2,200 respectively. However, the cultivators prefer the first type because they only have to spend money when the engine runs. The owner of an electrically-operated tubewell, however, has to pay for the meter rent. The installation of an electrically powered tubewell appears therefore to be more costly. Nevertheless, some cultivators have started to switch from diesel to electric engine because of the constant increase in the price of oil. This practice also has government approval in order to restrict the amount of imported oil. The state subsidizes all electric installation for agricultural purposes up to Rs 15,000. If the cost is higher, the peasant has to pay the exceeding amount.

Due to their high cost, the majority of tubewells have been installed on a share basis. Twenty-three tubewells are shared between different partners, while 10 tubewells are owned by a single cultivator. Five households possess and/or have shares in two tubewells. Usually, the shareholders are very close relatives, such as brothers, father and sons, or cousins. They may also be shared by non-relatives whose fields are adjacent. It is not difficult to find someone who wants to be co-owner of a tubewell.

The money required for the installation of a tubewell is usually gathered from various sources: a loan from a bank or from relatives which is added to the income from the sale of cattle and crops. Each cultivator contributes to the expense of using and maintaining the tubewell in proportion to the quantity of shares he owns in it. For example, a villager who owns a third of a tubewell has to pay a third of the total expenses every six months.

It is also possible to become a new shareholder many years after the installation of a tubewell. The new partner then has to pay his contribution to the other shareholders as if the tubewell had just been bought.

The majority of tubewell owners or co-owners are self-cultivators, while among owner-cum-tenants and peasants renting out their land, fewer and fewer tubewell owners are found, since the economic situation of this category of cultivators does not allow them to afford such an investment. Most of the tubewells were installed during the second half of the 1970s: 30 of them (79 per cent) between 1975–81.

Disputes over water do not occur because of its abundance. During the peak periods of irrigation, even if water is requested at the same time by all the shareholders of a tubewell, there is no competition over who should first irrigate his fields. The size of landholdings is so small that one can easily wait one's turn without damaging the crops.

Shareholders have to be on good terms with each other in order to avoid lengthy discussions and disagreements when paying the common bills. If a dispute occurs between two shareholders, a third person is called upon to arbitrate. He establishes the value of the tubewell and asks which of the two disputants is ready to buy the other's share. The evicted co-owner might install a new tubewell on his land or share another tubewell with new partners.

Today, tubewell water surpluses are sold. The majority of households of the categories owner-cum-tenant and renting-out landowner still cannot afford to own a tubewell even on a co-operative basis. But they nevertheless irrigate their fields and this greatly increases their production costs. It costs Rs 30 per acre to irrigate one's fields for a 24-hour period during crop growth, and at the time of harvest the cultivator also has to pay the man providing water one quarter of the production of wheat and fodder, and one-third of the production of rice and sugar cane. The share is higher for the rice and sugar cane because these crops require more water. To own a tubewell is thus a remunerative asset; the peasant takes this into consideration when purchasing one. Four per cent of self-cultivator households possess a tubewell just to sell water surpluses and not to irrigate their fields.

No cultivator owns a tubewell in Baranpur. The small farms do not yield enough to pay for installation, which costs more than in Chahiwala because of the depth of the water table and the rocky nature of the soil. The agriculture in Baranpur totally depends on the quantity and the timing of rainfall. It has to rain two to three times between the end of December and the end of February in order to obtain a good winter wheat. The summer monsoon rains fall during the months of the year with the least cropping intensity. Such dependency on rainfall has not, however, led to the development of techniques for the storage of rainwater.

Impact of the Green Revolution

Both villages began to show interest in the achievements brought about by the Green Revolution during the second half of the 1970s. However, the momentum of adaptation of these new methods of cultivation was determined by the irrigation facilities and therefore they were more rapidly practised in Chahiwala than in Baranpur. Another factor which conditioned the adoption of the new methods was the cultivator's ability to afford greater expenditures.

The new agricultural techniques were implemented through information provided by the government. The cultivators of Chahiwala are able to visit the government Agricultural Department in Pasrur, which provides free technical assistance. However, most cultivators want as little contact as possible with this official institution which they accuse of malpractice.

The peasants of Baranpur have assistance from two field assistants. One lives in Mandra, a town 5 miles from the village, but he does not have time to come to the village himself, since he has responsibility for a very large area comprising five Union Councils. The other field assistant is based in Gujar Khan. He used to visit Baranpur two or three times a year when his post was first created, but his visits have now ceased and he only takes part in the monthly meeting of the Union Council.

Factors which have motivated both sets of villagers to adopt the new agricultural methods include listening to agricultural radio programmes and the impressive results obtained by the first cultivators who used fertilizers and high yield variety (HYV) seeds.

The High Yield Variety (HYV) Seeds

Even before 1975, 30 per cent of the farmers in Chahiwala used HYV seeds. With the improved water supply during the second half of the 1970s, their number increased to 97 per cent. All but five of the cultivators' households without migrants sow HYV seeds, regardless of the size of their fields and the type of land tenure to which they belong.

Different varieties of wheat seeds are available, depending on the season of growth. Each variety costs Rs 175 per 100-kg bag. There are three periods of sowing:

- early sowing (1–15 October): the seeds are of the type Lyallpur 73 and Indus 79. The required quantity is 32–37 kg per acre.
- middle sowing (16 October–15 November): during this period the Sandal and Yakoora seeds are sown. A quantity of 40 kg per acre is recommended.
- late sowing (16 November–end of December): the wheat seeds are the Sona Lika and Bloo Silver varieties, and 45 kg per acre are needed.

As for the rice seeds, two varieties are recommended by the Agricultural Department in Pasrur. One variety is the Basmati 370; 4 kg per acre is required at a cost of Rs 85 per *maund*. The other variety is the IRRI 6, 5–6 kg per acre are recommended, and the price is Rs 55 per *maund*.

The sugar cane seed is of the SAMME variety: 40–45 *maunds* of roots per acre (equivalent to 70–80,000 roots) should be planted during the month of March. These seeds cost Rs 10 per *maund*.

During the *kharif* season, expenditure on seeds, fertilizers and diesel is twice as high as during the *rabi* season.

By contrast, in Baranpur only 81.5 per cent of the cultivators' households buy the improved seeds. The difference is even greater when one compares the size-class category 1 between the two villages. Barely two-thirds of this category of landowners in Baranpur use HYV seeds while almost all of them in Chahiwala do. In Baranpur the peasants also began to sow improved seeds at a later date, namely at the end of the 1970s. Here too, poverty explains the cultivators' difficulties in following this innovation.

The varieties of wheat seed are the *Pothohar* and the *Barani* 70. The seed rate is 28–32 kg per acre for each variety. The sowing time is 10 October–25 November for the Pothohar and 15 October–15 November for the Barani 70. The peasants do not use improved seeds for the cultivation of ground nuts.

Fertilizers

Traditionally peasants are aware of the necessity to regenerate the natural fertility of the soil. They used domestic compost and farmyard manure for this purpose. The village women also mixed farmyard manure with straw as a binding material to plaster the house or make dung-cakes for fuel to avoid paying out for other types of fuel, like kerosene oil (wood being almost non-existent in these rural areas). As a consequence, organic manure which could be used as fertilizer was in short supply until the Green Revolution. This led to a radical improvement with the arrival of nitrogenous and phosphatic chemical fertilizers (the soils in Pakistan are particularly deficient in these two nutrients).

The average price of fertilizers increased by 52 per cent between 1977 and 1982 (from Rs 64 to Rs 97.5 per 50-kg bag). In 1981, Niterophos, Di Am. Phosphate and Urea Large cost Rs 85, 103 and 105 respectively. The absence of a market with fair commercial practices (where it is necessary to have an extensive network of personal relationships to avoid being the victim of black marketeering and adulteration) means that the cultivators have no choice but to pay the asking price. Villagers from

Chahiwala confirm that a 50-kg pack of fertilizer purchased at the government Agricultural Department is adulterated with 10–15 kg of earth and stones. The fertilizer filtered off is sold on the black market. Complaints to senior officials are fruitless, since bags containing the correct weight of fertilizer are always displayed during official inspections. Private dealers do not offer a better service since they also cheat with the weights and sell the embezzled quantity on the black market.

The use of fertilizers is more widespread in Chahiwala than in Baranpur: 97 per cent and 83.5 per cent respectively of the cultivators' households without migrants. The remaining peasants do not have the economic means to buy them and instead use domestic manures. This is particularly true of small landowners of Baranpur: only 67 per cent of the size-class 1 can afford chemical fertilizers as opposed to 92 per cent in Chahiwala. The size of landholding affects the variation in the use of these fertilizers more in Baranpur than in Chahiwala because of the greater uncertainty of the agricultural output in the rainfed area. On the other hand, the type of land tenure does not make a difference in Chahiwala, where the percentage of peasants using fertilizers on their fields is almost the same among the categories of self-cultivators and owner-cum-tenants.

Two-thirds of the Chahiwala cultivators began to use chemical fertilizers in 1975, while the others started at the beginning of the 1970s. In Baranpur chemical fertilizers were not in use before 1978 because the cultivators' dependency on rainfall made them afraid of combining them with domestic seeds. Many households could not afford to purchase both fertilizers and improved seeds. They also feared spreading fertilizers in case the rains failed, losing both crops and fertilizers. They changed their opinion, however, when they saw the first positive results of the more daring cultivators.

Whatever the variety of improved seed crops, the same fertilizers are recommended in both villages.

Pesticides

The protection of crops against diseases and pests is not widespread today; only 11.6 per cent of the cultivators in Chahiwala and none at all in Baranpur spray pesticides in their fields. This is not surprising, since many cultivators cannot pay for an adequate quantity of improved seeds, let alone for pesticides. In Chahiwala, the Pasrur Agricultural Department used to spray pesticides twice a year during each cropping season but this practice has stopped. Consequently, villagers have to risk damage to their crops, which would lead to an increase in household expenditures through the purchase of more food from the shopkeepers in the market-town.

The Mechanization of Agriculture

Another component of the Green Revolution is labour-saving technology through the use of agricultural mechanization. This has had a different impact in each village.

Thirty-three per cent of the non-migrant peasant households in Chahiwala and twice as many in Baranpur regularly hire the service of tractor owners. Although these are very few in number (3 and 4 respectively in Baranpur and Chahiwala and their immediate neighbourhoods) through this practice they have radically transformed the method of cultivation. Tractors have been purchased with remittances sent by relatives working in the Gulf and the Middle East. Their owners sell their services without social discrimination as long as the customer can pay up front. The rate is Rs 50 or Rs 60 per ploughed acre and is indexed to the increase in the price of diesel oil. The rate is also established according to the nature of the soil. Two ploughings are necessary but some peasants make the first one with a tractor and the second with their bullocks so as to save Rs 50.

Sometimes a peasant hires a tractor because his bullocks are ill just at the period of ploughing. For the poorest families Rs 50 is a big expenditure and the peasant hopes that he will be able to save this money in the next cropping season.

A tractor is a source of income not only through the ploughing of others' fields but also through short-haul work in the village vicinity. The cost of transportation of goods, such as bricks, mud, earth, sugar cane, rice-bags, etc., is established according to the distance:

- Chahiwala–Pasrur: Rs 30 (7 miles)
- Chahiwala to a place before Pasrur: Rs 20
- Chahiwala–Gujranwala: Rs 100 (40 miles).

In Chahiwala, the only agricultural machines used are tractors for ploughing while the other agricultural tasks, like cutting, threshing, winnowing and sowing are carried out manually. No one possesses sophisticated implements like a mould-board or disc plough.

The cultivators from Baranpur, however, can hire a privately owned wheat thresher. Its owner, who lives in another village, goes to each of the four threshing grounds of the village when required. He charges Rs 100 per hour for threshing 25 *maunds* of wheat. If the quantity is less, the cultivator pays for the time spent. The threshing grounds are parts of the common land (*shamlat* land) and each landowner owns a share which is proportional to the amount of his production rather than the size of his landholding. This system allows a fairer distribution when plots of land are barren or uncultivated.

Farmers prefer to pay for mechanized threshing instead of doing it with bullocks as in the past. Far too much wheat was wasted when it took two weeks or more to thresh it. Rain, storms or birds could destroy part of it since the villagers could not protect their crops against damage. In reality, they were losing more through the value of destroyed wheat than they have to pay for threshing nowadays.

The greater spreading of agricultural mechanization in Baranpur across all categories of landholding is related to the unsatisfactory physical environment of the rainfed area. As we shall see below, agriculture is no longer the main source of income for the landowners. They want to devote less time to the tillage of the fields because it simply does not pay, and in this situation, agricultural machines are very welcome. They also reduce the number of traction animals which in turn leads to other savings for the household: a saving of labour since the feeding of cattle is time-consuming, and an economic saving through avoiding the purchase of fodder.

However, tractors have not been purchased by cultivators who operate larger than average farms. The economic input of these landowners originates from non-agricultural activities, namely the money remitted from foreign countries. Without this supplementary income, the modernization of agriculture would have occurred at an even slower pace. One could say that labour migration has speeded up the mechanical technology in agriculture, albeit on a small scale.

Patterns of Cultivation

In both villages, two seasons characterize the agricultural production: the winter season (*rabi*) from October to March, and the summer season (*kharif*) from April to September. The two peak periods of work in the fields take place during the sowing from June–July before the beginning of the monsoon, and during the harvest in September–October.

Chahiwala lies in the sub-humid zone where a cropping pattern was traditionally practised with winter crops depending on the moisture in the soil from the monsoon rains. In this system, called *dofasli dosala*, two crops are cultivated over two years on the same plot of land. The rotation was wheat/food grain/fallow/fallow.

Today, land is not generally kept under as long a period of fallow since irrigation ensures that the moisture is sufficient for the regeneration of the soil. At the time of this study only eight households left land fallow and this was only for a period of two months because the soil was particularly sandy.

The cultivators practise a crop rotation according to the following patterns (where (R) stands for *rabi* and (K) for *kharif*):

- wheat (R)/ pulses (R)/ rice (K)/ two weeks fallow/ sugar cane (K)/ cotton (K)/ one month fallow/ fodder: millet and sorghum (K).
- wheat (R)/ oil seed-fodder: Indian rape, mustard and colza (R)/ barley (R)/ rice (K)/ sugar cane (K)/ maize, also used as fodder (K).
- wheat and oil seed-fodder (R)/ rice (K). This is the most common cropping pattern.

Another reason for the difference in cropping rotation is the cultivators' distinction between subsistence crop (wheat in the winter) and cash-crop (rice in the summer). The staple diet is the *chapati*, a pancake-like bread made of wheat flour. Rice is consumed on special occasions, like social ceremonies, religious festivals, and visits from relatives and friends. Therefore, the peasants are reluctant to sell a large part of their wheat at the marketplace. Conversely a great quantity of their rice production is marketed through the crop-agents. The rice which reaches the market is of the best quality, namely the *Basmati* rice, while coarse rice is cultivated for the consumption of the household.

The production per acre of almost all the categories of owner-cum-tenants is higher than that of the corresponding groups of self-cultivators because parts are given to the landowner and the man providing the irrigation water. This division of the yield obliges the owner-cum-tenant to cultivate his land more intensively to obtain a larger output from his labour.

The average production is 15.1 *maunds* and 19.7 *maunds* per acre for wheat and rice respectively. Compared with Baranpur, the cultivators of Chahiwala have a much better chance of meeting their basic needs. Even though the cultivators always complain of lacking money to buy more fertilizers, irrigation has increased the cropping intensity and allows a production of wheat per acre which is three times higher than that in Baranpur. In addition, the cultivators of Chahiwala now have a permanent income through the cultivation of rice varieties which are highly cash intensive. This new economic resource could affect the interest in labour migration.

Fodder is cultivated by the majority of landowners only during the winter season in the sugar cane and cotton fields so as to make use of a maximum acreage from the paddy fields, which give them a large part of their income. When a cultivator increases the size of his holding, he does not proportionately increase the share of land used for the cultivation of fodder. Instead he cultivates more wheat and rice. However, it is very costly for the landowners with the smallest holdings to feed cattle since a fifth of their property is reserved for fodder fields. Land tenure does not influence the size of self-sown fodder either.

In short, even though some households are involved in cattle business, this economic activity only leads to a change in the cultivation pattern in a few cases. Just one cultivator sows a third of his fields with fodder crops. As we shall see below, the villagers own cattle mainly for their private consumption of dairy products and for their use as draught animals.

The wheat season starts in October. The preparation of the wheat seed bed requires four ploughings within a month so as to weed out and to reap the maximum benefit of the moisture of the soil. Few cultivators, however, have enough time and money to do the adequate number of ploughings. The majority of them (67 per cent) use a plough pulled by a pair of bullocks. Two to eight acres can be ploughed in a day with a tractor, depending on whether the soil is soft or not. It is five times faster than when the first ploughing is done with animal traction but the cost is Rs 50 per acre.

The next operation is sowing. The technique of sowing is either by dropping the seeds through a funnel and a tube attached to the plough, or by throwing them. One acre is sown in a day. Then the field is ploughed again, this time twice, and levelled. Four acres of ploughed land

Table 3.1: The agricultural cycle in Chahiwala

Month	Planting operations	Harvesting operations
Chet mid-March–mid-April	planting of sugar cane and sowing of cotton	*rabi* oil seed-fodder
Baisakh mid-April–mid-May	sowing of cotton; irrigation of *kharif* crops	wheat harvest starts
Jeth mid-May–mid-June	sugar cane and cotton weeded and watered; ploughing of paddy fields	wheat cut, threshed and winnowed
Asarh mid-June–mid-July	ploughing of paddy fields; planting of rice; sowing of maize; sugar cane and cotton watered	*rabi* fodder cut
Sawan mid-July–mid-Aug.	sowing of maize; sowing of *kharif* fodder; maize, sugar cane and cotton weeded and watered; start of ploughing of *rabi* crops	grass and weeds are cut for fodder
Bhadon mid-Aug.–mid-Sept.	watering of *kharif* crops; maize and sugar cane weeded; ploughing of *rabi* crops	cutting of grass and weeds
Asuj mid-Sept.–mid-Oct.	*rabi* crops ploughed; wheat sowing	rice and maize
Kartak mid-Oct.–mid-Nov.	wheat ploughing and sowing; *rabi* oil seed-fodder crops sowed	rice cut and threshed; maize cut; cotton picking
Maghar mid-Nov.–mid-Dec.	wheat sowing; *rabi* crops watered	rice threshing; sugar cane
Poh mid-Dec.–mid-Jan.	*rabi* crops watered	sugar cane
Magh mid-Jan.–mid-Feb.	weeding of *rabi* crops	sugar cane and *kharif* fodder cut
Phagan mid-Feb.–mid-March	plough for sugar cane and cotton	

are rolled by a flat plank in one day. After rolling, two men, who operate a ridge-maker, divide the field into small compartments by small ridges of earth in order to facilitate the circulation of irrigation streams. Afterwards the field is watered. Irrigation occurs three times during the growing season (3 hours per acre). The fertilizers are added when the stalks are 5 cm high.

The harvest takes place in April and May. Male kin, friends and hired labourers sit in a squatting position from morning to evening cutting the crops with a sickle. One acre is harvested by four men in one day. The threshing is done by bullocks trampling the sheaves and pulling a wooden beam so as to separate the grain from the sheath. Next comes the winnowing and cleaning of grain, which is done by throwing it up and shaking it in winnowing baskets in order to let the wind blow away the lighter chaff.

The paddy fields require more preparation than the wheat fields before transplanting the seedlings. An average of two months of preparatory work is necessary since more ploughings are required. After paddy-transplanting, the fields are irrigated every 4–5 hours for two months and again for another month after a month's break. During the period of crop growth, the men regularly go and hoe the paddy fields by cutting the wild grass.

The harvesting begins in October and is completed in the second half of November but the agricultural labourers are busy with the threshing until the end of the month by beating bundles of stalks against metal drums or timber beams lying on the ground. A lot of rice and wheat is wasted by this archaic method of threshing. Afterwards, the grain is rattled and swept from the threshing place. Before it has dried in the sun, the rice is brought to the rice dealer at the marketplace. Members of the poorest households collect the wasted stalks and rice from the paddy fields and the threshing places. Traditionally the calendar year begins around the middle of March and the agricultural operations follow the local division of time.

In Baranpur the winter crops are principally wheat and barley (for the flour), oil seeds: mustard and colza (for the oil and fodder), and pulses: lentils (*Lens esculenta*), field peas '*gram*' and '*mattar*' (*Pisum larvers*). The crops are more diversified during the summer with the groundnut, which is cultivated as a cash-crop, food grains like maize and millet which are also given as fodder to the cattle either green or as dried stalks, and pulses such as '*mung*' (*Phaseolus mungo*) and '*mash*' (*Phaseolus radiatus*).

The pattern of cropping is left to the cultivator's choice but almost all of the fields are reserved for wheat during the *rabi* season because it is the villagers' staple diet all year round, while the division is more even between the *kharif* crops. Besides ecological conditions, the cropping pattern also depends on a combination of diverse factors, such as the number of members in the household, the size of the landholding and future costly expenditures such as the marriage of a child. The majority (59 per cent) keep their fields fallow for half a year; others use shorter fallow periods of varying lengths, and only one household does not let their fields lie fallow at all.

The length of the fallow period depends on the quantity of rain and on the time the soil requires to regenerate. When the rainfall is sufficient and at the appropriate time, the peasants keep the fields fallow for a longer period.

In the case of a six-month fallow period, different patterns of crop rotations are followed:

- either the fields are divided into two equal parts. The *rabi* and *kharif* crops are alternately cultivated on the same half portion of land while the other half remains fallow (F = fallow, R = *rabi* and K = *kharif*).

1st year	R+K	F
2nd year	F	R+K

- or the fields are divided into four parts. The *rabi* and *kharif* crops are then tilled on turn.

1st year	R	F	K	F
2nd year	F	R	F	K
3rd year	K	F	R	F
4th year	F	K	F	R
5th year	R	F	K	F

According to this pattern, the fields lie fallow every two years and the total cycle of the crop rotation takes four years. The greatest part of the arable plots is reserved for crop cultivation for domestic and animal consumption for the household.

Farmers' incentive to produce more is not determined in this village by higher market prices for their crops but by lower input expenditures. They primarily want to increase the production for their subsistence, before considering to be cash-crop growers. Only in one household was the production of wheat found to give a marketable surplus. Otherwise, groundnut, which is the cash-crop *par excellence* in the village, is only cultivated by 15 households (25 per cent) on one-quarter to one-fifth of the size of their holdings. They cannot afford to devote more land to this crop which is sold for Rs 200 per 20-kg bag.

There is an inverse relationship between land productivity and farm size. Due to the absence of irrigation, the ecological conditions are identical for all the villagers. Any discrepancies in the average yields are consequently caused by differences in the cultivators' input, both in working hours and in money. However, in the rainfed area more intensive farming does not necessarily give a greater yield. Agriculture is not a profitable activity and some landowners neglect their fields because they prefer to concentrate their efforts on more lucrative sources of income. Nevertheless, for the households with hardly any land and no off-farm activities, the only way to survive is to intensify cultivation. Therefore the quantity of produced wheat per acre is highest on the smallest landholdings.

Today the average yield of wheat per acre is about 5.6 *maunds* (207 kg). This quantity does not cover a household's yearly needs. At worst, a family has wheat for only four months. However, on average, production represents seven to eight months of flour consumption. It all depends on the quantity and timing of the rainfall. When their own production has been used up, the households have to purchase flour from the market-place for the remaining months of the year. Although this yield is still insufficient, the use of fertilizers has greatly improved the situation. The production has increased by at least one-third and in many cases has doubled.

Dry-farming cultivation is based on a technique which aims to obtain optimum use of the soil moisture. Therefore the fallow fields are regularly ploughed during the rainy season. Cultivators pay special attention to their wheat fields and less to other crops.

Table 3.2: The agricultural cycle in Baranpur

Month	Planting operations	Harvesting operations
Chet mid-March–mid-April	ploughing for *kharif* crops	colza; *rabi* pulses
Baisakh mid-April–mid-May	ploughing for *kharif* crops	wheat, barley, mustard
Jeth mid-May–mid-June	ploughing for *kharif* crops; sowing of maize	wheat cut, threshed and winnowed
Asarh mid-June–mid-July	sowing of millet, *kharif* pulses and groundnuts	wheat harvest completed at the end of June
Sawan mid-July–mid-Aug.	sowing of *kharif* pulses and groundnuts continues; *rabi* crop ploughing	grass and weeds are cut for fodder
Bhadon mid-Aug.–mid-Sept.	*rabi* crops ploughed	cutting of grass
Asuj mid-Sept.–mid-Oct.	wheat, barley and *rabi* pulses sown	millet and maize
Kartak mid-Oct.–mid-Nov.	wheat and barley ploughing and sowing; oil-seeds sowing	millet, maize, *kharif* pulses and groundnuts
Maghar mid-Nov.–mid-Dec.	late wheat sowing if no rain at proper time	groundnuts
Poh mid-Dec.–mid-Jan.	wheat fields weeded	
Magh mid-Jan.–mid-Feb.	wheat fields weeded	
Phagan mid-Feb.–mid-March	wheat fields weeded	colza and *rabi* pulses

The cultivation of wheat requires three ploughings with the first two immediately following each other, and the third one after two to three days. The clods of earth are broken with spades.

The sowing of wheat is done manually or with a seed-drill three times, whilst hoping for rainfall in between. It starts in October and after two or three weedings, the crop is left to grow. April and May are the two harvesting months for wheat, followed by the threshing and winnowing operations using the same traditional techniques as in Chahiwala.

During the wheat harvest, the villagers go to the fields at 6.30–7.00 a.m. and remain there until noon. Then they rest for one or two hours while the heat is at its highest. At this time they either return home or they eat food in the fields which has been brought by a woman of the household. Afterwards, they continue to cut the crops until it is too dark to see. The women go home a little earlier because they have to fetch water and prepare dinner.

In both villages, the agricultural season has two peak periods from mid-April to mid-June and from mid-September to mid-November when sowing and harvesting operations coincide.

Livestock in the Villages

Besides land, livestock is the other important asset held by the villagers. Cattle is used for draught power in agriculture, for domestic consumption of dairy products and in a few cases for the sale of milk. Donkeys and mules transport goods and carry harvested crops to the house. Almost half of the households keep hens for the private consumption of eggs and to sell to hawkers who regularly visit the villages. Poultry is kept on a free-range basis and is fed on some of the household waste. Finally, the most common domestic animal in the villages is the dog. It has a role of defence and protection, and functions as a scavenger through its consumption of garbage and manure.

The difference in the economic situation between the two villages is also illustrated by the quantity of animals and the combination of species owned by the households. The poorer cultivators of Baranpur consider it advantageous to own both cows and goats because each animal provides milk and in addition the cows can be used as traction animals in the fields. The decrease in the production of cow's milk is then compensated by goat's milk. When the economic situation is even worse, one goat or one cow is owned for the consumption of milk only.

As a rule, households which own one buffalo also keep goats and at least one cow. If the household can afford to purchase a buffalo, it can also afford to keep other animals. Consequently, the households with the largest landholdings also have the most numerous and diverse livestock.

Figure 7: Goats returning from the fields at the end of the afternoon (Chahiwala)

Besides its use value, a prestige value is also attributed to each animal. It explains the villagers' preference for certain types of cattle, one that is not based on economic considerations. The owner of a buffalo is considered to have a higher social rank and to be wealthier than the owner of several cows because of the smaller quantity of milk yielded by cows, especially when they are engaged in agricultural tasks, and because of the low percentage of fat in their milk. A cow with a calf produces 2 litres milk daily as opposed to 6–7 litres for a buffalo. This low quantity is due to the villagers' inability to afford the best species and to their difficulty in providing fodder.

In other words, the villagers of Baranpur own poor men's animals like cows, goats and sheep while an average of 88 per cent of the Chahiwala cultivators possess a buffalo. The cow population is four and six times larger in Baranpur than in Chahiwala for the landowners of size-class categories 1 and 2 respectively.

Another expression of the villagers' economic difficulties is reflected in the number of bullocks, the animal *par excellence* for agricultural tasks. In Chahiwala, only 21 per cent of the cultivators' households with the smallest landholdings own a bullock. This highlights the economic importance of the reciprocal service of ploughing, since only up to 13 per cent of these households hire a tractor. In Baranpur, the absence of bullocks is compensated for by a wider use of tractors.

The purchase of an animal is very costly for a family which has only Rs 600 a month to cover all its expenses. It is especially difficult to find the money for a newly established nuclear family or when an animal has died suddenly. Sometimes the first animal may be offered by the bride's family as part of the dowry but in most cases it has to be purchased. The poor villager then has to borrow money from relatives and friends. He may also try to save money by breeding a calf himself but ignorance concerning hygiene, particularly a lack of knowledge about the dangers of filthy water, combined with the absence of veterinary stations in the rural areas, can lead to the death of the animal.

Once they have an adult cow and/or a female buffalo, the villagers try to increase the size of their herd whilst spending as little as possible. While the male calf is sold at a very young age, the female calf is commonly kept with its mother for 2–3 years until it becomes an adult. Then the mother is sold or reinseminated up to six times. The use of bulls for reproduction is free while artificial insemination costs Rs 20 per shot. Genetic improvement does not occur.

Although the soil is more fertile in Chahiwala than in Baranpur, the quantity of milk produced by each animal is similar in both villages. On average, a buffalo gives 6–7 litres of milk every day which a large-size family will consume. The women make clarified butter (*ghee*) and butter milk (*lassi*) with any surplus. Very few families who own buffaloes use the milk as a source of revenue (1 litre milk is sold for Rs 3 at the market). They obtain just enough milk for their personal consumption.

Meat is very rarely eaten in the villages. It is only consumed at social ceremonies and religious festivals. Goats are the animals which villagers can afford to slaughter, unless several related households jointly purchase a heifer and offer it to God on important religious festivals, especially the *Idd-ul-Fitr* festival.

The livestock is also beneficial for its manure, either as fertilizer or when it is mixed with dry straw for building material to plaster the house or as domestic fuel for daily cooking and heating the house in winter. An adult buffalo gives around 15 kg of manure every day, of which 8 kg are used by the household for preparing the daily meals. The rest is stored for

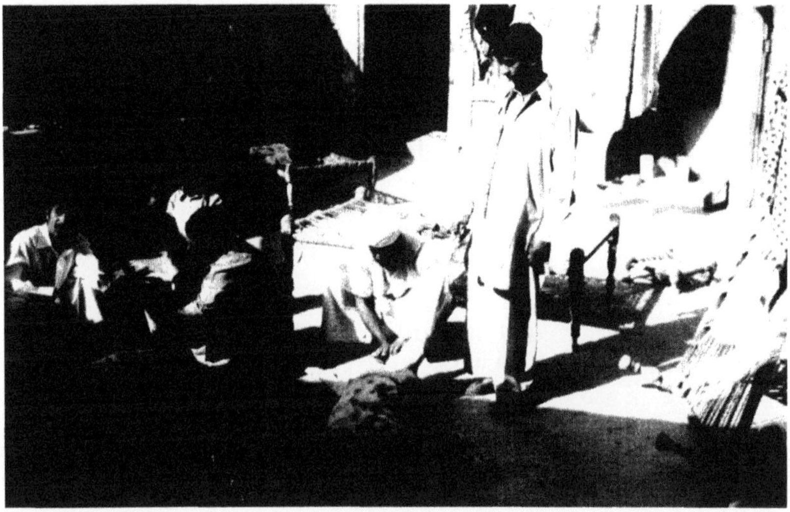

Figure 8: *Idd-ul-Fitr* festival in the house of the leader of the Virck *biraderi* (Chahiwala)

the rainy season since it is more difficult to have ready-made dung-cakes during the monsoon because they require four days to dry on any wall surface or on roof tops. Surplus dung-cakes can also be sold to households without cattle and this brings in a few more rupees.

Some villagers of Chahiwala trade in buffaloes and regularly participate at weekly cattle markets. The trade in livestock is a supplementary and very irregular source of income for the household. Sometimes the trader earns Rs 700–800 in a week, but at other times he might lose as much if, for example, he was cheated by purchasing an animal with an undetectable disease, like a dry udder.

The villagers treat a sick animal with their native medicine. The most common disease is ulcers of the throat, and during the months of May, June and July the neck inflates. Another ailment, haemorrhagic septicaemia (locally called *Gal Ghotu*), is cured with a liquid mixture made of the leaves and flowers of a plant named *haq*. When the cattle have digestive problems or when they are struck by paralysis, the villagers give them a three-day dose of a powder composed of dry ginger, and black and white salt mixed in equal quantities. The daily dose of 2 to 6 ounces is absorbed after the fodder.

When it is noticed that there could be difficulties in giving birth, raw sugar is given both before and after the delivery. Afterwards, the animal

Table 3.3: Prices of domestic animals in both villages

	Prices		
Types	**Low quality**	**Medium quality**	**High quality**
Bullock	(14–15 years) Rs 1,500–2,000	(6–7 years) Rs 3,500–4,000	(6–7 years) Rs 6,500–8,000
Cow litres milk daily	(10–12 years) 3–4 litres, Rs 1,200	(5–6 years) 6 litres, Rs 2,500	(4 years) 7 litres, Rs 4,000
Calf (cow)	(1 year) Rs 300–500	(1.5– 2 years) Rs 500–800	(2–2.5 years) Rs 1,000
Buffalo (male)	(6–8 years) Rs 4,000	(6 years) Rs 6,000	(4 years) Rs 8,000
Buffalo (female) litres milk daily	(7 years) 8 litres, Rs 4,000	(5 years) 10 litres, Rs 6,000	(4 years) 14–15 litres, Rs 7,000–8,000
Calf (male buffalo)	(1 year) Rs 500	(1–1.5 years) Rs 800	(2 years) Rs 1,200
Calf (female buffalo)	(1 year) Rs 300	(1–1.5 years) Rs 600	(2 years) Rs 1,000
Donkey	(6 months) Rs 2,000	(1 year) Rs 2,500–3,500	(4 years) Rs 4,000
Goat (Sindi) litres milk daily	(1 year) 2–3 litres, Rs 250	(2 years) 4–5 litres, Rs 350	(3 years) 6–8 litres, Rs 500
Sheep (Afghani)	(1 year) Rs 200	(2 years) Rs 300	(3 years) Rs 500

eats normally for a week, and then domestic *ghee*, which is considered to be a nutritious diet, is given to the animal for another week.

Enmity is also considered to be a possible cause of illness. The villagers believe that needles, human nails or hair can be mixed with the fodder or spread on the grazing fields and provoke the death of an animal. Amulets and other remedies protect against the supernatural evil powers, but the villagers did not want to discuss them because, as they said, 'to be superstitious is against the behaviour of a good Muslim'.

The cattle graze together freely on common lands. No shepherd supervises the animals during the day. Children or women take the animals to these natural pastures in the morning and they come back to the village by themselves at dusk. The villagers did not mention any quarrels caused by the destruction of crops by the cattle.

This democratic access to the grazing areas is not enough to provide an adequate quantity of forage for all the grazing animals in Baranpur. The grass is not rich enough because these pastures are located on infertile soil. No scientific improvement of coarse-grain production has been adopted. During the dry season the necessary fodder has to be cut daily from fields and pasturelands by the villagers. This is a strenuous task, especially for the women. In fact, the tending of cattle is almost exclusively women's work, and more particularly the task of the female head of the household. However, the fodder-cutter, like all the other agricultural machines, is an implement which is solely operated by men.

In Baranpur, the headwoman in 69 households feeds, milks and cleans off the cattle manure. If she is too old, the daughter-in-law does the job, as is the case in eight households. When a man participates in this work, his tasks are limited to the feeding of cattle and the cleaning of the cattle-shed but he does not milk the animals. Children also take part in these activities in some households.

An extra burden for the women of Baranpur occurs during the periods of drought. The grazing areas are without water during the hot and dry months of May and June and the women are compelled to fetch water from the wells for the animals. It is very time-consuming and arduous. They might have to go more than ten times a day to the water-points to provide the 40 litres of water necessary for an adult buffalo. The human consumption of water also increases during the same period. Fortunately, this extra work does not coincide with the harvest of the *rabi* crops, which finishes just before the start of the dry season.

On average, a minimum of 40 kg of fodder is required daily in each household for the maintenance of stock:

- 30 kg of specific green fodder (mustard, colza and barley) in the *rabi* season; maize and millet during the *kharif* season, added to husk of pulses in Baranpur and sugar cane leaves in Chahiwala).

- 10 kg of dry fodder which is made of sun-dried chopped stalks of the crops from the preceding year, as well as seed cakes, i.e. the residue of cotton seeds after one has extracted the oil in Chahiwala.

The fodder is cut with sickles (since the majority of the villagers are too poor to own a fodder-cutter) and poured into clay troughs. Fodder-cutters are time-saving implements. In half-an-hour two men can cut five days' worth of fodder for their cattle, consisting of two buffaloes, two buffalo calves, one goat and one donkey. As a rule the feeding of cattle is very costly for the household with very little land. In Chahiwala, the majority of the landowners have to reserve between 15 and 20 per cent of their fields for the cultivation of fodder. The use of crops is another means of providing more fodder without having to use specific plots to cultivate it.

Consequences of the Green Revolution in the Two Villages

The adoption of the Green Revolution technology has led to a scholarly controversy over its resultant impoverishment for a majority of cultivators. Supporters of an economic costs-and-benefits analysis have been criticized for arguing that all types of cultivators, irrespective of the size of their farm and the land-tenure system, could take advantage of the modernization of agriculture. Their opponents have emphasized the social costs of these new agricultural techniques by arguing that only the better-off landowners could afford them. Consequently, they claim that the relations of production in the rural areas underwent dramatic changes. Since the Green Revolution relies on capital-intensive technology, it follows that it should lead to the eviction of tenants from their land by landowners who start to cultivate mechanically by themselves and/or reduce the tenant's share, and to the urban migration of an increased number of small landowners who have become landless labourers. On the whole the distribution of rural incomes has deteriorated and the availability of social improvements like better health and educational facilities, reduced fertility and infant mortality is unfairly shared between social classes.

This study confirms both arguments of the controversy. It shows on the one hand that the Green Revolution has been accessible to the smallest cultivators of different land tenures during the second half of the 1970s. All of them have augmented their production through the increase, not of arable land, but of yield per acre. On the other hand, however, the cost of the new technology prevents them from adequately using it. The farmers use it according to their economic possibilities. Because the vast majority cannot afford the required inputs, the agricultural yield is still insufficient to cover the household's yearly consumption needs. Moreover their farms are too small to yield a marketable surplus: they are still in a subsistence economy.

Table 3.4: Average expenditure for fertilizers and HYV seeds in the two villages (Rs per year)

Class-size and type of land tenure	Fertilizers	HYV seeds	Total	Spent per acre
Chahiwala				
Self-cultivating 1	820	452	1,272	340
Self-cultivating 2	1,720	800	2,520	252
Self-cultivating 3	4,200	2,628	6,828	364
Self-cultivating 4	5,000	3,600	8,600	229
Owner-cum-tenant 1	694	421	1,115	298
Owner-cum-tenant 2	1,766	669	2,435	243
Owner-cum-tenant 3	3,800	2,060	5,850	312
Owner-cum-tenant 4	5,150	2,400	7,550	201
Landless tenant 3	4,000	2,400	6,400	341
Baranpur				
Self-cultivating 1.1	300	65	365	745
Self-cultivating 1.2	550	195	745	500
Self-cultivating 1.3	508	352	860	345
Self-cultivating 1.4	550	370	920	263
Self-cultivating 1.5	525	250	775	172
Self-cultivating 1.6	500	310	810	147
Self-cultivating 1.7	472	314	786	85
Average for S.C.1	486	265	751	120
Self-cultivating 2	983	689	1,672	89

Table 3.4 illustrates that the total yearly expenditures for fertilizers and improved seeds are more proportional to the size of landholdings in Chahiwala than in Baranpur.

The largest size-class categories of self-cultivating farmers in Chahiwala spend almost six times as much on fertilizers and eight times as much on HYV seeds than the smallest self-operated farms. The corresponding figures for the owner-cum-tenant operated farms are 7.4 and 5.7 times. In Baranpur, the ratio is 2 to 1. However, when one looks at the amount spent by acre, one notices that the expenditures of the smallest cultivators are very high compared to those of bigger farms. In Baranpur, the amount spent per acre is eight times greater for the size-class category 1.1 than for the size-class 2. In the rainfed area, agriculture is a rather hazardous activity for owners of very small holdings and the possession of a few more acres does not necessarily lead to a greater output. For the same reason the agricultural input does not increase concomitantly with the size of the cultivated area but depends on the cultivator's individual choice to devote more money and labour to the tillage of his land because he does not have any other sources of income.

The low rentability of agriculture in Baranpur is also highlighted by lower expenditures than in Chahiwala for the same category of landholding: 1.7 and 1.5 times less for the S.C.1 and S.C.2 categories respectively.

In both villages, the cultivators' scarce economic resources oblige them to make a choice in their input. They prefer to spend more on fertilizers than on HYV seeds. However, 33 per cent of the self-cultivators' households of size-class 1 in Baranpur were not at all able to purchase chemical fertilizers. I was curious to know the reason why, since the economic discrepancies between these petty landowners are not of a sufficient magnitude to explain this phenomenon. Everyone lives at subsistence level. The cause of extreme poverty in some households had to lie elsewhere; it is always provoked by a specific unforeseen crisis. If the main income earner of the household suffers from an accident or an illness, the family is thrown into a crisis. There is no form of state social security. Medical treatments are very costly and people have to rely on their relatives and friends. Other typical problems which can ruin the household are disputes between people which end up in the courts. The corruption of the police and judiciary system leads to heavy expenditures for the villagers. This unexpected economic burden uses up the money which could have been spent on agriculture.

The table also shows the importance of the type of land tenure in Chahiwala regarding the impact of the Green Revolution. Less is spent per acre in farms of a similar size when they are operated by owner-cum-tenants or landless tenants than in the ones operated by self-cultivators. This confirms the low incentive for cultivation of the sharecropper when half of his produce has to be given to the landlord after the deduction of various payments to the craftsmen and for the irrigation water.

These figures confirm the bias in favour of the adoption of the Green Revolution. It is the size of farm more than the tenurial system which leads to differentiation in the cultivators' implementation of the new technology. These dissimilarities do not relate to the percentage of peasants who use fertilizers and HYV seeds but rather the amount spent on agricultural inputs. Peasants from both areas are motivated to adopt new farm management but are inhibited by their limited economic means. Larger farms reap more of the benefits of the new technology than the small ones. In other words, advancement of the Green Revolution is not restrained by the farmers' conservative attitude towards change but merely by their lack of resources.

The smallest cultivators are those who spend the most per acre, especially in Baranpur where their expenditures are two to three times above that recommended by the Agricultural Department. Apart from these, all the other cultivators are far from using adequate doses of fertilizers and improved seeds. They follow the agricultural advisers' recommendations to the limits that their incomes will allow. Thus if a cultivator can only afford one pack of chemical fertilizer per acre when a double quantity is required, he mixes it with an equal amount of cattle manure; the same is true of the improved seeds which they cannot afford to buy fresh every year. Instead, they usually mix them with grain from the previous harvest, although the absence of adequate storage facilities (which consist of mud bins and/or a separate room in the house) leads to the destruction of part of the stock by pests and predatory animals.

On the positive side, a new market of services has appeared in the villages. Through the selling of irrigation water and the hiring of tractors, Green Revolution technology has become accessible to the households who could not afford to purchase tubewells and agricultural machinery.

Mechanization of agriculture has also been blamed for a structural change in the composition of the farm labour force, with the resulting eviction of tenants and the reduction in the demand for wage labourers.

H. Alavi writes: 'One tractor is estimated to displace a dozen (or more) of bullock-drawn ploughs' (R.D. Stevens *et al.* 1976: 324). So far these consequences are not visible in the two villages because they are situated in the old settled districts of Pakistan with a high area of fragmented holdings. Here, sharecropping has never been on a great scale. The land cultivated by tenants has not covered a significant area in Baranpur after independence since the landowners cannot afford to rent out a piece of their holding. However, as we shall see in the following chapter, a change in the agrarian relations has occurred because of the higher cost of this new capital-intensive farming.

The Administrative Frame of Rural Economy

Adequate implementation of the Green Revolution is too costly in the two villages and the cultivators do not have the means to increase the number or improve the quality of their cattle. They are unable to finance the modernization of their farming without financial credit, since the size of their landholding does not allow them to produce a marketable surplus which could increase their income.

Rural Credit

The state of poverty among small landowners in the old settled district of the Punjab is not new. The Punjabi peasants have always been in debt since colonial rule. The Hindu moneylenders' compound system of interest was an important cause of poverty in the rural areas before independence. In 1947, Pakistan was created in order to give Muslim people from South Asia their own nation. The Islamic ideology, upon which the foundation of the Pakistani state is based, forbade any form of usury.

Changes in the credit policy were also caused by the departure of professional moneylenders to India. Thus a vacuum in the rural credit facilities was created, although the peasants' demands for financial support remained the same after the 1959, 1972, and 1977 land reforms, which did not give them a more sound economic basis. As a consequence, new sources of credit were established through the mercantile practices of local shopkeepers, crop-selling agents and fertilizer depot-holders. Interest is indirectly accumulated by these commission agents (*arhtiya*s) through their tricky operations of buying and selling agricultural commodities at different periods of the year. They extend credit to farmers for the purchase of agricultural inputs and as reimbursement the cultivators are compelled to sell their produce to their creditors at the low harvest price.

Such is the case in the two villages. The peasants of Chahiwala do not have the economic resources to pay cash for the seeds, fertilizers and diesel oil for the tubewell. They therefore buy these commodities on credit from the rice agents, who take a 2-per-cent commission but who, unlike the banks, do not require any form of guarantee such as a specific size of holding. The peasants pay the rice agents back with enough crops to cover the debt and are then free to sell the rest of their harvest to other agents. However, these private rice-dealers have a marketing policy which is disadvantageous to the petty landowners. The dealers sell rice to rice-mills but they are only paid when they have sold Rs 100,000 worth. Then they remunerate first the landowners, who are not their debtors, and only then the peasants who are indebted to them. However, the peasants are badly in need of money to purchase agricultural equipment/items at the appropiate time to start the new cropping season. They therefore have to buy what they need on credit since they cannot wait for the money which the rice-agents owe them. As a result, they are again tied for another year.

In Baranpur the villagers are also dissatisfied with fluctuations in the prices of crops according to the offer–demand mechanisms, and with the corruption involved in the marketing of their crops. There are no government wheat-dealers in Gujar Khan to whom the peasants can sell part of their produce. Only private dealers are available. Various methods are used to falsify the quantity of crops which the peasants bring to the marketplace. For example, wheat is weighed in kilograms but the weight is entered in *seers* (0.93 kg) in the record book. Moreover, 2 kg of stones, sand and mud are deduced for each 37 kg-bag.

The peasants must also pay other charges when they sell their wheat at the marketplace: Rs 5 per *maund* for the transport from the village to Gujar Khan, Rs 1 per 2.5 *maund* bag as an octroi, 5 per cent of the sale profit as a market tax, and the wages of the broker, the weigher and the coolies unloading the bags. All these factors discourage the small farmers from producing more for the market.

The fixed price set by the government of Rs 62 per *maund* for the wheat flour is not respected in retail shops. It is sold for Rs 70–80 per *maund* just before the harvest, i.e. when the household has to purchase it as its storeroom has been empty for weeks. After the harvest, the wheat is bought from the peasant for Rs 60 per *maund*.

In other words, when the villager sells part of his produce at harvest time, his income does not cover the price fluctuation in the slack period some months later. Moreover, the difficult road access to Baranpur compels many households to purchase flour at the village depot, where the price is Rs 82 per *maund* because of the supplementary expenditures on transport.

The cultivators suffer from the private dealers' intermediary position in the market mechanisms and from the weakness of the authorities who do not put an end to this practice. Certainly the cultivators complain about this type of *laissez-faire* policy.

The villagers' poverty leads to their inability to afford the daily consumption needs. Almost 18 per cent of landowners' households without migrants in Baranpur and 9.5 per cent in Chahiwala have to buy food and clothes on credit from the shopkeepers. At most they would borrow Rs 1,500 yearly for this type of expenditure and it is paid back after the harvest. The poorest households, however, have to buy on credit again when the agricultural produce has been eaten up. It means that some households constantly remain in debt. In Chahiwala some cultivators' households purchase goods with grain, since they do not have the required cash. The local shopkeepers accept payment in kind but at a lower exchange rate than the one followed in Pasrur or other market towns.

The state could help the villagers' indebtedness by improving the existing credit facilities in the rural areas. Several forms of credit for agricultural investments are provided by the Agricultural Development Bank of Pakistan (ADBP), the commercial banks and the co-operative societies. The ADBP has a local branch in Pasrur city which provides loans for any form of agricultural expenditure. The loans are advanced for eight years and are repayable in yearly instalments with an 11 per cent rate of interest per year. The peasant who wants to borrow money has to show his 'Agricultural Passbook' (*Agripass*) which is prepared by the Revenue Department. All the peasant's property is recorded in this *Agripass*, such as his landholding, his cattle, his buildings, his machines, etc. The maximum loan he can obtain is equal to 80 per cent of the value of these properties.

For a loan to purchase agricultural machines a minimum security of 12 acres of irrigated land or 25 acres of *barani* land is required by the bank. To finance a tubewell installation, the required guarantee is a landholding of at least 6.25 acres, which may be either irrigated or rainfed land.

The local branch of the ADBP is able to give loans of up to Rs 150,000. For a higher amount, a cultivator must apply to the regional branch. For a higher loan still, he must send his application to the head office in Islamabad. The ADBP contacts the peasants through newspapers, radio programmes and field staff who go on tour in the villages. It provides information on bank loans, loan conditions and the functioning of a credit system.

In both villages, the prevailing ideology means that the peasants are not prepared to make use of this form of finance. They do not want to pay interest. They are not sound enough economically to face this extra expenditure and the number of years for which the loan is advanced is too limited. They do not consider a loan as a service offered by the bank but only as an additional burden. They also consider that the procedure for obtaining a loan is too bureaucratic, too slow, too costly (here the peasants refer to the cost of photocopies of their documents) and too exclusive. It is necessary to have the proper backing and go through the right channels. Moreover, the appellant often cannot provide the required guarantee for taking a loan since his landed property is too small. In other words, it is normally only the economically and politically strong peasants who can obtain loans. As an elder villager from Chahiwala said:

> Nowadays, the credit facilities exist only verbally, not in reality. Just like during the British rule when co-operative banks for landowners were opened in urban areas where the poor peasant could not afford to go.

Consequently, the villagers continue to rely upon their traditional sources of credit. Relatives and friends provide interest-free loans with no deadline for reimbursement. Some 26 per cent and 36 per cent of the landowners' households without migrants are in debt in Chahiwala and Baranpur respectively. The percentage is twice as high for the self-cultivators than for the owner-cum-tenants and also higher for the smallest farms.

Loans are taken out to fulfil two objectives. The first objective refers to productive investments, land transactions, or the purchase of agricultural inputs or cattle. This accounts for 10.5 per cent of households in Baranpur and 62 per cent in Chahiwala that are in debt. It is not surprising that the landowners of Chahiwala borrow more for agriculture, since this activity is more profitable than in Baranpur.

The second objective relates to expenditures for non-productive purposes, such as the reparation or construction of a house, the treatment of illness, and payment for social events. It was found that 89.5 per cent of the households in Baranpur and 38 per cent in Chahiwala have borrowed money for such purposes, especially for the financing of marriages (for daughters as well as sons). Marriage is the most costly social expenditure of the households and its degree of ostentation is a measure of prestige among villagers.

The amount borrowed averages Rs 4,000–5,000, or the equivalent of approximately ten months' salary for an unskilled worker. As a rule, it takes five years for a household to pay back the loan since very little can be saved from the low monthly income.

The creditor does not exert pressure because he is aware of the economic situation of his debtor. In most cases, creditor and debtor are relatives either as consanguine kin (48 per cent in Baranpur and 55 per cent in Chahiwala) or affinal kin (24 per cent in Baranpur and 19 per cent in Chahiwala). Personal friendship ties are also important channels of credit. In Baranpur and Chahiwala, in 28 per cent and 26 per cent of cases respectively, money was lent by friends. However, even though taking out a loan is productive, like the purchase of a share in a tubewell, or of a bullock-cart in order to work as a conveyer, it does not mean that the debtor's income increases to the extent that he can easily repay the debt. After some years, quarrels may occur.

When a very high amount of money is needed, the strategy is to borrow from several creditors instead of asking the bank. For example a landowner of Chahiwala borrowed Rs 80,000 from 17 different people to purchase 6 acres of land. One can easily imagine the intricate network of relationships this kind of transaction requires. It is hardly possible to solve such difficulties if one does not occupy an important social position in the village. In this particular example the debtor was one of the village *lambardar*s.

In Chahiwala, besides borrowing from a private creditor, the purchase and immediate resale of cattle is another means at the peasant's disposal for the rapid earning of small amounts. It might also happen that a peasant sells all the yield after harvest and his wife sells some of her gold jewellery in order to purchase a tractor. He then buys wheat and rice on credit for his household consumption until he earns some money through the hiring of the tractor. In this case, the peasant must be ready to take some risks since he cannot be certain that the new ownership of a tractor will immediately result in sufficient income to cover the subsistence expenditures.

Another possibility for the purchase of expensive agricultural equipment is to do it jointly. We have already seen that more than 73 per cent of tubewells are owned on a share basis. The situation is similar regarding the purchase of a tractor, although it has not yet happened in Chahiwala. In a village situated 2 miles away, however, there are four tractors which are jointly owned, not necessarily by members of the same family. Each man has an equal share and the expenditures and gains are also equally divided. In other words, peasants may become partners in a joint project if they have confidence in one another and are able to control their desire to outdo each other, a type of behaviour which is often at the origin of competition and conflict in the village.

Land Reforms

Another instrument through which the government could improve the cultivators' situation is by the implementation of land reform in order to create holdings of a viable size for small farmers and to protect the tenant's rights. Between Partition and the beginning of the 1980s, three land reforms were launched in Pakistan. Irrespective of loopholes and the government's laxity of enforcement due to the big landlords' manipulations, neither Baranpur nor Chahiwala should be concerned by these land reforms. The problem of land here does not concern the existence of large land concentrations but rather the extreme fragmentation of holdings. These two areas of the Punjab have had a long and continuous history of settlement, and the fields have become very small and scattered, especially after independence and the introduction of Muslim Family Law. This replaced the customary law with the Shariat Law of Inheritance, which prescribes the division of a father's properties between daughters and sons after the widow's entitlement has been allocated.[1] In consequence, the sub-division of land has greatly increased.

The efforts of the authorities have therefore concentrated upon the creation of larger arable fields through a consolidation of land in order to make cultivation a more attractive enterprise. More adjacent plots were also expected to be incentives to agricultural investments. The consolidation operations were implemented in the area of Baranpur in 1959–60. However, the peasants were afraid of being tricked. They thought that only people with enough money and with the proper connections would be able to receive the best portions of land through their bribing of officials. Consequently, the project failed and the cultivators continue to be handicapped by the fragmentation of their fields. This scattering impedes efficient agricultural farming; for example, they are unable to build shelters for the storage of their crops.

In Chahiwala, the land consolidation was realized in 1965 but did not take place on a fair basis. Powerful landowners bribed and exerted pressure on the administrators responsible, not so much to obtain a higher arable acreage (although this happened in some cases) but rather to receive land of better quality. They acquired fertile and easily irrigated plots near the village in exchange for the sandy plots without proper irrigation near the canal. The law also said that a landowner should be compensated with a larger plot when he received land of lower quality, but this did not occur. As a consequence, disputes from that time still poison the social life of the village. All in all, the land consolidation has not meant that the peasants now have joint plots of land, but that their estate is less scattered than before.

Following this introduction of the global economic situation in the two villages, we shall now turn to its impacts upon the social classes and to their inter-relationships within each village.

Note

1 However, most daughters leave their share of land to their brother or a close male relative after the death of the father; to do otherwise would lead to social conflicts and ostracism. In compensation, they receive a portion of the harvest.

4 THE LANDOWNERS

This chapter and the following one will analyse the socio-economic situation of the two social classes found in the villages, namely the class of landowners and the class of craftsmen. Only those households which have no migrants have been taken into account. They will be used as control units to compare with the changes caused by international migration.

The Agrarian Structure in the Villages

For generations land has been a very scarce commodity in both villages but the situation has been aggravated since independence with the population increase and the technological changes in agriculture.

In Baranpur, the majority of the refugee households who arrived after independence left the village again in the 1950s (Table 4.1). However, their departure did not reduce the competition for land since the number of native landowners increased 1.6 times over the period 1956–82. As a consequence, all the farms are owner-operated today and no land is given out to tenants. The cultivators need to keep all the production from their fields themselves when it is so limited and they are therefore not in a position to remunerate tenants with a share. In other words, the people who left were from the most impoverished households who could not ensure their subsistence from agriculture. Consequently, they would not have been able to benefit from the Green Revolution.

In addition to this rural–urban migration, since 1956 some 23 per cent of the cultivators' households have become landless. The proportion among refugee households is almost twice that of native landowners. In this situation, the competition for increasing landholdings is very fierce.

Table 4.1: Evolution of the landowner population in Baranpur (no. of households)

Origin of landowners	1956	1982
Native landowners	31 (9.25%)	50 (43.8%)
Refugee landowners	304 (90.75%)	59 (51.7%)
Moved from another area in Pakistan	–	5 (4.5%)
Total	335 (100%)	114 (100%)

The majority of cultivators (65.7 per cent) belong to the size-class 1 category, and their status as either natives or former refugees plays hardly any role in the size of their landholdings. Both groups have control over almost the same quantity and quality of land. There are no absentee landlords.

In 1982, 76 households (66.6 per cent) of the total 114 landowners' households in Baranpur were not involved in the international labour migration. In order to analyse the impact of migration, the size-class 1 category of self-cultivator is divided into seven sub-groups, as detailed in the Introduction. The majority of landowners without any migrants in their households (68 per cent) own plots of land which are 12.5 acres or less, i.e. a size which cannot cover the subsistence of an household according to official estimation even if these landholdings are mostly arable. The uncertainties of dry-farming, the archaic methods of cultivation, and the pattern of land inheritance mean that it is impossible for these landowners to fulfil the needs of their families.

Due to better agricultural conditions in Chahiwala, there are fewer international migrants than in Baranpur. The number of households without any migrants represents 91.5 per cent of the total number of landowners' households (109 out of 119).

There are four categories of landowners in Chahiwala:

- the self-cultivating landowner (S.C.): here 51 households (or 46.8 per cent) of the total landowner population are without any migrants;
- the owner-cum-tenant (O.C.T.), i.e. the landowner cultivating his own fields plus some rented-in fields: here 42 households (38.5 per cent) of the total landowner population are without any without migrants;

- the landowner renting out all or part of his land: here 15 households (13.7 per cent) of the total landowner population are without migrants;
- the cultivator who has lost his land but who nevertheless is still considered as a member of the class of landowners. In this case, the cultivator is a landless tenant. It concerns only one household (0.9 per cent) of the total landowner population without migrants.

Although the agricultural structure is here more favourable than in Baranpur, it does not impede competition between cultivators to consolidate their holdings. In Chahiwala too, the landowners cannot rely solely upon their landholdings. This is not surprising since more than 41 per cent of them cultivate fields which are smaller than the minimum size required for subsistence farming in semi-irrigated agriculture, i.e. 12.5 acres. Consequently, they try to increase their production by working as tenants for others. The competition for a small additional strip of land is very severe and leads to disputes, quarrels and sometimes even murder.

The preceding chapter revealed that new acreages of land open for cultivation are not available, whilst barren land has almost tripled in the last 50 years and is now equivalent to 12 per cent of the total area. The number of fields dropped from 2,178 in 1918 to 1,361 in 1981. However, this is due not to a reduction in the number of cultivators but to the land consolidation of 1965. The fields are now less fragmented but there has not been an increase of acreage for each cultivator.

Plots of land are only very rarely for sale because land is looked upon as a *mother* and therefore is not a commodity to be easily disposed of. The landowner sells it only as an extreme solution when he is in a desperate economic situation, for example upon the marriage of his children. However, in most cases he prefers to borrow money from relatives or friends, or perhaps to mortgage a plot of his property.

Another difficulty in purchasing land is its very high cost compared to the average yearly income of a cultivator who does not usually have the adequate guarantee required by the banks to obtain a loan. Therefore the easiest solution for a cultivator in search of supplementary land to cultivate is to rent fields from another landowner.

More than 38 per cent of landowner households in Chahiwala have chosen this strategy. The rented area is very small with an average size of 3.2 acres for size-class 1; 5.7 acres for size-class 2; and 11.7 acres for size-class 3. The renting of land allowed 13 owner-cum-tenant households to enter a size-class category higher than the one to which they would have belonged if they did not work on others' land. In other words, the owner-cum-tenant is able to manage better economically but he does not generally till a large landholding.

Organization of Agricultural Tasks

The difference in the potential for irrigation between the two villages influences the organization of agricultural tasks and the place occupied by agriculture in the household economy.

The Labour Force within the Household

In Chahiwala, a cultivated plot can be jointly owned and tilled by a father and his sons even if it is very small. This is the case for 20 per cent of landowner households. Usually, only one son becomes a full-time cultivator when his father's holding is very small. No preference like primo- or ultimo-geniture is made among the sons for the taking over of the farm. It mainly depends on their individual interest in agricultural work. The other sons then have off-farm activities and participate in agricultural tasks during peak seasons.

Similarly, a plot of land can be jointly rented. This always occurs between very close kin. Expenditure on cultivation and production is then equally divided between the partners. The co-owners jointly decide agricultural issues and often follow the decision of their elder, who may be either the father or the eldest brother. Traditionally, the father's authority is decisive but he can no longer determine everything. He cannot forbid his sons from using modern agricultural techniques. They can have the last word over the father's stubbornness.

Sometimes a son who cultivates jointly with his father is not treated fairly. He does not receive his due share of the production even if he has to support his own family. This is particularly the case in extended families with a joint economy where the elders, backed up by the unmarried daughters, exercise a social and economic pressure on the married son and his wife. It means that the son works without payment for his father and without the economic possibility to start his own nuclear family. Endless internal quarrels result from these frustrations, especially between daughters-in-law.

Women also participate in agricultural tasks, traditionally only those belonging to the households of craftsmen. It reduces the prestige of a landowner when poverty compels the women in his family to work outside the house. He tries to solve the shortage of family labour during harvest time through hired labour.

In Baranpur the absence of irrigation means that agriculture is only one of the economic resources at the disposal of the household, regardless of whether the family structure is nuclear or extended. This has various consequences for the organization of the agricultural work.

Joint cultivation is very rare. It is not a compulsory practice for people who live in an extended family; in fact only two out of 18 extended households follow this form of labour organization. Usually households with extended families have one male member who tills land and the others are engaged in all kinds of jobs outside the village.

The majority of fields is thus tilled by households consisting of a nuclear family and the organization of work is based on a gendered division of labour. In each household, the women participate in the work in the fields, not only during the agricultural peak seasons but also daily all year round. The only agricultural task which they do not take part in is ploughing. Otherwise, their labour is necessary because it allows the men to have off-farm activities.

The Employment of Hired Labourers

The employment of labour from outside the household increases the household's prestige. It indicates that the landowner has a good harvest and that the women of his family do not work in the fields, even during peak periods.

In Chahiwala, there have been changes in the availability of labourers over the last 20 years. The tasks of planting and harvesting rice and sugar cane were mostly carried out by the families of craftsmen for those landowners who could afford to pay them. Many village artisans have, however, moved to towns because they faced increasing difficulties in finding work in the village. Due to the increase in the cost of agricultural production, the landowners have started to do more work in the fields themselves. The small size of the landholdings does not allow them either to spend more on inputs or to give away a share of the production as payment, even when yields have improved. The need for labour during the peak season is solved through another means, even though it has consequences for the family's honour. In this case, all the family members of both genders are involved in the harvest. Another means used by the household to avoid the employment of external manpower is to cut the crops slowly. This can easily be done since they do not all ripen at the same time.

The change in the relations of production has another origin too. The relative economic progress of the country during the 1960s created new job opportunities in the towns and cities. The traditional form of payment characteristic of the *seypi* system could not compete with the daily salary that a man could earn in the city, even if he was unskilled. Finally, the awareness by craftsmen of their social status has increased, although actions of solidarity against the gross exploitations exercised by landowners are not common. Nevertheless, some individuals want to escape the servitude of being permanently at the landowner's disposal and by moving to a city they can become anonymous and lose the feeling of humiliation and any discrimination due to the label 'servant' which they always wore in the village.

Nowadays many landowners also work outside the village. It can lead to a shortage of manpower if they cannot take leave from their jobs during the agricultural peak period. If this happens, people from other non-irrigated areas close to Pasrur district may be called upon to help out with harvest.

Economic pressures have therefore entailed a re-evaluation of agricultural work. Landowners have changed their mentality. The shortage of land is the reason why some landowners work for other landowners in order to earn extra crops. Similarly, there is a general lack of adequate forage and this explains why the landowners help each other to cut and thresh wheat and rice. For this, they receive stalks of the crops as payment. Otherwise, a member of the class of craftsmen would normally fulfil this subordinate role. The cutting of crops is now regarded in the same manner as any other kind of work, whereas it used to be considered servile. Landowners share the opinion that they have two seasonal labours, one in the town and one in their fields.

There are two types of contract between extra labour force and the landowners: one with casual labourers and one with seasonal labourers. Casual work is based on the principle of reciprocal service (*mangi* labour). A landowner who needs help may call on any members of his *biraderi*. It does not matter if someone cannot reciprocate the service during the same season: he may do it the year after. But all labour within the *mangi* system framework places an obligation on the demander. Casual labourers do not receive a fixed payment but they might be served food. This is an individual matter depending on the generosity and the social status of the petitioner.

Craftsmen may also be asked to help. It is then considered by the landowner to be part of their duties within the *seypi* framework. He requires help from all the households of *kammi* (such as the blacksmiths and carpenters), and not just from those that are traditionally related to agricultural work. In other words, the landowner disposes freely of the *kammi*'s labour force on demand (*begar*). Labourers are also employed according to their speciality. For example, members of the Christian community have a good reputation for their dexterity to winnow crops but they do not cut them. The villagers are informed of a cultivator's need for an external workforce through announcements on the loud-speaker of the mosque of his *patti*. People come to his fields on the specified morning and the cutting of crops begins when enough people have turned up.

The type of tasks performed by casual labourers are:

- ploughing of fields. This is based on a reciprocal exchange of service. The villagers call it *mangi hal*, which means 'to ask a plough for request'. When the fields are ploughed with a tractor, they call this arrangement *mangi* tractor, even if this is not really a reciprocal service since the tractor owner does not need the help of other people for this task, and the demander pays for this work
- spraying of fertilizers
- preparing the beds in irrigation fields
- cutting of fodder, for example, if the landowner cannot be present during this period. Two daily meals are served or Rs10 per day are given to each labourer
- planting of sugar cane. In this work, a large team of up to 30 men are involved who are relatives, friends and *kammi*s. They can plant 1 acre a day
- peeling of sugar cane.

The other form of external help is seasonal labour. The landowner is not obliged to use the same seasonal labourers from year to year, but if he is not satisfied with their performance, he is not allowed to send the team away before the harvest is over.

Figure 9: People of the class of craftsmen harvesting rice under the supervision of the landowner, seen smoking a water-pipe (Chahiwala)

Neither is the *kammi* forced to work for a landowner. The social life of the village affects the ease with which to find craftsmen for seasonal labour. In fact, the village is split by fights between factions and a powerful faction may put pressures on craftsmen so that they do not dare to work for anyone apart from the landowners of that faction. It is very difficult to remain outside the conflicts, especially for the craftsmen who have no power in the decision-making processes. Consequently, the landowner households from the minority factions find it difficult to recruit manpower.

Wheat sowing is always accomplished by the cultivator without external help but the organization of labour for other agricultural tasks and its payment vary with the type of crop. For cutting wheat, there are two types of remuneration, always without food. The most common form is a bundle of wheat stalks per man and per acre. Each man makes bundles which weigh the heaviest they can carry on their head, usually 40 kg. The labourers work in teams of four and the cutting of 10 acres is completed in 10–15 days stretching from 8 a.m. to 5 p.m. The other form of payment is fixed beforehand. The team receives 3 *maunds* of wheat (111 kg) for the cutting of 10 acres.

For threshing wheat, 1 *maund* of wheat is paid for 8 *maunds* threshed. Some extra people may also help and they only receive food.

Transplanting paddy requires more work and more ploughing than the wheat-fields. The landowner pays between Rs 50 and 80 per acre to the team, which consists of four to six men. Their number varies according to the size of the field but the payment remains the same. They can plant one acre per day. Food is served twice a day, in the morning and in the evening. There is no special food, just whatever has been cooked in the house on that day. However, a sweet dish is compulsory. The landowner's wife and daughters are extremely busy during this period.

For cutting and threshing rice there are also two forms of payment. One form is for the labourer to take the rice stalks which he has threshed. On average, one man goes home with 1 *maund* of stalks on his head after 3–4 hours of work. This is given as fodder to the cattle and this quantity is the minimum required for one day. The other form of payment is 1 *maund* of rice for a team of 4–5 men for every 6–7 *maunds* cut. In this case, the owner keeps some of the rice stalks for himself and sells the rest. If the cutter has a *seypi* relation with the landowner, he receives one meal a day in addition.

The labourers prefer to take the stalks because fodder is not available at the marketplace and because they have their own rice if they also are landowners. Villagers are always short of fodder and they do not have time to cut for longer hours, although they do not have enough foodstuffs for the cattle. They could easily keep a surplus of fodder since it can be safely stored for six months.

Some landowners employ qualified people, generally Christians, for the cleaning of rice. They are paid 2 *dropas* (7.4 kg) for every 6–7 *maunds* winnowed. They may also be paid in cash. The rate is Rs 25 per day for a couple. However, in most households this task is carried out by their own womenfolk.

For cutting and peeling sugar cane the labourers receive the leaves which are used as fodder. They may also take home 8–10 stalks of sugar cane. When raw sugar (*ghur*) was made in the village, the labourer was given daily 2 kg of *ghur*, sugar cane juice and the cut stalks.

In Baranpur, seasonal and/or casual labourers are not usually required. The holdings are so small that there is no shortage of manpower even when the men work outside the village. They make their holidays coincide with the peak agricultural periods. During the rest of the year, they are busy in the fields before and after their working day. Moreover, jobs outside the village are not always permanent or full-time and so the cultivators can combine two activities without much difficulty.

Figure 10: Old landowner couple harvesting their wheat fields (Baranpur)

If external help is required, the landowner calls on the members of his *biraderi* on the basis of the *mangi* system. The payment is three meals a day, a sweet dish and as much water as needed. This form of remuneration is very strenuous for the women of the household because of the lack of running water or handpumps in most houses.

When the seasonal labourers are not kin, the payment is one-tenth of the quantity cut by each man. Food is served twice a day, as well as water and a sweet dish. Only five households have this kind of arrangement.

The Rules of Tenancy

In Chahiwala, the rules regarding tenancy and the villagers' relations to land, water and each other in the process of production have been slightly transformed since independence through the land reforms, which have given greater security and rights to the tenant-at-will. Occupancy tenants are not found in the villages and two customary forms of tenancy contracts are practised.

The first type of tenancy is the *thekha* tenancy through which the landowner and the tenant fix the amount of production (crops or money) to be given by the tenant after each harvest. The average payment is 10 *maunds* of wheat and 7 *maunds* of rice per acre and per year, equivalent to Rs 600 for each crop. The rate is similar for irrigated and rainfed fields. The landowner does not pay a share of the cultivation expenses, nor does he interfere in the agricultural operations. Only the tenant decides the quantity and type of crops which are cultivated.

There is further a distinction between the *katcha thekha* tenancy, where the land is rented out for a short period – one or two years according to the mutual agreement between the two sides – and the *pakka thekha* tenancy, where land is rented out for a fixed period of five or ten years and the tenancy contract is recorded in the court.

The landowner does not have the right to take back his land before the agreed period is over, but the tenant may vacate it at any time. Under the *pakka thekha* form of tenancy, the landowner immediately receives the three-to-four-years' payment when the contract is signed.

The landowner chooses this type of leasing when he needs a large amount of money quickly. However, this practice is rare since only three households of the village have rented out land on this basis. Many landowners do not like this type of tenancy because they do not know what the quantity and quality of yield will be when they fix the amount to be paid. It may be that the tenant will earn more than his patron in case of a very good agricultural year and the landowner's pride would find this hard to bear. The reverse situation is also possible and the tenant is the loser in case of bad harvest.

The other type of tenancy is called *hissa* tenancy. It is a share-cropping payment (*batai*) where agricultural inputs and yields are supposed to be divided equally between the landowner and the tenant after deductions for the services of the *kammis* or other agricultural labourers. The tenant is, however, solely responsible for remunerating the blacksmith-carpenter.

Expenditures for the agricultural inputs are not equally shared in irrigated cultivation. The quantity of distributed product is different according to the status of the person who provides water. There are three rates of payments in the *hissa* form of tenancy. The first pattern of payment involves three partners: the person providing the water, the landowner, and the tenant. Remuneration for the cultivation of wheat is 25 per cent of the harvest for the person who provides the water for irrigation, while the rest is divided equally between the landowner and the tenant. For the cultivation of rice the production is equally divided between the three partners involved.

The second type of payment concerns only two partners: the landowner who provides the water for irrigation, and the tenant. Their respective shares of the harvest are two-thirds and one-third, both for wheat and rice.

In the third form of payment, the tenant provides the water. The production is then divided equally between the tenant and the landowner regardless of the type of crop.

It is therefore always more expensive for the tenant to irrigate than for the landowner, since he receives less from the produce. Many disputes occur over reciprocal accusations and failure to respect the initial agreement.

It is also possible for brothers jointly to cultivate the rented land. They divide the produce equally after having paid the share for the water if they do not provide it themselves.

Forty households (95 per cent) of owner-cum-tenant category till land according to *hissa* tenancy rules because of the landowners' refusal to rent out their land on a *thekha* basis for a five-year period. They feel insecure following the land reforms of Z. A. Bhutto's administration and have misunderstood some of their consequences. The landowners believe that a tenant can become the owner of his rented plot if he cultivates it for many years and pays his share regularly and fairly. Therefore, landowners prefer to rent out their land for just one year at a time.

Tenants, on the other hand, would rather rent the land for a period of five to ten years because it allows them to cultivate it more effectively.

Under this type of tenancy, the tenant has to ask the landowner's permission to use HYV seeds and fertilizers, for the variety and quantity of crops he may sow, and for the installation of a tubewell. The landowner undertakes to buy the tubewell when the tenancy period is over. It is not necessary to obtain permission to hire seasonal labourers.

The landowners also try to get free use of their tenants' labour. They want them to work on plots of land which they do not rent out. When a tenant refuses, the landowner takes another tenant the following year. Then, both the tenant and landowner complain of each other's behaviour and dishonesty.

To summarize, the tenant is only guaranteed a year's tenancy when he rents a holding, and he has to remain on good terms with his landlord. The latter is in a stronger position since he can always easily choose a new tenant, while the tenant has great difficulty in finding land because of the competition with other cultivators who want to increase the size of their holdings.

The tussles between factions in the village also play a role in the access to rented-out land since the strongest faction exerts pressure on a landowner if he is willing to take a tenant from another faction.

Fifteen households in Chahiwala rent out all or part of their land. It represents an area equivalent to 79.5 acres, which is a very small area for the 46 owner-cum-tenant households, including the households with migrants. It is equivalent to 1.7 acres of land for each household, assuming that each household rents an equal size of land. The rented holding is usually irrigated. In order to better understand the pressure on the land, one should also take into account those landowners who have not been successful in becoming owner-cum-tenants. In addition, the cultivators also rent land in neighbouring villages, where they are in competition with the other villagers.

Widowhood, illness or having occupations outside the village are the three main reasons for a landowner to rent out land. In the case of a widow, her in-laws may cultivate her late husband's land and may or may not take their own share of the production, depending on the type of relationships they have with each other. However, widows often face great social and economic difficulties, especially when there is no adult male child in the household, i.e. when no man can defend her interests. Everyone in the village tries to snatch her land through all kinds of means, including physical pressure and violence. Both men and women may use accusations of illegitimate sexual relations to ostracize the widow and make her give up the rights to her land. She cannot trust her in-laws' *biraderi*, her tenants, or members from other *biraderis* who want to protect her from her tenants' bad deeds. She is aware that no help is given for free and wonders what price she will have to pay her protectors one day. Her life is ruined by permanent worries, insecurity and court actions.

Illness is the second reason for renting out one's land. The lack of and/or the high cost of medicine combined with inadequate nutrition make recovery slow and difficult when a cultivator becomes very ill. If he does not have a grown-up son or a brother to cultivate his fields, he may be forced to rent them out.

Finally, some landowners have chosen not to till their diminutive smallholdings and to rent them out. They know that off-farm activities will usually bring in a higher income.

In Baranpur, rented-out fields are very rare even if non-agricultural employment is the primary source of income in the majority of households. Fields are only rented out when there are no male members in the household to till the land, either because of illness, old age or death. Then land is rented on a *hissa* basis.

As for the ease of finding a tenant, the villagers are of differing opinions. Some state that it is very easy because every landowner is ready to increase his cultivated area. However, others believe that the cost of production is too high and the work content is too great in comparison with the harvested yield, which moreover has to be shared with the landowner. For this reason, when the output does not reward the input, some landowners prefer to leave their fields uncultivated instead of renting them out.

Besides the discussion on social costs and benefits, the Green Revolution is also a controversial issue regarding the change it brings to the structures of land ownership and the tenure system. Transformations have occurred in the two villages even though there are no capitalist farmers, apart from one household in Chahiwala with two migrants in the Gulf. However, their economic position has not modified their social status because they do not traditionally belong to the class of landowner but to the barber *zat*. In Chahiwala and Baranpur, the higher costs of agricultural production, accompanied by the impossibility of cultivating more extensively have led to a significant rural–urban migration (for instance the total number of households in Chahiwala only increased from 208 to 216 between 1961 and 1982) and to an increase in the number of owner-cum-tenant and landless cultivators. Even though the landholdings are very small, there exist socio-economic drawbacks which are similar to those provoked by the Green Revolution in wealthier areas of Pakistan. The technological changes have radicalized the economic discrepancies.

The Non-Farm Employment of Landowners

In many landowner households, the income from agriculture is not sufficient to cover the subsistence of its members. Consequently, it is necessary for at least one of its male members to work outside the village (Tables 4.2 and 4.3).

In Chahiwala, 57 households without a migrant (equivalent to 45 per cent of the total number of households without migrants) have an economy based on agriculture complemented by an occupation outside the village. The size of holding does not have any influence on the need to have several sources of income. However, the type of tenure affects the dependence of the household on off-farm activities. The owner-cum-tenant's obligation to give half of the harvest to his landlord leads to a less intensively cultivated holding. We have seen that his economic input per acre is less than that spent on owner-operated farms. However this form of tenancy obligation leaves him less time than self-cultivators to engage in non-farm employment.

In Baranpur, poorer agricultural conditions and the loss of land for many families lead to a higher percentage of households with a pooling of income. Here 75 per cent (68 households) have members with non-farm employment, including five households which live exclusively from employment outside the village. Moreover, *zakat*[1] is distributed to three extremely poor women. The current situation differs from that existing a generation ago. Just before Partition and during the 1950s, agriculture was still the main occupation of the cultivators. When a sample of 63 men from the generation of middle-aged cultivators were asked about the profession of their fathers, 51 answered that they solely cultivated land, 4 that they had another source of income besides agriculture, and 8 said that they did not till their fields at all but instead worked outside the village. The cultivators have become increasingly compelled to look for other sources of income as a direct consequence of the inheritance pattern, the absence of irrigation facilities, and the impossibility of financing the costs of modern agriculture and livestock breeding.

Although the following tables illustrate the change in cultivators' occupations, they do not show the rate of unemployment, i.e. those cultivators who could not find a job outside agriculture. This might explain why only one household among the self-cultivators of category 2 in Chahiwala earns a non-agricultural income.

Work opportunities offered to the peasants are very few, with the army and the police being considered as the most secure possibilities. In Chahiwala, almost a quarter of the men working outside the village have enrolled in the army or the police, while 44 per cent (35 out of 80 wage-earners) have done so in Baranpur. The others have taken on diverse jobs. For instance in Baranpur, 12 men work in the construction sector, 15 in the service sector, 5 in industry, and 6 are petty-traders. The only small industries available around Chahiwala are brick factories, private and government rice-mills and the Pasrur sugar cane mill. The agro-technical sector offers only seasonal jobs to non-permanent employees. Con-

Table 4.2: Distribution of households in Chahiwala according to source of income

Type and size of land tenure	Agriculture only	Agric. + job outside	Agric. + migration	Total
S.C.1	18	20	2	40
S.C.2	7	1	0	8
S.C.3	2	3	0	5
S.C.4	1	0	0	1
S.C.5	0	0	1	1
O.C.T.1	12	8	2	22
O.C.T.2	8	5	1	14
O.C.T.3	5	4	0	9
O.C.T.4	1	0	0	1
Renting out	7	8	1	16
Landless	0	2	0	2

sequently, the villagers work for only six months of the year without the guarantee of being rehired again the following year. They join their workplace after the harvests of wheat or rice and leave the care of the land to the other male members of the household. The majority of these labourers (64 per cent) in Chahiwala have not yet established their own family. They are bachelors who still live in their parents' house. They keep only a part of their earnings as pocket-money and give the rest to their parents. In this way, they slightly improve the general standard of living of the household.

In Baranpur, however, both father and son(s) are busy outside the village. Most of their jobs do not require specific qualifications, or if they do, the labourers have not been trained as such but rather learnt it on the job. Such jobs are at times unstable, especially for the younger unskilled labourers.

It is also common for a cultivator to occupy two different professions in his life. First he works in a faraway city and regularly remits a part of

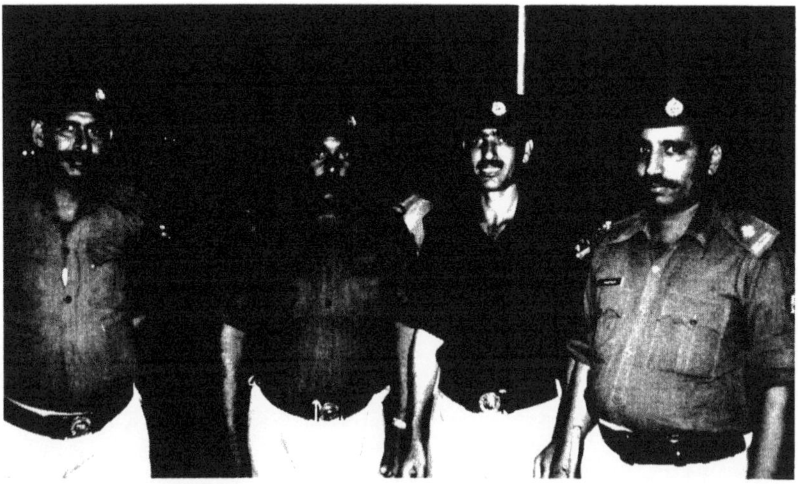

Figure 11: Police and army forces are common job opportunities for the villagers

Figure 12: Private rice-mills in Siranwali offer some of the few remunerated jobs to villagers

Table 4.3: Distribution of households in Baranpur according to source of income

Type and size of land tenure	Agric. only	Agric. + job outside	Zakat	Agric. + migration	Total
S.C.1.1	0	2	0	1	3
S.C.1.2	1	4	0	2	7
S.C.1.3	0	11	0	5	16
S.C.1.4	0	9	0	3	12
S.C.1.5	0	4	0	1	5
S.C.1.6	0	9	0	4	13
S.C.1.7	2	10	0	7	19
Total for S.C.1	3	49	0	23	75
S.C.2	1	6	0	4	11
S.C.3	0	0	0	0	0
S.C.4	0	0	0	2	2
Landless	0	14	3	9	26

his wages home and is therefore a migrant in his own land. Twenty-two per cent of the wage-earners in Chahiwala and 25 per cent in Baranpur had to move to large cities like Lahore, Karachi, Gujranwala, Rawalpindi and Islamabad in order to find work. They do not come home very often, sometimes not even for the religious festivals or for the harvest. When they get older, the labourers come back to the villages and start a new job in the surrounding area.

Wages are very low. Sixty-one per cent of the Chahiwala villagers earn between Rs 400 and 550 a month and 77 per cent in Baranpur earn between Rs 300 and 700. For instance, a man who loads and unloads a truck at a government rice-mill is paid Rs 20 per day for carrying 200 bags of 40 kg. A casual labourer earns Rs 15 a day for eight hours' work, and he works six days a week.

Even with this extra income, a household still cannot meet sudden expenditures like illness or social investments like marriages. As a consequence, every member of the household tries to contribute to the improvement of the budget through all kind of small jobs here and there. For example, women make embroidery which is sold at market; or boys in the poorest households start working under highly exploited conditions at the age of 12, as helpers in tea-stalls or restaurants and as shop-assistants. Others are involved in the agricultural tasks of the house and it is difficult to say whether these activities should be considered as components of the socialization process or as an unpaid use of their labour.

Some parents send their sons to technical training centres. They know that the share of holdings inherited by each of them will be so small that 'it will just be sufficient for the family's shit', as one woman bitterly put it. By receiving a skilled training, many young men also expect to have a better chance of obtaining a work-contract abroad.

The household's need for money does not lead to the engagement of female labour in income-generating activities outside the village. However, the women's daily tending of cattle and participation in agriculture releases the men from strenuous and repetitive work and allows them to be busy outside the village.

Another aspect of the social organization which makes this pooling economy possible is the extended family structure. It facilitates the accomplishment of the agricultural tasks and solves the problems of manpower shortage and the difficulty for the labourer in getting leave during the harvesting months. It is usually the father who tills the land while his grown-up sons are busy in towns.

The Budget of the Cultivators' Households

It is difficult to establish the budget of each household precisely. Therefore the following information is not conclusive evidence but offers data which gives some insight into the villagers' economic situation. One should be aware that some of the figures in the tables are obtained from a very small sample of households. Therefore, the calculation of the average budget might differ from similar studies conducted in other villages.

The cultivators only have an approximate idea of the amount of their monthly expenditures and are even less precise about their monthly income, especially when agriculture is their only source of revenue. The crops are mainly cultivated for their private consumption and the small surplus is sold on the market. In order to make a budget for each household, all the crops have been considered as marketed, in order to establish with greater accuracy the agricultural income of each family. The price of crops fluctuates according to the local economy, and to the speculative practices of the commission agents and their intermediaries.

The installation of tubewells in Chahiwala has added a source of income to those households that provide water to other cultivators' fields. The following calculation was made in order to find the equivalent in cash of the one-third and one-quarter yield received for the sale of water.

1 The average production for each crop (15 *maunds* and 19.7 *maunds* per acre for the wheat and rice respectively) is multiplied by the number of irrigated acres and the result gives the total production for each crop in the households which pay for the water.
2 The total production for each crop is multiplied by the harvest price of crops in the marketplace to arrive at the total income for each crop.
3 This total income for each crop is divided by 3 and 4 in order to obtain the price paid for the irrigation of the paddy- and wheat-fields.
4 The individual water income is obtained by dividing the total water income by the amount of the co-owner's share in the tubewell.

Some expenditures concern all the households, regardless of their income, such as taxes, cesses and remunerations of the *seypi* tasks. The landowner pays a land tax with an assessment made on a soil basis and this varies with the quality of the crops. However, it does not increase progressively with the size of land and earnings from the farm. This means that small landowners pay the same rate as medium farmers every six months, namely Rs 2 and 6.25 per acre in Chahiwala and Baranpur respectively. The water rate amounts to Rs 25 per acre every six months and the tubewell tax is Rs 60 yearly. The village artisans are remunerated both in cash and kind and even though the amount is fixed by the traditional *seypi* system (the payment is based on the number of ploughs owned by the household), the amount fluctuates according to the agricultural production. The greater quantity and variety of crops harvested in Chahiwala allow a higher rate of payment. The blacksmiths and carpenters receive 1 *maund* of wheat, 1 *maund* of rice, 10 kg of cotton and 10 kg of sugar cane a year for each plough owned by the landowner's household. Those in Baranpur are only paid 1 *maund* of wheat by each household. The tailor and the barber receive 1 *maund* and 20 kg of wheat respectively in Baranpur, while the barbers' payment in Chahiwala is not fixed. The landowners give them wheat and rice according to how much they can afford. The watchman receives Rs 2 from each household every six months.

The agricultural income is calculated on the basis of the selling price of the crops which a household has at its disposal for its yearly consumption after the deduction of these various payments which are evaluated at harvest price.

Tables 4.4 and 4.5 present the general trend of the domestic economy according to the size of holding and the category of land tenure. Here, the following points should be made:

- *Agricultural income* is the value of the total produce of the farm. A part of it is consumed by the household; another part is used for the remuneration in kind of the *kammis*; and a third part is sold on the market.
- *Other income* refers to wages received for non-farm employment.
- *Agricultural expenditure* is calculated on the basis of the specific conditions for each farm. These expenditures cover the purchase of improved seeds and fertilizers, the cost of maintenance of working animals, the hiring of tractors, the buying and repair of the farm implements, the land revenue tax, the payment for the irrigation water, the wages of casual and seasonal workers, the remuneration of the *kammis*, and the rent paid by the tenant to his landlord.
- Since the households are not self-sufficient, they have to buy food products much of the year. *Consumption expenditure* refers, then, to the value of the farm products consumed by the household on the basis of harvest prices and to the money spent on the main components of the villagers' diet after they have consumed their own production. (Other domestic expenditures are for clothing, housing, education and medicine.)
- The result of total income less total expenditure (final column – 'Budget surplus/deficit') indicates the economic position of the household and its possibility of saving money.

The budgets confirm that the agricultural incomes across all categories of holding size are less in Baranpur than in Chahiwala. The difference increases proportionately with the size of landholding and also

Table 4.4: Average monthly budget of the landowners in Chahiwala (in Rs)

Land tenure/ income source	No. of households	Av. members in household	Gross agric. income.	Other income	Total income	Agric. expenditure	Consumption expenditure	Total expenditure	Budget surplus/ deficit.
S.C.1									
- agric only	18	6.8	978	–	978	270	492	762	+216
- mixed	20	6.8	702	657	1,359	256	515	771	+588
S.C.2									
- agric only	7	8.3	1,558	–	1,558	530	673	1,203	+335
- mixed	1	8	1,333	450	1,783	707	630	1,337	+446
S.C.3									
- agric only	2	6.6	2,944	–	2,944	1,174	895	2,069	+875
- mixed	3	6.5	3,416	637	4,053	1,658	961	2,619	+1,434
S.C.4									
- agric only	1	9	3,100	–	3,100	1,800	1,063	2,863	+237
O.C.T. 1									
- agric only	12	5.5	917	–	917	188	336	524	+393
- mixed	8	8	860	581	1,441	304	572	876	+565
O.C.T. 2									
- agric only	8	6.8	1,095	–	1,095	443	500	943	+152
- mixed	5	9.2	1,500	437	1,937	364	582	946	+991
O.C.T. 3									
- agric only	5	6.4	2,086	–	2,086	789	529	1,318	+767
- mixed	4	9	2,083	537	2,620	708	819	1,527	+1,092
O.C.T. 4									
- agric only	1	10	3,000	–	3,000	1,308	1,030	2,338	+662

with the availability of a non-agricultural source of income in the household economy.

The Green Revolution has improved agricultural performances but at the same time it has made the cultivation of fields relatively expensive compared to the income they yield. The ratio of agricultural income/agricultural expenditure is equal to 2:7 in Chahiwala, and 1:9 in Baranpur.

Table 4.5: Average monthly budget of the landowners in Baranpur (in Rs)

Land tenure/ income source	No. of households	Av. members in household	Gross agric. income.	Other income	Total income	Agric. expenditure	Consumption expenditure	Total expenditure	Budget surplus/ deficit.
S.C.1.1									
- mixed	2	5	408	175	583	96	603	699	-116
S.C.1.2									
- agric only	1	6	593	–	593	138	511	649	-56
- mixed	4	4.8	321	430	751	108	537	645	+106
S.C.1.3									
- mixed	11	6.8	136	614	750	95	667	762	-12
S.C.1.4									
- mixed	9	6.5	120	541	661	123	677	800	-139
S.C.1.5									
- mixed	4	7	155	500	655	67	504	571	+84
S.C.1.6									
- mixed	9	7.1	104	802	906	190	800	990	-84
S.C.1.7									
- agric only	2	7	240	–	240	50	495	545	-305
- mixed	10	6.2	239	441	680	97	677	774	-94
S.C.2									
- agric only	1	7	338	–	338	173	624	797	-452
- mixed	6	8.7	285	441	726	198	1,176	1,374	-648

The peasant has to work hard in the fields and invest heavily in crops, fertilizers and irrigation, whilst the produce market prices have not risen proportionately. When the cultivator sells a portion of his production immediately after harvest, he is forced to part with it at the shop of the commission agent from where he has obtained agricultural inputs on credit. Because of the middleman's policy to take commission, the harvest price of the peasant's produce is actually less than the purchase price of the seeds. In addition, he is not insured against destruction of his crops due to floods, storms, predatory animals, etc. In Baranpur, the abject agricultural conditions do not make this occupation attractive. Due to the small size of their plots and the poor quality of land, some cultivators have deliberately 'chosen' to reduce their agricultural expenditures (these represent up to 21 per cent of the total expenditure) even if it means a decreased agricultural income. In rainfed areas, agriculture and cattle-rearing have become secondary activities and contribute about 30 per cent of the total household income. The cultivators are less and less motivated to till their land. Here non-agricultural activities contribute more to the budget than agriculture both on small and medium-sized farms.

However, even though off-farm earnings reduce the discrepancy in the economic conditions between the two villages, the peasants of Baranpur are still in a worse economic situation. These landowners have great difficulty in making ends meet. In most cases, their total income does not cover their total expenditure. Landless households are able to manage better because their agricultural expenditure is limited to the foodstuffs for their livestock, which provides them with a higher income than the marketing of crops through the selling of milk and dairy products.

The economy of the village continues to run because the income of each household fluctuates at different periods. In an acute situation, one always borrows from one's relatives or buys on credit. Here the international migration plays a decisive role as a secure source of credit. Selling the women's gold jewellery is another means to deal with difficult economic periods. The situation becomes more severe when there are successive bad harvests, since all the cultivators are not able to find jobs in towns and cities to compensate for their economic loss. Peasants then have to reduce their consumption expenditures and very little is spent on modern agricultural inputs.

The budgets also confirm that self-cultivators spend more on agricultural expenditure than owner-cum-tenants, but the latter group's greater labour investment is rewarded with a proportionately higher output. Nevertheless, their economic situation is not improved because of the share-cropping payment. It follows that the Green Revolution is still too expensive for medium-sized farms. We saw that less is being spent per acre for the use of new technology on medium-sized farms than on the smallest farms, but the total agricultural expenditures are proportional to the size of holding. Cultivators have to make a choice on the items of expenditures, some of which, such as water and fodder, cannot be reduced. In fact, apart from the common ecological variables which condition agriculture, the quantity of input in the tillage is an individual decision. Some households are ready to spend more than others in order to obtain a greater yield. Therefore, agricultural expenditure varies from household to household and from year to year according to the landowner's ability to buy fertilizers and improved seeds, and to hire the service of a tractor owner.

The economy of the household relies more and more upon the pooling of several resources. The following combinations are found:

- agricultural income plus income from one male member working outside the village;
- agricultural income plus incomes from several male members working outside the village;
- income from one male member working outside the village, and
- income from several male members working outside the village.

Consequently, the monthly resources at the disposal of the household may vary greatly. The class of landowners does not constitute a homogeneous social class but contains many socio-economic discrepancies. In the majority of cases the self-cultivator remains in a better economic position than the owner-cum-tenant, regardless of the pooling of incomes.

It is interesting to note that there is only a small difference in consumption expenditures between the categories of cultivators. The amount depends on the number of members in the household but it does not increase proportionately with income. In Chahiwala, the wealthier self-cultivators and owner-cum-tenants spend only twice as much as the poorer ones, although their income is 4.5 and 3 times higher respectively. In other words, the landowners do not spend above a maximum limit on their consumption even if they can afford it. They do not change their consumption pattern or invest more in their children's education. Their income is still insufficient for productive investments in the village or outside, such as the purchase of more fertile land in other areas of Pakistan – even if they were interested and able to adjust to a new social environment. Instead, they give priority to another type of expenditure.

The social ceremonies of the life-cycle and the religious festivals are expected to be held with pomp. Competition between families over the display of presents, the quality of food served and the number of invited guests is the rule. In return, these social investments increase one's prestige and simultaneously lead to many social, economic and political advantages in the village. The poor cultivators mind very much being kept out of this race and not being able to afford a decent wedding party for their children. In Baranpur too, the general tendency is to moderate the consumption pattern. Even if a household could better cover its basic needs, it limits the purchase of more consumption goods. Poverty should not be a hindrance to following traditions which are part of the villagers' cultural identity.

To summarize, the economic possibilities of these petty landowners are very limited and fragile. Agriculture is still geared more to the satisfaction of the household's needs than to producing a marketable surplus. Many households cannot pay cash for food and clothes because of the bad agricultural production and the absence of job opportunities outside the village. The low level of wages in Pakistan, and the high unemployment and/or under-employment do not allow the people to become much better-off. They have no access to sources of credit to improve their agricultural production and their general living standards. Moreover, whatever money is saved is used for social investments which are necessary for the constant reaffirmation of the villagers' cultural identity, even if their cost is a burden for the domestic economy. In this situation, the peasant does not have many possibilities for financing a productive investment, and work in a foreign country is considered to be the most reliable solution to the economic problems.

Note

1 *Zakat* is one of the five pillars of Islam. It refers to the compulsory alms which each Muslim has to give annually for charitable purposes.

5 THE LANDLESS VILLAGERS

The previous chapter concentrated on the landowners of the village. This chapter deals with the landless villagers. The latter do not constitute a homogeneous social class and one may distinguish between two categories of landless villagers, each with its specific social status. On the one hand, there are the people who have lost their land for a variety of reasons but who still consider themselves and are referred to as members of a landowner's *zat*. On the other hand, there are the craftsmen who have never traditionally owned land.

The Landless Villagers of the Landowners' *Zats*

In Chahiwala there are only two households of landowners which have lost their holdings. It is therefore more relevant to look at Baranpur in order to ascertain the economic situation of this category of villagers since 26 households (22.8 per cent) of the landowner class do not own land in this village. In nine of the households one of the members works in or has tried to obtain a job in a foreign country. These will be discussed later on in the study.

In order to set the actual situation in a more accurate dimension, it should be borne in mind that the landowning population has diminished by 66 per cent between 1956 and 1982 (see Table 4.1). The actual landless households of the landowner class are those who have been able to remain in the village because of this important rural–urban migration.

The majority (12) of the remaining 17 households came from Kashmir. The independence led to the loss of their landed property and of their profession as cultivator. Two generations ago the headmen of these households tilled land. Only one man was engaged in other activities, both as a soldier and a traditional medicine man. A change occurred during the following generation after the departure from Kashmir. The men started to work in all kinds of jobs outside the village, often in faraway cities. The sort of work in which the third, and newest, generation of those who left Kashmir will engage remains to be seen. Most of this generation is still too young to work.

Concerning the native households, their members were already landless two generations ago. Some of them worked as tenants for the Hindus and Sikhs. The others had off-farm employments.

The possibility to obtain work outside the village is limited and often temporary, especially in the construction sector where labourers are paid on a daily basis. Moreover, wages are very low. In this climate of unemployment, the army is considered as a desirable occupation. Two men were soldiers before Partition, five after 1947, and two from the latest generation. The early age of retirement (35 years) allows the start of a new profession, sometimes with the added advantage of having acquired a skilled qualification whilst serving in the army. The premium paid at the time of retirement is also an advantage which is very much appreciated, together with the medical facilities offered in military hospitals.

The poverty which characterizes these landless households often leads to the pooling of incomes earned by several male members. This situation occurs in 12 households where all the labour force resources are mobilized. However, the women do not participate in jobs outside the village or in any kind of income-generating activities at home. The villagers' ideology prevents the women's contact with the larger society. It is also very unusual for a woman to take the initiative to work outside the domestic sphere.

The households of landowners with very small holdings in Baranpur have a budget which is almost identical to that of former landowners. This confirms that agricultural work does not reward the efforts of cultivators when it cannot provide a satisfactory subsistence level. The difference between the two categories of villagers is not economic but social. Land ownership gives a higher social status but is not necessarily an economic asset.

Landless households try to compensate for the lack of cash-crops by selling milk, preferably the more costly buffalo milk which is sold for Rs 4 per litre. This increases the monthly income by at least a third. However, the absence of land is a further difficulty for collecting fodder which is partly cut by women from different fields and partly purchased at the marketplace or from other villagers. The monthly expenditure for fodder ranges on average from Rs 60–100.

To summarize, the loss of land does not mean that one no longer belongs to the class of landowners. Socially, landowners continue to marry each other and not with the class of craftsmen. Nevertheless, their economic status is taken into account in the matrimonial transactions and the poorer families are excluded from establishing affinal ties with the better-off landowning families.

The Class of Craftsmen

The class of craftsmen does not constitute a homogeneous social class. Economic discrepancies arise according to how much the skill traditionally practised by each *zat* is in demand by the modernization of the national economy. Cultural changes and the poverty of landowners have led to a transformation in the village economy during the last decades. The work of village craftsmen outside the spatial boundaries of the village is an indicator of the increasing integration of the village economy into the global Pakistani economy. The village is not able to offer job opportunities to all its specialists. Some have to make a living by working in towns and might eventually have to change their profession.

This happened to the water-carrier and the pot-maker in Chahiwala with the sinking of individual handpumps. The pot-makers manufactured, among other items, clay buckets for the wells. Moreover, they were Hindus and consequently left the village in 1947.

The washermen (*dhobi*) have also disappeared. Some have moved to towns; others have died without issue. In the *dhobi* households the men washed the landowners' clothes every 8–12 days all year round. However, many *zamindar* women washed their families' clothes themselves. The washermen were paid one *maund* of wheat per household every year. On special occasions, such as a marriage in a landowner's family, they received additional wheat and rice, cooked food and second-hand clothes. They started to leave the village in the middle of the 1960s because they could earn more by practising their trade in the towns. The landowners could only remunerate them with crops while they could now earn money by moving to a town.

The weavers' fate was similar. In Baranpur, three weaver households of the Khokar Qutab Shahi and Rajput Janjua *zat*s were settled in *dhok* Dihmal before Partition. In Chahiwala they belonged to the Goundel *zat*. They shifted occupation for different reasons. Today some of them like to be considered as descendants of weavers.

Barkat Ali from Chahiwala relates the history:

> When this village was created, the landowners called for the weavers but I don't know where they came from. My father's grandfather and my grandfather's grandfather were settled with their family in this village. We are six brothers in my family. Only my eldest brother and I took up this occupation. Later I learnt tailoring because it demands less work than weaving and I could earn more money. My eldest brother inherited our father's tools, but it was not the rule that the eldest son should inherit the sewing-machine. I was just too young at that time. Later on, I bought my own sewing-machine. I have *seypi* relationships with 15 households which I took over from my father.

In both villages the weavers produced bed sheets, cotton clothes and a type of insulating material (*khaddar*) on horizontal looms. The weaving patterns were made by the women. Clothes were provided to the three religious communities but only when they were ordered. Customers came to Baranpur from far away, up to 8–10 miles, since there were no other weavers in the area. They were paid 4 *ana*s per bed sheet (the most expensive ones cost Rs 3), and 4–5 *paisa*s per yard of *khaddar*. The customer had to provide the raw material. Some weavers worked on a *seypi* basis. They received between 2 and 5 kilograms of wheat yearly for each weaving of 20 yards of cloth.

With the change in the villagers' mode af attire, the profession of weaver disappeared. Some moved to the cities, others remained in the village and learned the skill of tailoring. Today only the households of four brothers from weaving families are left in Chahiwala. Two are tailors; the third is the village watchman (although his two sons work as weavers in a textile factory); the last one is a cultivator.

Scavengers from the Adawa *zat* and many Christian families also departed from Chahiwala in the 1950s. After independence, the Muslim landowners did not need to employ Christian labourers. They possessed enough manpower amongst themselves. As a result the Christian families gradually became poorer and began to leave the village for cities, where some continued to work as garbage collectors and other defiling services while others took up jobs as coolies, masons and unskilled agricultural labourers. Their children could receive free education in Christian schools and this slowly improved their economic condition.

Another cause of the rural–urban migration of the Christian population is the improvement of agricultural facilities. The cost of this modernization made it more and more difficult for the landowners to remunerate the *seypi* payments and consequently many landless villagers lost a source of income.

A third reason for the decrease in the Christian population is the unfavourable localization of their settlement. They built their compound on plots of the common land (*shamlat*) which were originally provided by the Muslim landowners. This area is the first to be flooded during heavy monsoon rains and many houses were destroyed in the violent floods of 1954 and 1956. Instead of rebuilding them, many families moved to the cities. Only four Christian households are left in the village today. They carry out menial tasks for the landowners.

Chahiwala now has 97 households of craftsmen, belonging to 11 different *zat*s. Eleven households have some experience of work outside Pakistan.

The disappearance of craftsmen has been more radical in Baranpur than in Chahiwala because of the mediocre agricultural yield, which makes it difficult for the landowners to pay the craftsmen in kind. The customary payment of craftsmen has barely increased over the last hundred years. In 1886 a blacksmith-carpenter received (on the basis of *seypi* relations) 8 *choha*s (14 kg) of wheat and one bundle of crop per plough twice a year. By 1947 this payment had fallen to 10–12 *seer*s (11 kg). This decrease continued until 1956 with a half *maund* yearly. In 1982 the payment was 7 *maund*s (37 kg) from each family yearly.

In 1947 a tailor received (under *seypi* relations) 32 *seer*s (29 kg) of wheat from each family every half year and some tips on the occasion of any villager's marriage. In 1982 the rate was 32 kg of wheat from each family twice a year, 7 *maunds* (37 kg) of barley once a year and Rs 50–100 in tips for marriages.

At the time of Partition a barber was paid (under *seypi* relations) 6–8 *seer*s (7.4 kg) of wheat from each family every half year and 1 kg wheat and Rs 75 in tips for marriages. In 1982 he was paid 10 kg of wheat and 10 kg of maize or barley from each family yearly; Rs 10–20 for each circumcision; Rs 5–10 and raw sugar for cutting a baby's hair; Rs 200–300 and second-hand clothes on the occasion of marriages.

The consequences of these unsatisfactory rates of payment are apparent when one looks at the new professions taken up by craftsmen in the last two generations. Only for the professions of barber, blacksmith-carpenter and tailor has it been economically viable for at least one son to continue the father's skill. They are also the only *seypi* occupations left in the village. The other village craftsmen have experienced diverse transformations in their activities.

Apart from the weavers previously mentioned, two families ceased working as printers and dyers (*lelatti*). They used to buy tins of coloured powders (green, red and yellow) in the market. The women collected the fuel for lighting the stove and mixed the colours with glue in big pots but it was the men's job to dye the material. The same colours were also used for printing motives carved in wooden blocks which were purchased from expert craftsmen in Chekwal or Rawalpindi.

The printers and dyers did not have *seypi* relations but worked for anyone. They were paid 4–8 *anas* per cloth and Rs 2 for 12 dyed shawls (*chadars*). These two professions disappeared many years before independence because of the development of textile industry in the cities.

The servant of the mosque (*khadme mashad*) also ceased to exercise his activities. He provided water to the mosque and lit the oil lamps in the evening. He was paid one *topa* (about 2 kg) of wheat for every plough owned by each family.

The last *zat* of craftsman found in the village before Partition was the *zat* of shoemakers. Their duty was to repair old shoes for the families with which they had *seypi* relations. They were paid 10 *seers* of wheat and 5 *seers* of maize or barley from each household every year. They made new shoes too, usually one pair in a week. Shoes for adults cost 8–12 *anas* and shoes for children 4 *anas*.

This profession has totally disappeared from the village during the present generation. Today none of the sons of the shoemakers' families has continued their fathers' skills. The type of labour based on the obligation to be at the landowners' disposal and the low rate of payment led to the diversity of jobs by the members of this caste.

In 1982 only 21 craftsmen's households were left in Baranpur. Among them five had been affected in some way by international labour migration. Two households were settled in the centre of the village, eight in *dhok* Ghazi and eleven in *dhok* Dahmial. This localization was similar to the one which existed before 1947, since most of the *kammis* were members of the Muslim community. They did not leave the village at Partition and the refugees who arrived from India in 1953 were landowners except for two households.

These landless people belong to six different *zats* – the Awan, the Awan Qutab Shahi, the Khokar Qutab Shahi, the Goundal, the Rajput Janjua and the Moghul. No traditional profession is specifically related to any particular one of them any longer. In all these households, the male members are engaged in different types of work. The army continues to provide important job opportunities. Twenty-five per cent of the households have or have had one of their members working as a soldier. At the time of retirement, a soldier may choose either to receive a monthly pension for the rest of his life or to take a lump sum of all this retirement money. The villagers prefer the second option because they may then have several thousand rupees at their disposal. When it is so difficult to save money, they consider this as a very advantageous opportunity. They use this amount for the financing of costly projects such as the marriage of a child, the reparation of the house and, in some cases, the financing of labour migration.

Notwithstanding these economic transformations, some professional services are indispensable for the landowners and are therefore still present in both villages.

The Blacksmith and Carpenter (Lohar-Terkhan)

The blacksmith-carpenter *zat* is one of the most important occupational *zats* for agricultural production since it manufactures and repairs the cultivators' tools. There are 19 blacksmith-carpenter households in Chahiwala and one in Baranpur.

Mohammed Ismael from Chahiwala, who was born in 1914, related their history:

> All the blacksmith-carpenters living in this area came from Chura, a place near Rawalpindi, before the British rule. They settled, for example, in Kotli Lohara, Torkhana Wali, Chrind Mrind and Ramguer. In this village, they received land from the Moghul government when they arrived, altogether 32 acres. They call themselves Moghul, not *lohar-terkhan* because they consider that they are the children of Moghul rulers.
>
> There was a religious *pir*, called Shura Sharif, who said to his Muslim followers that they should travel to different parts of the Punjab so as to

convert people to Islam. The blacksmith-carpenters were among his followers. All the population of this area were Hindu of the Blagan and Virck castes. This happened at the time of Mohammed Ben Kasseem's arrival on the subcontinent. He was sent by Hajad Ben Yusaf, ruler of Saudi Arabia, who had heard of a Muslim woman who had been raped by Hindus on her way to India.[1]

My father's grandfather arrived from Ranguer in this village to teach Islam. He came after a battle between Muslims and Sikhs by Attock after the last Moghul ruler.[2] But I don't know whether it was before or after the destruction of the village.

Some blacksmiths were already Muslim before coming here. They were the followers of Shura Sharif. Others were converted in the village. Some of them were not blacksmiths by profession but cultivators.

The activities of blacksmith-carpenter are not separate. These craftsmen have knowledge of both skills. Their relationship to the landowners is based on a *seypi* contract. Eight households have *seypi* relationships with landowners who reside either in Chahiwala or in other nearby villages. The 'Book of Rights' shows the evolution of their duties and payments since the beginning of the century.

In 1912–13 it was mentioned that the tasks of the blacksmith are to make iron tools (for instance the plough, sickle, trowel and spade) for the landowners who provide them with iron and coal for the forge. In the case of tenancy, these expenditures are paid by the tenant.

The carpenter is responsible for manufacturing the wooden elements of ploughs and yokes and other agricultural implements, and for repairing the wooden mechanisms of the wells. He also makes beds, windows, doors and all kinds of wooden household items. The landowners have to provide the wood.

The definition of the blacksmith-carpenter's tasks was not modified for 60 years. It was not until the 1972–73 'Book of Rights' of Chahiwala that there was mention of their occupation again. The only change was that there was no longer the wooden structure of wells to repair because of the more widespread use of private handpumps.

Although the type of payment is identical for both crafts, the amount has always been more limited in Baranpur due to the less favourable agricultural conditions. Here the half-yearly payment was only 10–12 *seers* of wheat for each cultivator's plough. In the case of a bad harvest, the landowners paid less and promised to give more the following year. The government rate was 16 *seers* but the actual payment was determined by the field production.

Table 5.1: Rates of the annual *seypi* payment for the blacksmith-carpenter in Chahiwala

Period	***Kharif* crops**	***Rabi* crops**
1912–13	one bundle of maize per plough owned by the landowner; 2 *seers* of raw sugar; one big pot of sugar cane juice	one bundle of wheat per plough owned by the landowner; one bundle of fodder; one *topa* of wheat at the time of winnowing wheat
1918–19	one bundle of maize	one bundle of wheat
1923–24	1/2 bundle of maize; 2 *seers* of raw sugar one big pot of sugar cane juice; one bundle of husk	1/2 bundle of wheat; one *dropa* of husk for each plough owned by the landowner
1931–32	1/2 bundle of maize; 2 *seers* of raw sugar; one big pot of sugar cane juice	one bundle of wheat; one bundle of wheat stalks; one *dropa* of husk
1936–51	Same payment as before	Same payment as before
1954–55	1/2 bundle of maize; 2 *seers* of raw sugar; one big pot of sugar cane juice	2 bundles of wheat; one *topa* of husk
1962–63	1/2 bundle of maize; 2 *seers* of raw sugar; one big pot of sugar cane juice	2 full bundles of wheat; 2 *dropa*s of husk
1979–80	one bundle of rice	2 bundles of wheat; 4 *topa*s of husk

Measures:
one *topa* = *c*. 2 kg
one *dropa* = 4 *seers* or 3.7 kg
one bundle contains max. 20 kg of crop

Even though the *seypi* payment has increased in accordance with the improvement in the agricultural production over the last 70 years, the blacksmith-carpenter is still not remunerated with a sufficient quantity of crops to satisfy his family's needs. As a rule, a nuclear family with two children consumes 1 kg of wheat and 0.5 kg of rice daily. Such payments under the subsistence level are one of the reasons for the shift from their traditional *seypi* relationships to wage-labour in the cities where they can earn up to Rs 50 a day. Another source of income is to own a landholding jointly and receive a share of the crops.

From these rates of payment, one can also see the changes which have affected agricultural production with the substitution of maize cultivation (maize fields were cultivated until the middle of the 1960s) by paddy fields due to the easier access to the underground water. The local production of raw sugar also stopped in the 1960s and 1970s because of the construction of a sugar-mill in Pasrur.

The Barber (Nai)

The seven households of barber caste in Chahiwala belong to the Kaloo *zat*. Kaloo is the name of a village near the town of Chowinda close to the Indian border from where their ancestors came. The villagers call them barbers because of their occupation. Only in one household did the head of the family fail to learn this profession because of his dislike for the job. Baranpur has only two barbers' households of the Goundel *zat*.

The barbers have *seypi* relationships with landowners. They think that there is enough work for all of them. In Chahiwala, the amount of payment was fixed in the past. Each family gave one *maund* of wheat and one *maund* of rice every year. Now the landowners give a quantity of crops according to their mood. The barber does not have the power to complain about unfair payments. Ghulam Rasool from Chahiwala was tired of this situation and tried to work in Lahore. He obtained jobs in different barbers' shops with Turkish baths, but he did not earn enough and decided to come back to the village.

When comparing the two villages, it appears that the situation has become more favourable for the barbers of Baranpur. Before independence they received 6–8 *seers* of wheat from each family every six months. Today the payment is 10 kg of wheat and 10 kg of barley or maize from each house yearly. The relationship between barbers and landowners is not hereditary and they are not bound to each other. Their customers may also be any other landless villagers. Either they exchange services or they pay the barber the same rates as the landowners. If they do not immediately pay him, the barber waits for a social ceremony in his family and then they give him a greater amount of tips.

The barber does not have a shop but goes from house to house with his scissors and razors. It is common to meet him in the middle of a street crouched down and shaving a customer.

The barber's duties are multiple – besides pulling out teeth, shaving the beard, the chest and under the armpits and cutting men's hair (it is considered incorrect for women to cut their hair and long hair is one of their criteria of beauty) – the barber informs the relatives of their *seypi* families about births, marriages and deaths or any other important social events occurring in their patrons' households. The receiver of the message has to serve him food for this service or to give him old clothes.

Following the birth of a child, the barber cuts the hair of the baby (male or female) after seven days. He receives tips (*laag*) of up to Rs 100 for this and a woven blanket (*khardan*).

Tips are also given when he circumcises a male child at a date chosen by the family. It generally takes place 7–8 days after birth but can also occur when the boy is 12 years old. Parents believe that a child does not feel very much pain when he is very young. However, if they wait for many years, it is in order to save enough money to arrange a prestigious ceremony with many guests.

The barber himself prepares the ointment for the circumcision. It is a mixture of *patkri* and oil which is rubbed on to the penis after the operation. Other people, such as the midwife, assist him during the circumcision.

In the case of marriage, the women of the barber's household clean the dishes the day before and the day after the wedding ceremony. They grind chillies and other spices. They cook food in the village. They used to receive 1 kg of wheat and Rs 15 in tips for these tasks. Today the tips may amount to Rs 200–300 and are added to shares of cooked food for their household and to the old clothes of the married couple.

For funerals the barber prepares the water-pipes for the guests while the women of the barber's household cook and serve food. He receives a portion of the cooked food. This payment has not changed since Partition.

The Tailor

Before independence the tailors repaired old clothes for the villagers with whom they had *seypi* relations, and stitched new clothes which they sold to any customers. They made dresses for the three communities although very few Hindu and Sikh households gave them orders because many women from these two communities owned a sewing machine. In those days people owned at the most two suits made of coarse material. A hand-woven cotton dress was worn both in summer and in winter because of its insulating properties. The tailors received 32 *seers* of wheat

Figure 13: Barber's shop at the bridge over the Upper Marala-Ravi link (Chahiwala)

from each family every six months. The quantity of dresses to be stitched was not fixed. The tailoring price for one *khaddar* suit was 2 *anas*. Nowadays the villagers prefer to buy material from the market and as a rule they have four suits.

The tailor is called upon especially on the occasion of a wedding. He receives tips as a form of payment after the ceremony. Some people do not give sufficient tips in relation to the worth of the work. Otherwise, the tailor has *seypi* relationships with the landowners. They pay him the equivalent of the cost of a suit in wheat and rice. The rates are Rs 20 for a man's cotton suit, Rs 15 for a woman's silk suit, and Rs 10 for a woman's cotton suit. He keeps a record of the work carried out for the landowners until they can pay him after the two annual harvests. Some landowners also remunerate him in cash.

There are two possible forms of payment for the customers with whom the tailor has no fixed *seypi* relationships. He exchanges services with the other craftsmen, for example the blacksmith-carpenter provides him with furniture and iron items for the house (keys, locks, sickle, etc.). The other artisans pay him with money, and this happens without argument even if, unlike the landowners, they are poor. However, as one tailor said, 'God is the final judge. If a man does not pay me, he will have to pay in any case for his bad deeds at his death.'

Figure 14: Tailor stitching clothes before the celebration of the *Idd-ul-Fitr* festival (Chahiwala)

Besides these professions found in both villages, there are several others only practised in Chahiwala due to the better economic situation of landowners and the more self-centred village economy.

The Fakir Zat

The first account of the settlement of the Fakir *zat* in Chahiwala was told by Chaukat Ali and his wife Umran.

> The Fakir *zat* is constituted of two *aals* called Joya and Ghuman, according to the name of two brothers. The Fakirs originally came from the Bahawalpur area. There were 20 famous Joya villages there. They were *jats* (landowners). One of the elders in these villages married a Fakir woman of Chahiwala. From that day, the Joya people have been called Fakirs. This man was very poor when he arrived and the *zamindars* helped him to settle down. He begged in the village. The *zamindars* said that he should perform different duties in the *dira*[3] instead of begging, so he could get one *chapati* and some flour daily. Each *patti* has a *dira*. It was a building with large rooms where the *zamindars* gathered to chat at least once a day. Birth, marriage and funeral ceremonies were performed there. The Fakir's duties were to light a fire in the room in the evening during the winter and to light the *zamindars'* water-pipes in the morning. He collected wood or any other kind of fuel from different places.

The second account was given by Ser Mohammed:

> The Fakirs arrived in two waves to Chahiwala from two nearby villages. The first came from Barapur where the Fakirs lived among the Sikh community but they were not allowed to mix with them. So they thought it was better to leave. The second wave was from Mundaki and was related to the Fakirs of Barapur.

Talian Bibi, widow of Bohar Shah, gave a third account:

> The traditional occupation of Fakirs was begging. In the past, people thought it was their duty to support the Fakirs. They did not work and depended on charity. My family still lives from the alms given in the name of the Holy Prophet. On different occasions villagers distribute food to us. Every thursday, they give us some money. There is the grave of a *pir* in the village. We are his descendants. We accept any gifts as a token of respect.

Chahiwala had four *dira*s – one for each *patti* – and a specific Fakir household took care of each of them. This task was not considered as *seypi* work. In the morning the duty was to clean the room, to arrange the beds (*charpoi*s) so that the men could sit comfortably and chat, to light the fire and the water-pipes. Before ceremonies with many guests, the Fakir household had to lay mats of wheat- or rice-stalks (*prali*) on the floor so that there were more sitting-places available. The payment was some flour given in the morning by each landowner's household in the Fakir's *patti* but not by the households of the other occupational *zat*s, even if the *kammi*s were also allowed to sit in the *dira*. The total amount of flour was one or two *seer*s daily. In the evening each landowner's household provided a *chapati*.

Sometimes, at the funerals of elderly people, the Fakir household received money or new clothes. In the event of marriages, the payment was in the form of cooked food and money.

At the end of the 1960s a change occurred. People stopped sitting in the *dira* because their relationships begun to differ. According to various informants:

> People respected each other more in the past. They listened to each other and were not reluctant to help each other. They also obeyed the powerful villagers more because they depended on them economically. Now they feel more free. They think that they can earn money without the help of influential people. Consequently, they do not so easily accept the domination by the landowners. Since the *dira* was a place where these influential villagers could exercise their power through meetings and discussions, people stopped going there.

The lack of leisure time is another reason given for the disappearance of the *dira* as a social centre. Villagers are busier with their work or rather they have to spend more time on the maintenance of their families.

Today Chahiwala has 23 Fakir households (15 Joya and 8 Ghuman). Collectively the Fakir *zat*s do not master a traditional professional skill. They did not have to fulfil any specific tasks for the landowners (except for the four households involved in the maintenance of the *dira*s) and begging was their traditional occupation. They used to receive *chapati*s and flour, not daily but according to the landowner's good will. With the passage of time, the landowners began to dislike this situation and became less and less generous. Moreover, along with the stop to the work in *dira*s, all the Fakir households started to make a living through a combination of different kinds of labour throughout the year, such as selling vegetables in the village and in large cities (Sialkot, Pasrur, Lyallpur, Lahore and Karachi), cutting rice and wheat, and working on construction sites in towns and cities. Since the beginning of the century, the Fakirs have also been trading buffaloes. Today, six households earn their income through this activity and another is involved in goat-rearing. However, being landless makes this trade a costly affair since the village lacks common grazing ground and fodder has to be purchased.

Only two households are engaged in agriculture with their members working as *hissa* tenants. However, during the harvest seasons all the men of the other Fakir households provide labour in the fields so as to obtain wheat and rice for their families. Another pattern of household economy is the pooling of several incomes. For example, one man runs a small tea-shop on the main road near the village with the help of his grandson, while his son works as an unskilled labourer in a cotton mill. In five households the income is earned by two members, and in two cases there are three income earners. The women's incomes, earned from extra domestic activities such as midwifery or Qur'an teaching to children, are pooled in the household economy. Embroidery is also a source of modest earnings which is often kept by the women for their own private consumption of 'luxurious' goods such as soap, or to spend on the children.

The Kashmiri **Zat**

The Kashmiri *zat* which settled in Chahiwala with Butt as a sub-name does not have a traditional occupation. Their ancestors came from Kashmir, but three generations ago they could no longer speak

Figure 15: Friday cattle market in Siranwali, where people of the Fakir *zat* are involved in buffalo trading

Kashmiri. However, contacts with Kashmir were maintained and marriages still occurred with relatives remaining there until independence.

The Kashmiri people are engaged in different kinds of labour, mostly outside the village. These activities may change from one generation to the next. For example, Mohammed Ali has been a mason all his life, while his father traded buffaloes and his grandfather wove clothes.

The Kashmiris have never had *seypi* relationships with the landowners. Their work in the village before Partition consisted of:

- the trade of buffaloes, often between partners who shared expenses and gains equally. This type of partnership is called *pachar*;
- the carding of cotton. Wages were very low with a maximum of 8 *anas* for carding the cotton needed for an eiderdown;
- the weaving of clothes and bed-sheets. At Partition, the weaving of six eiderdowns earned Rs 10;
- the reaping of crops for landowners. The payment was two bundles of wheat and two bundles of rice (when it was cultivated) for each plough owned by the landowner.

The professions of the Kashmiris are even more varied nowadays. There are three shopkeepers in the village; a retired mason; a petty army officer with a son who is a carpenter in Lahore; a machine-fitter in Lahore; and a father who sells nuts at an important bus-stop near the village with two sons who are motor-fitters in workshops in Gujranwala city. All their wages are rather low.

Figure 16: Hussain from the Kashmiri *zat* prepares sweets for a landowner's household where a wedding is taking place

The Awan Zat

The villagers refer to the people of the Awan *zat* by the name of their traditional occupation *mochi* or shoemaker, even though some of them no longer work in this trade. The Awan people found in Baranpur are all related to each other.

The shoemaker is not involved with all the leather items used by the villagers. He only repairs and makes shoes. The skinning of animals was the duty of the Christian community. The hides were sold at the hide-market in the village of Koralri where the dyer treated them. The shoemaker did not have anything to do with the treatment of skins, which was considered to be a very defiling and disreputable occupation. Conversely, slaughtered animals are not regarded as bringing defilement. However, nowadays, with the departure of the majority of the Christian community from the village and the absence of a proper source of income, some of the shoemakers do skin animals. In fact they still have less work now because the villagers no longer wear leather shoes. Before Partition only the well-off people could afford to buy shoes; the others walked barefoot. There was only one pair of shoes in the household, worn by various male members in turn when visiting the town. After the Hindus' departure, the villagers' economic situation slowly improved and they began to buy shoes. At that time a pair of shoes cost Rs 1–2. If families could not afford this amount in cash, they paid in wheat and raw sugar. Nowadays, only the landowners can afford leather shoes, while the majority of the villagers buy plastic shoes and sandals from the market. They are cheaper but they only last three to four months.

A pair of leather shoes takes two days to make, and ten pairs in a month is the maximum order for a shoemaker. The material (skin and thread) costs Rs 100 for these ten pairs. For new shoes, the shoemaker is paid in cash by both the landowners and the other craftsmen. When he repairs shoes, he works on a *seypi* basis for the landowners. However, Alam Din says:

> Some families with which I don't have *seypi* relations may come and get their old shoes repaired. I won't charge them because I can't refuse them. We live together in this village and we have to respect each other.

Another reason for not refusing is the neccesity of asking the landowners for permission to cut fodder in their fields. In fact, the work of a shoemaker is seasonal. It is not practised during the harvest months when the shoemakers supplement their income by reaping wheat and rice for the landowners. Each man receives a bundle of wheat, equivalent to a maximum of 20 kg, and one *maund* of rice for each harvested six *maunds*. On average they earn 10 *maunds* of each crop.

The yearly *seypi* rate of payment is one *maund* of wheat and one *maund* of rice from each landowner's household, irrespective of the number of repaired shoes. With the other occupational *zats*, the shoemaker exchanges services. Two shoemaker households have *seypi* relationships with 28 families. These relationships are not hereditary and the shoemaker is free to terminate them if a landowner does not respect the agreement.

The majority of the villagers no longer need the shoemaker's handicraft, which will probably disappear over the next 10 years. The fact that the landowners do not pay them the correct amount is another cause of their disappearance. Consequently, after years of hard work, many shoemakers have already moved to the towns, where they have opened up their own workshops. There was economic hardship at the start but at least in towns they were sure to be remunerated for their work.

All in all, the economic situation of the shoemakers has worsened during recent years because of the villagers' new habits and the landowners' unfair behaviour. Therefore, there are only seven shoemaking households left in Chahiwala. Two of them rely exclusively on incomes from outside the village. For the others, the payment in kind earned either through the *seypi* relationships or through harvesting for the landowners is essential for the subsistence of the family when the quantity of available cash is so limited. None of the crops earned can be sold on the market; all of them must be used for the family's daily consumption needs.

Other Types of Craftsmen

Finally two other *zat*s of craftsmen are found in Chahiwala. One is the Pathan *zat* whose traditional occupation was water-carrying. Today they sell wheat and rice which have been roasted by their women folk.

The other is the Qureshi *zat*. Besides diverse types of hawker jobs in the village and nearby towns, their members fulfil several functions for the landowners. They keep the genealogies of the *biraderi*s where they have *seypi* relations. In the past they also informed landowners about possible marriage partners for their children through collecting all kinds of information regarding the economy and reputation of the potential in-laws' families. This activity ceased when the landowners stopped consulting them. Finally they are professional musicians (*Merassi*) who play at parties in connection with their landowners' life-cycle ceremonies.

Household Budgets of Craftsmen

To establish the average budget for these households in order to determine the improvements brought about by foreign remittances presents the same difficulties as for the landowners' households because of the type of revenues. The income may be composed, on the one hand, of payment in kind from the landowners' and tenants' households with which *seypi* relationships are established, and on the other, the salary from wage-labour.

Villagers in households without *seypi* relationships make a living by being employed permanently or seasonally in factories. Due to the insecurity of employment, they are always ready to take whatever job is available. Therefore, irrespective of their traditional occupations, members of landless households are involved in the harvests. This work gives a supplementary income in kind which provides a part of the

Figure 17: Professional storyteller of the Qureshi *zat* (Chahiwala)

Figure 18: Professional entertainers of the Merassi *zat* playing in the households of landowners after the rice harvest. They are paid with small quantities of rice (Chahiwala)

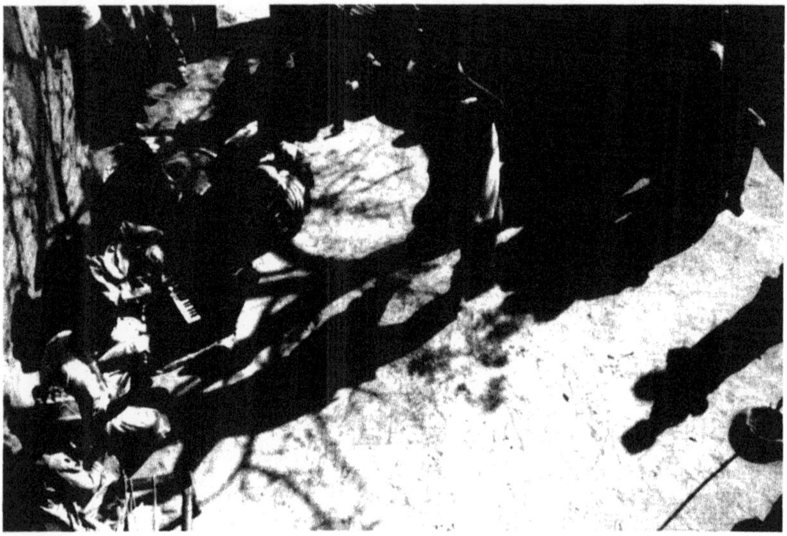

household's yearly consumption of rice and wheat. Every man tries to take leave from his work if he is employed in a factory, or stops his daily activity as hawker or street-seller during the agricultural peak season.

As a rule, craftsmen do not own land. If some households have a tiny plot of land – as is the case for three blacksmith-carpenter households and one Joya Fakir household in Chahiwala – this holding is a gift offered by landowners satisfied with their *kammi's* good services. This land, which is always cultivated by a tenant on a *hissa* contract basis, represents a slight economic improvement. When one operates with such a limited budget, any other possible sources of income are always welcome. It is not unusual for boys of 12–13 years to be taken out of school and put to work as hawkers or unskilled workers in a factory. However, no women are income earners outside the village.

The obligation to increase the economic resources of the household also explains why the absence of land ownership does not prevent the craftsmen from keeping cattle.

The type of cattle kept is influenced both by the prevailing ecological conditions and the economy of the household. Very few craftsmen own a bullock since this animal is mostly used for labour in the fields. Many households do not have a buffalo or a cow because of the daily problem of providing fodder for the cattle. Their owners have to cut grass from the landowners' fields with whom they have *seypi* relations and/or buy it from the market, especially for horses which cannot exist on greens alone. This costs the owner of a horse-cart Rs 15 daily or almost as much as he earns in a day. Consequently, craftsmen do not drink milk or consume any dairy products from cows or buffaloes in their daily diet. Some households drink goat's milk as a substitute, especially in Baranpur. Goats are cheap and particularly well adapted to the dryness of rainfed areas. Poultry is more prevalent in Baranpur, where the craftsmen tend to be more self-sufficient in their animal products than in Chahiwala. Their limited sources of income require a greater diversity of activities.

Other reasons affecting the size of cattle population in each household are the economic impossibility of buying more animals, or the sale of the household's sole buffalo when a large amount of money is demanded (such as in the case of illness or repairs to the house). Cattle actually represent the only form of savings owned by this category of villagers.

The incomes are so low that it is impossible for these villagers to save money. The average monthly wage is Rs 644. In several households (8 in

Table 5.2: Monthly budget of craftsmen in the two villages (in Rs)

Zat	Av. members in household	Gross agric. income.	*Seypi* income.	Other income	Total income	Consumption expenditure	Agric. expenditure	Total expenditure	Budget surplus/ deficit
				Chahiwala:					
Fakir	5.9	221	–	435	656	377	144	521	+135
Shoemaker	6.1	–	73	550	623	666	–	666	-43
Kashmiri	6	–	–	–	600	414	–	414	+186
Barber	6.6	–	160	545	705	500	–	500	+205
Blacksmith -Carpenter	5	356	291	1,046	1,693	538	150	688	+1,005
				Baranpur:					
All craftsmen's *zats*	5.9	–	174	644	818	499	147	646	+172

Notes:
(1) *Seypi* income is calculated from the selling price per *maund* of each crop.
(2) Agricultural income and expenditure refer to the tending of cattle. Buffalo milk is sold on the market for Rs 5 per litre and ghee for Rs 35 per kilogram.
(3) The villagers do not exactly know how high their consumption expenditures are because in reality they operate within a barter economy. When this was the case, I reasoned that the expenses were equal to the total income, as was the case for other households.

Baranpur and 25 in Chahiwala or 50 per cent and 29 per cent of the total number of *kammi*'s households without a migrant), there is more than one wage earner and they pool their salary together. Even then the economy is very fragile because of the high number of people who live under the same roof. As for the poorest landowners, the revenues barely cover the expenditures. Debts and credits are unavoidable in many households. Income earners with a daily wage are in a particularly difficult situation. It may happen that they remain jobless for many days and then the only solution is to buy food and clothes on credit from the local shopkeepers or to borrow money. Reparations or extensions to the house, the illness of a household member, funerals, and the marriages of children are all very costly affairs for the villagers. The only source of credit at their disposal is the family. Both affinal and consanguinal relatives may be asked for help when money is needed for the improvement of the residential property or for the purchase of agricultural land, tools or livestock. This economic support is not a normative obligation but depends on the individual choice of the people who are asked. Several thousand rupees are lent until the debtor is able to pay the money back. The creditor knows that it could take years and is not even sure that the debts will ever be reimbursed. These transactions occur in a climate of reciprocal solidarity. Both the creditor and the debtor know that they may have to count on each other's help.

Ideological Transformation of the Craftsmen

Dealing with unemployment and underemployment is a permanent driving force among the villagers. They are hard workers and consider it shameful not being able to cover the needs of the household, even if the absence of job opportunities is not their fault.

The economic problems become even more acute when one does not own land. In fact, to be landless is a real economic handicap because land is still the surest means of income for the villagers. The yield may vary from one harvest to the next but it represents economic security. No one of the landowner's household goes to bed hungry, as may be the case for the poorest landless families. As a rule, the incomes of the landless villagers are so low that they are unable to save money. They are then confronted with severe problems when an unexpected expenditure has to be faced. However, the situation is not the same for all the people of the class of craftsmen. Belonging to a craftsman's *zat* and mastering a skill needed by the national economy is an advantage which the villagers are becoming increasingly aware of. Some of them (especially the blacksmiths and carpenters) have greater opportunities to improve their economies in the long run because of the actual demand for their craftsmanship both in the domestic and international labour markets. They are on a similar economic footing as the landowners, or even slightly better-off than the poorest among them.

The villagers' new awareness of the importance of specialization is due to a change in their mentality. Over the last 15 years they have broadened their knowledge and their worldview is less and less limited to the confines of the village. Improved means of transportation, the general progress of the Pakistani economy which demands and facilitates contacts between people, and access to more information have all led to an individual being able to think differently. Therefore, the possibility of technical training could be a way of improving the poorest villagers' situation. However, two obstacles still exist which hinder the implementation of such a programme.

The first obstacle is the combination of the policy of low-wage labour practised in Pakistan, the absence of social security allowances and the arrogant behaviour of the ruling classes. As long as Pakistani society tolerates the conditions of the work market, the villagers will continue to consider emigration as their only solution.

The other obstacle is ideological. In spite of greater access to information, elements of a feudal ideology still survive in the villages. In medieval Indian societies, even though the *seypi* system was not egalitarian, it traditionally allowed all categories of villagers to make a living. Each group had its specific responsibilities and obligations towards the others within a subsistence economy based on an archaic technology. Irrespective of the attitude of superiority exhibited by the landowners towards landless people, both classes shared the feeling of belonging to self-sufficient productive units. Socially, the *zamindar/kammi* relations were based on centuries-old co-existence principles. Exploitation was camouflaged under a paternalistic ideology. With the subsequent transformation of the village economy and its integration into a market system, many traditional relations of production became unnecessary and vanished. Those which still remained through being indispensable have changed in nature. From being interpersonal, relations between economic categories of villagers have become more impersonal and can be replaced by wage-labour instead of payment in kind. In other words, the progress of the productive forces through the Green Revolution has been accompanied by a concomitant change in the relations of production. Even though the landowners cannot manage without the craftsmen, they do not treat them fairly. For instance they do not respect the agreements of the *seypi* system or increase the *seypi* remunerations to a level which could ensure the landless villagers' subsistence. They still think that they have a higher social status and increasingly consider the craftsmen to be their servants. In the past the *kammis* had no means of protesting and/or defending themselves against landowners who abused their rights. The situation was one of 'take-it-or-leave-it'. Today the economic improvement brought about by the Green Revolution has meant that more and more craftsmen are refusing to be considered as subordinate to the landowners. It is no longer necessary to be totally dependent on the landowners' fluctuating goodwill to assure the basic needs of one's family, particularly when a member of the household is a migrant. Craftsmen do not organize themselves in protest movements; their class consciousness is not developed to that level. Rather, solutions are considered as individual. Many craftsmen left their *seypi* relationships and started work as wage-labourers in towns. They did not necessarily find the work well paid but at least they felt that it was possible to keep their honour. They became their own masters. Others have learnt another skill.

Nowadays, many *kammi*s consider moving out of the village. They no longer accept the humiliations and frustrations. Labour migration increases this awareness with the new possibilities it offers of becoming economically better-off while still being considered of a lower social rank.

This ideological transformation leads to new, sharper conflicts in the villages. In response to this opposition to their authority, which is considered as a lack of due respect, the landowners embarrass the *kammi* families through all kinds of prohibitions. For instance, they forbid the *kammi* women to cross the fields when they fetch water: they have to use the public paths along the fields, which means a much longer walk.

Jamal Din of the water-carrier *zat* in Chahiwala says:

> Nowadays the patterns of relationships in the village have changed. Villages have become like cities. This is the reason why the *kammi*s leave their *seypi* relationships. There is no respect for them. In the past, it was the landowners' belief that the *kammi*s must have a share of their production and they gave it happily. This does not happen any longer. We have only two things: no food (*bhook*) and no clothes (*nang*).

The situation is similar in Baranpur. Here the relationships between landowners and craftsmen have also deteriorated as a result of quarrels, even if they are less frequent than in Chahiwala. One landowner said:

> There should not be conflicts because the *kammi*s are a part of the *zamindar*s' community. The *zamindar*s should give the due share of crops to the *kammi*s because they are very poor.

The following story gives an idea of the type of conflict which can arise if the *kammi*s become able to compete with landowners economically. A member of the Awan *zat* in Baranpur told his story:

> The *zamindars* do not consider the Awan people as landowners but as *kammis* because we took up the profession of shoemaker when we arrived here. The land which we received was too small, and therefore we had to learn this new skill.
>
> After Partition, I worked as a tenant for a Nangial family. One year the production was very good. The landowners could not accept seeing me better-off, and one night they burnt my stable. They threw kerosene oil through the ventilation windows and lit a fire. Thirty-five hens and two bullocks were burnt to death. All the agricultural tools and the building were totally destroyed. The landowners advised me not to report the matter to the police. They threatened to kill me and my family.

Possibly other unknown elements played a role in the *zamindars*' anger. However, one should not underestimate the jealousy and the violent reactions felt by villagers who no longer respect the status-quo of the social organization.

Confronted with all these transformations in village life, the departure to a foreign country – mainly an Arabic one – is considered as a miracle solution to the economic difficulties. This phenomenon has become integrated into the popular culture in the 1980s under the expression '*Dubai chalo*' , which means 'let us go to Dubai'. 'Dubai ... has come to mean in Pakistan a modern-day El Dorado or Shangri-La' (A.S. Ahmed, 1990: 173).

Notes

1 The informant expresses the popular explanation of the Arab invasion of the Indian subcontinent. He is not concerned with whether other motives could explain this historical event.

2 This might refer to the battle in 1827 between the troops of the Muslim reformer Syad Ahmad and those of the Sikh ruler Ranjit Singh.

3 Meeting-place of the landowners.

6 INTERNATIONAL LABOUR MIGRATION

The previous chapters have shown that the economic situation in the two villages is precarious, irrespective of the inhabitant's economic class, and there are no signs of improvement within the village boundaries for the near future. Working in a foreign country seems for many villagers to be the immediate solution to their economic difficulties and this opinion is strengthened by the relatively improved economic situation of the migrant households.

The Households without Migrants and Labour Migration

For the majority of households in the two villages, out-migration is an unattainable goal mainly because of its cost. These households without migrants are, however, daily influenced by the effects of remittances in their dealings with the migrants' families.

Tables 6.1 and 6.2 illustrate the villagers' intentions of working in a foreign country. Only the households without a migrant are taken into account, i.e. a sample of 184 and 91 in Chahiwala and Baranpur respectively. As can be seen in Table 6.1, 38 per cent of craftsmen's households as opposed to 55.5 per cent of households of landowners want to send at least one male member abroad. In fact, the landowners are in a better position to finance the international migration and this project therefore is not unrealistic.

Table 6.1: Chahiwala villagers' opinions on international labour migration (in households without migrants)

Social class	No. of h'holds	Interested	Not interested	Without opinion
	Landowners:			
S.C.1	37	19	18	–
S.C.2	8	6	2	–
S.C.3	5	3	2	–
S.C.4	1	–	1	–
O.C.T.1	19	13	6	–
O.C.T.2	13	6	6	1
O.C.T.3	9	3	5	1
O.C.T.4	1	1	–	–
Renting out land	15	8	6	1
Landless tenant	1	1	–	–
Total	109	60 (55.5%)	46 (42%)	3 (2.5%)
	Craftsmen:			
Water-carrier	10	3	5	2
Bard	6	3	3	–
Barber	6	1	2	3
Shoemaker	6	2	4	–
Blacksmith-carpenter	16	7	7	2
Kashmiri	4	2	2	–
Christian	7	4	3	0
Weaver – Goundal and Bhatti	8	2	6	–
Joya Fakir	15	6	9	–
Ghuman Fakir	8	3	5	–
Total	86	33 (38%)	46 (53.5%)	7 (8.5%)
Total landowners and craftsmen	195	93 (47.7%)	92 (47.2%)	10 (5.1%)

Table 6.2: Baranpur villagers' opinion on international labour migration (in households without migrants)

Social classes	No. of h'holds	Interested	Not interested	Without opinion
	Landowners			
- former landowners	17	8	9	–
- with land:				
S.C.1.1	2	1	1	–
S.C.1.2	5	4	1	–
S.C.1.3	11	10	1	–
S.C.1.4	9	5	4	–
S.C.1.5	4	1	3	–
S.C.1.6	9	6	2	1
S.C.1.7	12	7	4	1
Total S.C. 1	52	34	16	2
S.C.2	7	3	3	1
Total landowners	76	45 (59%)	28 (37%)	3 (4%)
Total craftsmen	16	10 (62.6%)	3 (18.7%)	3 (18.7%)
Total landowners and craftsmen	92	55 (59.8%)	31 (33.7%)	6 (6.5%)

As can be seen from a comparison of the two tables, the percentage of households interested in migration is higher in Baranpur than in Chahiwala for both classes. This difference can be explained by the poorer economic situation in a rainfed agricultural area. Here the craftsmen are particularly interested in out-migration because they suffer even more from a low agricultural production since their *seypi* remuneration is proportional to the yield, and furthermore the landowners cannot afford to employ them as casual labourers. For this social class, migration is perceived as the ultimate solution to economic difficulties.

Regarding the landowners, there is not a concomitant relationship between the size of landholding and the desire to work abroad. Even though it is obviously more advantageous to own more land, the size and the production of the cultivated plots are always insufficient to fulfil all the needs of the households. Consequently, the landowners' opinion is independent of the size-class category of land to which they belong.

If the villagers who are interested in working abroad could overcome the difficulties related to departure, there would be a further 47.7 per cent of households in Chahiwala and 59.8 per cent in Baranpur which would send their suitable young men abroad immediately.

The reasons for departure are often formulated in general terms. The villagers express the wish for a global economic improvement to the household – better food and proper clothes – and for the possibility of paying for expensive medical treatment when someone is seriously ill, as two villagers of Baranpur explain. First, a village mother:

> Two years ago, my eldest son got seriously injured in a bus accident. He lay in the hospital in Rawalpindi for more than a year. My husband had no money for his treatment. He had to sell 4 acres of land to Gholam, the head of a household with two migrants. The price was Rs 4,000. It was very little money for this size of land but there was nobody who could help us at that time.

Then, another villager:

> I have been ill for the last two years. Last year, the left side of my body became paralysed. I can't walk or stand. I borrowed Rs 6,000 for the treatment. I have been admitted for six months at Mirpur hospital. Now I am under treatment in Rawalpindi. I am very discouraged because of my illness. I cannot do anything to earn money. I have no money to send my sons abroad.

In other words, the villagers' immediate thoughts concerning the use of foreign remittances is to cover their basic needs. Their children's education is rarely mentioned as a priority. When the villagers have more precise ideas, they mention first the construction of a new house, second the marriage of the children and third the purchase of land. This choice of aims is due to the individual's own preferences and also to the atmosphere of competition between households.

> Last year, when my two granddaughters were married, we had no money to provide good food and valuable dowries. But last week, there was a marriage in a migrant's house and they spent a lot of money. It is the custom that the guests give money to the hosts on marriage. In the past it was Rs 2 but now at least Rs 20 are given. People with money can do this but not the poor.
>
> The first thing migrants do when they come back is to build a new house. If the previous residence was too small, they buy land and build a large house on it. The price of everything has increased due to migration. It is easy for the migrants to buy everything but not for the families without migrants.

When we look at the households where no one wants to go abroad (92 in Chahiwala and 31 in Baranpur), we see that there are only a few common reasons for this lack of interest:

- Talking with great lucidity about their situation, the villagers mention that they do not have sufficient money at their disposal to finance a departure. This is the main obstacle and in the majority of cases they cannot borrow money from friends or relatives. Some villagers who live from hand to mouth totally repress any desire to migrate as opposed to those who are just as poor but who still hope to realize their dream.
- The absence of any male member in the household who can make the journey, because all of them are either elderly or ill.
- There is no other male member who could protect the family in the absence of the migrant worker.
- The people are satisfied with their economic situation and happy with their occupation.
- Some villagers do not want to live in a foreign country and feel that it is possible to fulfil one's needs in Pakistan just as well as abroad.
- Finally, since a military career is one of the villagers' chief sources of revenue, especially in Baranpur, the man in the household who could be the migrant is a professional soldier and therefore bound to remain in Pakistan until his retirement at the age of 35.

Villagers who express no opinion on the subject are found amongst the poorest households. All their efforts are concentrated on the daily struggle for food. They do not feel concerned about migration and migrants. It is as if they do not have any energy left to think about anything other than their poverty.

Unsuccessful Migrants

If one looks at the households which have successfully overcome all the hurdles preventing one of their male members from going abroad, it is nevertheless possible that other difficulties may occur. The potential migrant may be the victim of a dishonest labour-recruiting agent who disappears with the deposited money without delivering the promised work-permit and plane ticket.

Twelve households, corresponding to 8.8 per cent of the total number of households of Baranpur, have been cheated in their attempts to obtain work abroad for one of their members. In Chahiwala, only one villager has been sold an illegal visa to Kuwait. Such exploitation cannot solely be attributed to the villagers' naivety; the villagers are no more naive than other people. They are all well aware of the existence and activities of fraudulous recruiting agents. Therefore, they are very careful when they contact an agent. As a rule, he has been recommended by a friend or a relative who knows him personally. He may be a professional agent or a man working abroad who has been able to secure a certain number of work-contracts. Nevertheless, recommendations alone cannot prevent villagers from being cheated by someone who is tempted to make easy money. As a villager who lost a deposit of Rs 8,000 in an attempt to obtain a visa to Saudi Arabia, said bitterly:

> Even if the agent is a member of my *biraderi,* it is not written on his forehead whether he will commit a fraud or not. There is no way to be sure that the members of one's own *biraderi* won't be dishonest.

The demand for work-contracts abroad is so high that the agent can charge prohibitive prices. Visas, too, are sold to the highest bidder. Thus even at this initial stage, migration strengthens the existing social inequality. Only a certain social category – it is difficult to call it a corporate social class – is allowed the opportunity to become better-off.

Two representative cases illustrate the different phases of unsuccessful migration.

Faiz Mohammed is a 40-year-old man who owns 2.5 acres of land and who has worked as a bus-driver for the last 20 years. He said:

> I tried to go abroad twice. The first time was in 1979. A man from Karachi came to the village and said that he had some visas for Saudi Arabia. I gave him Rs 6,000 but I could not get the visa. Only Rs 2,000 were returned. Now this agent has disappeared. In 1980 I gave Rs

> 14,000 to another agent, this time from Sialkot who has also disappeared. Twelve men from the village gave money to this man. My neighbour Aman knew him as a respectable retired army officer, and told us that we could be confident. He gave him money too. After the disappearance of this agent, some of us went to Karachi and waited for our visas there for two months. We have tried to find where he is and to which address his army pension is sent. But the army administration in Sialkot does not want to inform us about his army number. It is confidential. When we go to his family's house, we are told that no one knows where he is. We don't have the money to pay a lawyer since all of us are very indebted.

Another example is the case of Sher Mohammed who went to Spain in 1979:

> A friend of the village advised me to go to Spain and told me about an agent from Gujar Khan who could provide me with a visa. I was promised work from him as soon as I reached there and that my pay would be Rs 5,000. I obtained a 90-day tourist visa. I borrowed Rs 20,000. I tried in vain to get a job and, since I had a return-ticket, I came back to Pakistan after 17 days. The agent came with me to Spain. There, four other Pakistanis, whom he had sent before, waited for him. They were also jobless. They beat him severely and a case was registered against them by the police. They were all deported from Spain.
>
> When I came back to Pakistan, I travelled directly from Karachi to the village. Once here, I walked straight to my house and said nothing. Everyone started to cry – my parents, my wife, my children – and after a while I explained what had happened. My wife is still crying nowadays because she thought that we could have opened a shop, bought some land or repaired the house

Unsuccessful migration may cause a state of depression in the migrant household. Its members have hoped that they could at last begin to see an end to their economic insecurity and even if they had not made any specific plans for the remittances, they feel that a failed attempt shatters all their dreams. It also means that these households are indebted for amounts which they cannot reimburse. It is not possible for them to reduce their actual expenditures, therefore they do not cut down on their monthly consumption. The kinship and/or friendship relationships between the creditor and the debtor are obviously an advantage in this situation since it is difficult for the former to exert pressure upon the latter. However, the unsuccessful migrant feels a moral obligation to pay the money back and he might try to work abroad again since only a job in a foreign country would allow him to save enough money. Another alternative would be to borrow from another creditor if the first one could not wait any longer. All in all these households have become a lot poorer.

Socio-economic Background of the Migrant

So far 21 households in Chahiwala and 44 in Baranpur (9.7 per cent and 32.6 per cent of the total number of households respectively) have been directly involved with the international labour migration. Among these households, 12 in Chahiwala and 25 in Baranpur have at least one of their members working abroad; 4 households in each village are on the point of sending a migrant; 4 households in Chahiwala and 3 households in Baranpur have a migrant who has returned; and 1 and 12 households in Chahiwala and Baranpur respectively have been cheated by a recruitment agent. The total number of men working abroad is 12 in Chahiwala and 27 in Baranpur.

It is important to distinguish between the class of landowners and the class of craftsmen since the former represents an unskilled labour force which has difficulty in fulfilling the vocational qualifications required by the labour contractors. In most cases, the landowners only know about cultivation and the receiving countries do not need farmers. Cultivators are then hired abroad as unskilled labourers, mostly on construction sites. This situation is totally new for them. In the village they do not even build their houses by themselves. They require the assistance of *kammi* people who have some knowledge of masonry. Thus, even though they take on unskilled work in the construction sector, they still have to undergo some informal training beforehand.

On the contrary, craftsmen of the village can often get a job corresponding to their traditional occupation. It is therefore easier for them to obtain a work-contract.

Migrants of the Landowner Class

There are 10 landowner households in Chahiwala and 38 in Baranpur which have been or are involved with a job abroad. When examining the relationship between migration and land tenure, it appears that the migrant households belong to the average type of landowners found in the two villages, i.e. holding no special favourable positions which could have made their departure easier. These households' tilled plots are insufficient to cover the family's needs and outside employment is necessary.

In Baranpur the type of land tenure and the size of holding do not greatly influence the migration process. All the migrants among the class of landowner belong to the group of self-cultivator, and the majority of them are petty landowners of the size-class 1. As mentioned above, they have not been able to find land on a tenancy basis since vacant land is not available in the village.

In Chahiwala, the distribution of migrants is more widespread among the different categories of land tenure, but always within the smallest size group of each category. The average total income of a household before migration ranges there from Rs 900–1,100 monthly. Four migrant households own a tubewell and one household has a tractor. They are all using fertilizers and HYV seeds. But these methods of cultivation have not been influenced by an improvement in the economy of the household due to foreign remittances, since these cultivators began to adopt a more modern form of tillage many years before male members of the household went to work abroad.

Similarly, the international migration has not so far led to a radical transformation of agricultural production in Baranpur. Although some migrant households began to purchase fertilizers and improved seeds in the first years following the migration of one of their members, others still do not use them. Only one tractor has been bought with the remittances. In both villages, the quantity of chemical inputs used per acre in households with a migrant is hardly above that consumed by households without a migrant.

The migrant's level of education is often higher than that of the other villagers, especially concerning the number of years spent in school (see Table 6.3). However, the cultivators without schooling did not try to acquire technological qualifications before their departure in order to obtain better job opportunities abroad. They are often employed as unskilled labourers on road constructions. Job offers are more plentiful for those who have some kind of other specialization besides agriculture and this trend is increasingly common. In fact, many landowners are aware of the future economic difficulties which their sons will face if they only know about land cultivation. Many parents encourage their sons to acquire a technical skill with the hope that they will be able to get a good work-contract in a foreign country. Some of them even acquire this qualification for the sole purpose of going abroad and have discarded the idea that it is possible to make a living in Pakistan. However, such villagers do not take part in courses at professional training centres like those established by the Pakistani authorities.

It is certain that a large number of teenage boys will have to acquire a job outside their villages because the majority of the holdings which are under 7.5 acres will be divided once again between the children on the death of their father. The size of the inherited holdings will be so small that they will not be able to provide a subsistence for their households. One can therefore assume that the pressure on land will become fiercer with the social conflicts it entails; that the rural–urban migration will increase, and that the number of candidates for international migration will continue to rise. It will become increasingly necessary to cultivate new plots of land in other areas of Pakistan. Simultaneously, local industries will have to be created in order to retain the rural male population in the village.

This necessity of searching for a job outside the village is not a new phenomenon in Baranpur because of the agricultural conditions. Through the last generations, men of the village have had to take work in other towns or to enrol in the army or the police at a much higher rate than in Chahiwala, in addition to providing agricultural labour. Table 6.3 shows the consequences on the availability of jobs in the village brought about by the structural changes in agriculture over the last 20 years. More and more holdings have been tilled by their owners so that the need for tenants has dramatically reduced. It has also led to a shift of profession between generations. Many young men of the latest generation, among which the migrants are recruited, have had to take up new professional activities outside the village. In the case of households with land, only one son is engaged full-time in agricultural labour. He works with his aged father and they are helped by the other sons during the peak agricultural season. On the father's death, his sons will inherit their respective shares of the land but only one man will continue to till all the land on a share-cropping agreement.

In short, one may say that even though the international migration has barely affected agricultural production, nevertheless it has had an economic impact on the households. The foreign remittances are new

Table 6.3: Level of education and occupation of a sample of migrants from the landowner class

Years of primary schooling	Profession of father	Profession before departure	Profession abroad
Chahiwala:			
5	cultivation	cultivation + knowledge of carpentry and welding	unskilled labour
8	cultivation	cultivation + bus driver	private car driver
5	cultivation	cultivation + welding training	welder
–	cultivation	cultivation	unskilled labour
–	cultivation	cultivation	masonry
–	cultivation	cultivation	unskilled labour
–	cultivation	masonry	construction work
5	cultivation	cultivation	construction work
–	cultivation	cultivation	unskilled labour
Baranpur:			
10	army + bell-boy	army	sailor
10	unknown	cashier at Gujar Khan market and unskilled jobs	unknown by the informant
9	army	masonry	masonry
–	cultivation	masonry	masonry
5	cultivation	bus and truck driver	driver
–	tenant	army	construction work
7	cultivation	unskilled construction work	unskilled construction work
2	cultivation	cultivation	machine operator
10	cultivation	army	guard
9	army	secondary school student	factory worker

Table 6.3 cont: Level of education and occupation of a sample of migrants from the landowner class

Years of primary schooling	Profession of father	Profession before departure	Profession abroad
12	army + mill worker in England	secondary school student	mason
12	same father	secondary school student	mill worker
–	cultivation	driver	driver
6	cultivation	mason	mason
9	cultivation	secondary school student	construction work
5	cultivation	mason	mason
9	cultivation	army	mason and unskilled electrician
10	cultivation	electrician	electrician
5	assistant shop-keeper	unemployed	gardener
–	cultivation	cultivation	road construction

sources of supplementary income which far outweigh any previous possibilities offered to the villagers.

Migrants of the Class of Craftsmen

Eleven households in Chahiwala and five in Baranpur of the class of craftsmen are or have been directly involved with labour migration to Middle Eastern countries. As mentioned before, it is easier for the village craftsmen than for the cultivators to obtain work-contracts thanks to their knowledge of a traditional occupation. The oil-producing countries have a shortage of all kinds of skilled and semi-skilled workers in all sectors of the economy, service sectors included. For example, all the carpenters of Chahiwala working abroad are engaged in carpentry on different construction sites. Similarly, it is not difficult for barbers, cooks or tailors to obtain work-contracts. The transnational companies involved in construction projects in the OPEC countries need these skilled labourers.

The main difficulty for a potential migrant from this economic group remains the financing of his departure irrespective of the economic improvement which took place in the villages during the 1970s. Unlike the landowners, they are unable to raise a large amount of money through, for example, the selling of crops after the harvest or the borrowing of money, since they lack any commodities to use as security. This explains why only two households have managed to pay for the expense of migration in Baranpur. We have seen that very few households of craftsmen are still found in the village because of the economic changes since independence. The life of the village community was greatly affected by the rural–urban migration long before the international migration started.

However, when a skilled artisan succeeds in going abroad, he rapidly makes more money than a migrant who was a cultivator before leaving, since the former possesses better professional qualifications. This is a further reason why he finds it less acceptable to live in a village community which is based on traditionally unequal relationships between people.

Among the blacksmith-carpenter *zat* in Chahiwala, four households have a migrant. None of these households is involved in *seypi* relationships. Following their contact with foreign countries, their members are the most radical opponents of this form of labour relation with the landowners:

> We have no *seypi* relations in the village. In the past our forefathers had, but the *zamindars* wanted to dominate us. They did not respect us. We want to work independently without having limited relationships.

The tailor Barkat Ali had the chance while I was in the village to receive a free visa from a friend working in Saudi Arabia. His friend wrote to him: 'God has given to me some free visas, so God will help you too.'

A few days before this surprise, Barkat Ali told me:

> Only God knows whether I will go abroad one day. Although I am a skilled man, I never thought of leaving my country. Due to poor economic conditions, I am unable to go to a city to earn more, so how can I think of travelling outside Pakistan? Some people become rich but I am not able to change my own situation.

The income of Barkat Ali's household is Rs 300 every month – the salaries of father and son – and 10 *maunds* of both wheat and rice yearly through the *seypi* relationships. They possess no land and only own a cow. It was totally unrealistic for these people to plan to work abroad.

Table 6.4: Level of education and occupation of migrants from the class of craftsmen

Years of primary schooling	Profession of father	Profession before departure	Profession abroad
Chahiwala:			
5	barber	barber	barber
–	barber	barber	barber
–	carpenter	carpenter	carpenter
–	carpenter	carpenter + cultivation	carpenter
5	carpenter	carpenter	carpenter
8	carpenter	carpenter	carpenter
Baranpur:			
8	blacksmith	mason	mason
5	shoemaker	bus-driver	unskilled construction labourer

The visa sent from Saudi Arabia is a work-contract as a tailor in a shop. It is valid for five years. The only expenses which Barkat Ali has to pay are the fees for the government clearances (Rs 2,500) and the plane ticket (Rs 4,500). He borrowed from his cousin, his father's sister's son, and from friends living in another village. His monthly wage will be Rs 2,500, to which will be added free food and free accommodation. It means that he will earn ten times more than in the village. His son will continue to work as a tailor in Chahiwala, possibly to maintain the *seypi* relationships. But as Barkat Ali said:

> Any *kammi* going abroad does not have to think of the broken *seypi* relationships. He is free to go. But I worry about my death on my way to Saudi Arabia, how will my family be able to pay back these Rs 7,000? I have never borrowed money before.

By referring to a *Hadith*,[1] he adds:

> If a debtor dies before paying back his debts, the creditor may cancel them. But if he does not, the debtor's funeral will not be accepted by God. It is always compulsory not to have debts before dying.

With the remittances he plans to give back the borrowed money, to build a brick house and to marry his son. He will also try to assist his son to come to Saudi Arabia.

> I will do so because my son is not so young any more. He will be 24 years old if it requires 3–4 years of work before we have collected enough money to make a good marriage.

Some village craftsmen do not have skills which are marketable in the oil-producing countries and migration can lead to dramatic consequences, as these two examples show.

Koshard, a man of the shoemaker *zat* has tried to go to Iran. All the members – males as well as females – of his household supported his departure. He tells about his experience:

> I worked for two years in Teheran in 1978–80. Before I was a shoemaker in a workshop in Lahore. I was paid Rs 200–250 weekly. This was not enough for my family. I went illegally to Iran. It cost me Rs 2,700 which I borrowed from my eldest brother (Rs 700) and I sold my wife's jewellery for a value of Rs 2,000. I could not get a proper job in Teheran. I worked in a poultry farm, then in a toy-factory and finally on building sites. My pay was Rs 1,500 per month. I shared a room measuring 3 by 3 metres with seven other Pakistanis so as to save money. I could only save Rs 6–7,000 within these two years. I came back because my last job was temporary. With this saving, I bought a radio-cassette, two suitcases, two blankets, three watches and a leather jacket.

With an average income of Rs 600, it is not surprising that Yousaf of the Kashmiri *zat* was interested in the advantages of international migration. He went to work as a painter in Muscat for almost three and a half years. Before his departure, he was in the buffalo trade. He had saved money, but not enough. He had to borrow Rs 1,500 from friends, Rs 2,000 from his wife's sister, and his wife sold her jewellery for Rs 1,000. However his income abroad was too low to bring about an economic improvement. He only earned Rs 1,400 per month and it took him one year to pay back the borrowed money.

He returned to the village because of health problems. This was a great psychological shock for the whole family. All their dreams were shattered. It was difficult for him to readjust to the village life because he had planned to transform his family's economic situation. On his return, he had a transistor radio, ten sets of clothes and Rs 500. Yousaf opened a grocery store. For this he had to borrow goods worth Rs 3,200 from his brother-in-law's shop in another town. He gives his brother-in-law all the money he earns and keeps nothing for himself. He just takes the goods which he needs for his own consumption from the shop.

He also started another buffalo business with his previous partner on a *pachara*[2] basis. However, he had to borrow money from him. This trade did not flourish and his partner asked him to repay his debts immediately or threatened to close his shop.

These two examples are representative of the migrants who belong to the poorest socio-economic category in the village. They had to make a lot of effort to finance their departure and did not obtain any long-term rewards. In these cases, the families have lost their only source of saving, namely the wives' jewellery. Migration has only worsened their situation. Their hope now is to provide their sons with a good education and send them abroad. However, the eldest sons are still very young and there are grown-up daughters to marry soon.

In two other Kashmiri households, all the hopes are also centred on the sons' departure. They received a vocational training to help them to obtain an overseas work-contract. In one case, it was decided nine years ago that the son should go abroad. He was sent to the workshop of the brother-in-law of his aunt in Lahore when he was 13 years old to learn the profession of carpenter.

In 1980, his parents gave Rs 14, 000 to a relative – the son of his father's female cousin – who had contact with a labour-recruiting agent and also paid for a visa. The family trusted this agent but two years later no one has received any work-contract.

In the other case, the household has twice tried to send the son abroad. The mother says:

> My son received the training of a motor-fitter only for the purpose of going abroad. Two and half years ago, we gave Rs 8,800 to my eldest brother-in law [her husband's sister's husband] who in turn gave them to a friend working in Kuwait. But this man did not go back to Kuwait and reimbursed the money. With this amount we married our eldest son last month. I had to sell 7 *tolas* (1.12 kg) of gold worth Rs 4,500. I felt ill when I did it. We also borrowed Rs 4,000 from my brother-in-law. Now we want to try again to send a son for financing the marriage of our youngest son and our daughter. But we can give at the maximum Rs 4,000 and we have to sell the gold of my daughter-in-law since I gave

her my jewels. My youngest son will also try to leave after 3–4 years when he will have saved enough money.

This example is a good illustration of the place which migration occupies in the villagers' thinking. All their attention, efforts and dreams are focused on the hope of having a relative working abroad. They are under a permanent psychological pressure because they believe that there is, at last, a way to overcome their poverty if they simply obtain a work-contract in a foreign country. It is very frustrating for them to be so close to a goal without being able to reach it.

The Migrant and His Family Status

The family structure is one of the main differences between landowners and craftsmen in the two villages. There are more extended families among the craftsmen's households with a migrant in Chahiwala and among the class of landowners in Baranpur. There are economic reasons behind these patterns. Married men in the households of craftsmen do not have the economic resources to start their own nuclear family. Neither do they own a piece of land upon which to build their own house. An extended family structure enables the villagers to deal with economic hardship more effectively. The small size of landholdings in Baranpur necessitates a pooling of the various incomes of the household and this is facilitated in the extended family structure.

Extended families also make it easier to tackle the socio-economic problems caused by a man's absence. In this regard, the relationships between brothers and between fathers and sons play an important role when a man goes abroad. The migrant has to ensure the physical protection of his family through the help of a very close male relative. In fact, 85 per cent of the migrants in Chahiwala and 64 per cent in Baranpur are already married and have young children when they leave the village.

The ages of the migrants range from 22 to 55 years. However, the oldest ones have been working abroad for 18 years and it is very rare for a man older than 45 to leave his village for the first time. Villagers have a relatively short life expectancy. Many of them die between the ages of 60 and 65. Moreover, when the children are grown up, especially when they are all married, a father feels that the aim of his life has been reached. To marry one's children properly is actually a duty which requires a great deal of effort, both economically in order to finance the ceremonies, and psychologically so as to find a life-partner who lives up to one's

Figure 19: Extended family of a migrant working in Abu Dhabi (Chahiwala)

expectations. Therefore when all this has been accomplished, a man often considers that he has reached the last period of his life. He no longer has the desire or the energy to work abroad. He prefers to remain in the village amongst his family and friends, and to enjoy life and the mounting respect he receives as he grows older.

On the other hand, the migrants are not in their teens. This is understandable when the cost of going abroad is taken into consideration. It can take years to save the required amount of money and a very young man simply cannot afford to go abroad, unless his parents and other close relatives consider that he is the best candidate for migration and consequently finance his departure.

The structure and composition of the family also influence the choice of the migrant. The migrant is the head of the household in 57 per cent of cases in Chahiwala and 71 per cent in Baranpur. In extended families, the migrant is a son and has to obey his parents even if he is a married man. He normally occupies the second position in the line of brothers living in the household. However, the eldest son may also be the migrant when his younger brothers are too young to work abroad. The choice of the migrant can be explained by the traditional division of labour between brothers. It is the eldest son who remains on the family's land while his brothers are engaged in off-farm occupations. The authority of the oldest son over the younger ones is also reflected in the organization of the arranged marriages. Due to the high cost of these social ceremonies, each child has to wait his or her turn, according to their gender and age. The unmarried migrants are found amongst the youngest sons.

Strategy of Departure

Until the beginning of the 1970s England was the major country to consider for migration. When the British government implemented a radical change in its immigration policy, however, new countries in need of manpower had to be found. The oil-producing countries of the Middle East filled this vacuum after the 1973 Yom Kippur War which was followed by a dramatic increase in oil prices. By the 1980s, the villagers could expect to find short-term work in one of the Middle Eastern countries, even though European countries, not to mention the USA, Canada or Australia, were still considered to be the best destinations. Some Pakistanis were still trying, at their own risk, to illegally enter North European countries through complicated and costly channels, although no one in the villages had tried.

Thirty-three men left the villages between 1977 and 1982 (10 from Chahiwala and 23 from Baranpur respectively or the equivalent of 83 per cent and 92 per cent of the total number of migrants).

Neighbouring Iran used to be the cheapest and geographically most convenient destination for Pakistanis. It cost between Rs 2,500–3,000 to enter illegally. This amount covered the travelling expenditures and the introduction to an Iranian labour-contractor. Five men from Chahiwala went to Iran travelling overland, following a very complicated route in order to avoid the Pakistani police, who try to stop illegal migration. The migrants with their various Baluchi guides had to hide in trucks and wait for many days in different cities before continuing their journey. Under these conditions it is not unusual for the journey to take four weeks from south Punjab to south Iran. However, the political situation after the Iranian revolution has led to a reduction in the number of migrants going there, both legally and illegally. Therefore, the remaining possible recipient countries are the OPEC countries, but it is extremely costly to obtain a work-contract there and very difficult to reach the countries of the Persian Gulf illegally. Many villagers from all over Pakistan have lost their lives when they risked crossing the Arabian Sea in unseaworthy

Table 6.5: Yearly distribution and cost of migration by country

Year of departure	Village of origin	Cost (Rs)	Destination	Total no. of migrants for the year
1958	Baranpur	2,000	England	1
1963	Chahiwala	(sent by the army)	Dubai	2
1965	Baranpur	7,500	England	1
1969	Chahiwala	10,000	Kuwait	1
1970	Baranpur	20,000	England	1
1972	Baranpur	28,000	England	2
		15,000	Qatar	
1976	Baranpur	10,000	Qatar	1
1977	Baranpur	10,000	Abu Dhabi	5
		11,000	England	
		20,000	Dubai	
	Chahiwala	12,000	Kuwait	
		12,000	Kuwait	
1978	Baranpur	8,000	Abu Dhabi	8
		10,000	Libya	
		6,600	Libya	
		8,000	Bahrain	
		7,000	Saudi Arabia	
	Chahiwala	6,000	Dubai	
		11,000	Iran	
		11,000	Oman	

Table 6.5 cont.: Yearly distribution and cost of migration by country

Year of departure	Village of origin	Cost (Rs)	Destination	Total no. of migrants for the year
1979	Baranpur	6,000	Greece	
		15,000	Saudi Arabia	
		12,000	Saudi Arabia	
		10,000	Libya	
		12,000	Abu Dhabi	8
		14,000	Saudi Arabia	
		27,000	Abu Dhabi	
	Chahiwala	11,000	Oman	
1980	Baranpur	15,000	Libya	
		15,000	Libya	
		27,000	Saudi Arabia	
		10,000	Abu Dhabi	6
	Chahiwala	7,800	Kuwait	
		14,000	Dubai	
1981	Baranpur	9,000	Iraq	
		18,000	Libya	
		12,000	Oman	5
		8,000	Oman	
	Chahiwala	10,000	Saudi Arabia	
1982	Baranpur	35,000	Saudi Arabia	1

boats hired out by unscrupulous labour-recruiting agents. Luckily this did not happen to any men from the two villages. All the villagers working in the Gulf States went there with a work-contract in their pocket.

The migration process is circular and the employers benefit from the advantages of a mobile and consequently unorganized labour force. The hiring of labour is mainly in the form of work-contracts which are usually renewed every two years. The early migrants have experienced rotation up to seven times and the majority of them are now engaged in their second period of a two-year contract.

In addition to this rotation, the migration is characterized by employment stablility. The migrant returns to the same company and to the same job. The mobility of the manpower is ensured by a horizontal rotation between Pakistan and the receiving countries rather than by a vertical movement through an improvement in the migrant's professional qualifications. In the majority of cases, he is recruited on the basis of his traditional vocational knowledge. The changes experienced by the migrant will rather be provoked by the requirements imposed by a new discipline of work. He is not used to a process of work dictated by a capitalist organization of production.

A work-contract offers the advantage of job security for the migrant. He does not have to wait or look for a job but starts working almost immediately after he has arrived in the receiving country. The villager only faces unemployment when he has travelled to a foreign country without any real certainty of being employed.

Candidates for migration face two main problems: the financing of migration and the procurement of a work-contract.

The Financing of Migration

Through the years, migration has become more and more expensive. It increased from Rs 10,000–15,000 at the end of the 1970s to Rs 15,000–20,000 in the mid-1980s. The average cost of migration was Rs 12,720 irrespective of the target country for the period 1977–1981 (Table 6.5). Prices fluctuate greatly from one year to another and from place to place. Even within the same year, there can be vast differences between expenditures for travelling to the same country. For example, in 1979 a work-contract in Abu Dhabi cost one migrant Rs 12,000 while another paid Rs 27,000. The procurement of a cheap work-contract depends on the villager's good luck and appropriate contacts. In fact, more than half of the amount paid by the migrant is retained by the labour-recruiting agent and his collaborators, since, for example, a plane-ticket to Kuwait costs Rs 4,500 and the expenses for a Non-Objection Certificate and other official clearances from the Pakistani authorities amount to Rs 2,500, while the total cost of departure to the migrant can be up to Rs

12,000. The absence of governmental control over the private labour-recruiting agencies accounts for the prohibitive prices and exploitation of the villagers.

Since the level of income at the disposal of the household is very low, the villager has difficulty in financing his departure and takes great risks. His own savings are rarely sufficient unless accumulated during a previous spell of employment abroad. He does not own any valuable goods which can be sold. As is the case for other needs requiring a large amount of cash, the selling of land is not considered as a viable source of funding. Only one out of 37 migrant households in the two villages since 1970 has mortgaged one acre of land to finance migration. The migrant's wife can sell the jewellery from her dowry although this is difficult for her because of the sentimental value attached. Disputes may also arise if these jewels previously belonged to the migrant's mother. She might then oppose her daughter-in-law selling them, especially if she is jealous of her son's future economic betterment. Conversely, the mother might think that she can freely use her former jewels to finance the migration of another son.

Villagers can also sell some of their livestock and all their crops just after the harvest. In certain cases, this means that the household does not consume milk until it is able to buy a buffalo again, or it has to buy food on credit until the first remittances arrive.

The rest of the money has to be borrowed. The great number of factions in Chahiwala means that economic support comes mainly from friends and/or from in-laws. The *biraderi* is not an institution which the villager uses for this purpose. He knows that it would not be of any help because of the climate of jealousy, rivalry and desire to dominate each other among its members. Families of the same *biraderi* compete economically and politically with each other and consequently are not even willing to support the departure of someone from the same *biraderi*. In other words, the *biraderi* does not show any signs of solidarity in this matter in the same way as it does in the case of situations where individuals are in conflict with other *biraderi*s or with the authorities. Competition also occurs within the same household. This explains why only two migrants have been helped by their brothers.

In contrast, the more harmonious social atmosphere of Baranpur means that *biraderi* and household members are not opposed to helping each other financially; there is less jealousy. This economic support is given without any rate of interest and nobody has become a professional money-lender. The creditor knows that he will get the money back with the arrival of the first remittances. If the migrant has been unlucky enough to be cheated by a dishonest labour-recruiting agent, the creditor does not have much power to get his money back because the debtor simply has no external means of income which could allow him to repay. This type of financing is, then, very risky, since no one can be sure of getting a visa and the date of departure is unknown. For some households the attempts to migrate or an illegal departure have actually aggravated the domestic economy.

The Network of Contacts Used to Obtain a Work-Contract

For many villagers, the absence of economic resources transforms the international migration into an impossible dream, but those who can gather together the necessary amount of money know that there is another great difficulty to solve, namely the procurement of a work-contract.

Very few villagers leave the country through the governmental manpower recruiting organizations because these are not considered as effective as the private agencies. Moreover, since the candidates for migration are more numerous than the quantity of available work-contracts, villagers have to mobilize their network of relationships in order to get a visa. Friends and affinal ties are, in reality, the surest means of support a man can find in both villages. The parents of the migrant's wife are also interested in the improvement of the welfare of the household where their daughter lives. Any refusal to help could also lead to a more tense atmosphere between the wife and her in-laws, a situation which the wife's parents want to avoid. Another way of obtaining a work-contract is open to villagers sent abroad together with their army corps.

The strategies followed for the acquisition of a work-contract are diverse but almost always take place in two stages. One first asks a friend or a relative who is already working abroad or who has a good contact with a labour-recruiting agent for help. The second step is taken by this intermediary who undertakes to provide the visa and work-contract once the applicant has paid him the deposit. The middle-man is often blamed if the agent disappears with the money because the agent is expected to be a respectable person when he has been introduced by a friend or a relative. The villager always takes it to be some kind of guarantee if the agent is related to his family in one way or another, even if the ties are very loose. It is a naive feeling of security because the agent can easily disappear from his domicile with the villager's money. However, the villager somehow feels protected from any frauds because of this kinship relation.

The limited role played by the *biraderi* in the financing of migration in Chahiwala is confirmed by its absence from the principal means of support before departure. Only in four cases have *biraderi* members been instrumental in the procurement of a work-contract. These individuals are either working abroad themselves or are very religious and disinterested in the race to increase one's social status.

Many work-contracts have been obtained without the intermediary of a Pakistani recruiting agent, but directly through contacts with acquaintances in the receiving country. This explains the variation in prices and in the period of time required to obtain a work-contract. It also offers a greater guarantee against being cheated, which is a real risk as attested by the high number of fraudulent work-contracts sold in Baranpur.

If we look at the decision-making process before departure, it becomes apparent that migration is a collective affair. Only two villagers made the decision to migrate individually, while in the case of all the other migrants their closest relatives were involved in sending them abroad. It might even be that parents decide that one of their sons should apply for a work-contract without consulting him first.

As a rule, the household members arrive at a consensus without difficulty since migration is generally considered to be the only possibility of improving one's economic situation. If one of its key members is opposed to it, the other members will constantly exert pressure until an agreement is reached. The migrant's wife might not be well informed of the procedure through which her husband has obtained a work-contract. She only knows the outline of his plan and has been excluded from all the details of the transactions for gathering the money.

When a villager receives a work-contact and money for the plane ticket from one of his relatives abroad, it does not take more than six months to arrange the other formalities. However, it can take between six months (for those who travelled illegally to Iran) and two years (for those leaving for a Middle Eastern country). The variation in the length of time it takes between the decision to migrate and the actual date of departure depends upon the the importance of the social network which the villager has to mobilize to finance the migration. When the decision to migrate has been taken, the required amount of money should be collected immediately. It would be foolish not to have the money to pay for a work-contract if one suddenly becomes available.

Other Problems to Solve before Departure

Even if a work-contract were easily obtainable and the financing of the departure were not a difficulty, the migrant would not be able to leave his village at once. He has to make sure that his family will not face any new problems because of his absence.

Migration and Shortage of Manpower

Migration should not lead to a change in the sexual division of labour within the household, a problem which varies in scale depending on the economic class of the migrant.

The village craftsman temporarily withdraws his *seypi* relations with the landowners when he goes abroad. This is not a problem since the *kammi* is allowed to interrupt them at any time. It is then up to the landowner to find a new carpenter or barber. Since these activities are hereditary, a migrant always has a relative in the village to continue the *zat* duties. A village specialist can therefore leave the village without worrying about his professional responsibilities or a possible shortage of manpower in his household.

The situation is different for a landowner, especially when he lives in a nuclear family, because of the normative obligations towards women of the household. As we shall see at length in the following chapter, a man's ideal mode of behaviour towards his womenfolk is to give them the possibility of observing *purdah*. This means granting them all the means – economic as well as social – so as not to be involved in tasks outside the house. Every man tries to live up to this expectation, and his prestige and respect among villagers increase according to how strictly he can follow these norms. Therefore it is out of the question to let a wife take over the man's labour when her husband goes abroad. Arrangements for cultivation have to be made, so the migrant asks his father or a brother to take care of his land in return for a share of the yield equivalent to that paid to a tenant. If there are no male relatives available or if the migrant is on bad terms with them, he rents his land out to a tenant. The wife will have then have to make some decisions concerning the agricultural production if unexpected problems arise, and she will have to be present in the fields at harvest time in order to supervise the tenant. If she does not have full confidence in him, a male in-law sleeps beside the harvested crops during the night. Her own male relatives are not welcome in her husband's fields. Such increased participation of a woman in the agricultural production is, however, very rare because it is the maximum limit of non-observance of *purdah* which a man can accept. It is an unsatisfactory solution to a shortage of manpower and a man's social prestige will suffer from it.

To sum up, the shortage of manpower in a household does not lead to a diminution in the agricultural production because the migrant is always able to find someone to cultivate his fields. However, it costs him a third of the production of rice and a quarter of the production of wheat, but it is a loss which is easily compensated for by the remittances sent home.

Migration and the Physical Protection of the Family

The notion of honour of the family is a very important consideration in Punjabi villages. A migrant must make sure that it will be maintained once he is abroad. The women's observance of *purdah* is not only guaranteed by economic security; she also requires physical protection against anybody who could threaten her honour. A man only leaves the village if there is someone to take care of his wife and children. In most cases, it is a trustworthy male relative. However, women often complain that their in-laws are exceeding the limits of what they can accept as a form of protection. Instead this chaperonage becomes a new means for the migrant's parents to exercise traditional coercive pressures upon their daughter-in-law. They use their role as protectors as a pretext to reduce her personal freedom.

Migration and the Maintenance of Equilibrium in the Political Life of the Village

The core of the socio-political life in the village is the *biraderi.* A *biraderi* is strong if it has many male members. Therefore, if three or four men of the same family controlling the *biraderi* are abroad, the political balance in the village might change since another family will try to become dominant. This situation might also occur when the migrant is a *biraderi* leader, as in the case of the Virck *biraderi* in Chahiwala with the departure of their leader, Amir.

Amir is the man around whom the consensus regarding lineage matters is realized. His decisions are respected by the other *biraderi* members even if they disagree with them. Amir left the village for Saudi

Arabia with a very clear idea of his collective responsibility. He naturally wanted to provide economic support for his wife, children and closest relatives. He also wanted his *biraderi* to remain the strongest in the village. Amir's father, up until his death, imposed his domination on the villagers by the use of coercive means, sometimes even terror. His sons have tried to imitate his methods but have not been able to achieve the same authority. Therefore, since the *biraderi* needs to use physical and psychological pressure to maintain its leading position in the village, it must compensate for this weakness by increasing its economic position. Amir will be the first in the village to combine a strong economic position with a strong political position. In fact, if the leader of a *biraderi* is well-off, he automatically becomes stronger politically through the use of money for obtaining political allies. The dominating group within the *biraderi* will then as a whole take advantage of his improved economic situation. It will be able to pay higher amounts of bail when one of its members sits in jail, or higher bribes to policemen, judges, and government officials to try to win court cases concerning, for example, disputes between landowner and tenant. One should remember that the shortage of land means that everyone is keen on increasing the size of their holdings. In other words, all the relatives of Amir will benefit from his absence in the long run and they will strengthen their domination over the other villagers with new economic sources.

This is well perceived by Amir's enemies who are also trying to go abroad. One of them expressed it in these terms: 'Enemy should be in front of enemy's eyes.' However, Amir is aware of the temporary political vacuum which might occur while he is away. There will be fights within the *biraderi* over the selection of a new leader since the *biraderi* members disagree over who this should be. Amir was only able to leave when all the political intrigues were to his faction's advantage. He is, however, not naive enough to believe that his closest relatives (brothers) and friends will follow all his instructions, either given before his departure or sent from Saudi Arabia. In this matter his wife could prove to be a more reliable ally than his own brothers, who are involved in intrigues and double-dealings. However, her illiteracy will make it difficult for her to find someone who will not misuse the content of the letters sent by Amir for his own interest against her and her family.

Another factor, which could have consequences for the political life of the village, especially in Baranpur, concerns the ethnic composition of the community. We have seen above that the class of landowners is a very

Figure 20: Amir, headman of his *biraderi*, surrounded by his relatives (Chahiwala)

heterogeneous social category due, on the one hand, to its internal economic differences, and, on the other, to its various geographical origins. The opposition between native and non-native villagers is the main cause of clashes in the village.

The proportion of migrants among the landowners is approximately the same among the native villagers and those who migrated to Baranpur after independence. Migration should not then be perceived as a further reason for conflicts between the two groups. The difference in the standard of living between landowners is not based on their origin since neither of the groups has better economic abilities to finance migration.

Migration and Its Consequences for the Villages

The villager leaves his village with the hope of realizing specific plans to improve the economic situation of his household and simultaneously increase his prestige. The question remains whether the actual effects of migration correspond to these expectations.

The Economic Consequences of Migration

In this section, we shall examine whether migration leads to the economic security and betterment anticipated by the household.

The Level of Wages Abroad and of Remittances

The majority of migrants receive a monthly salary of between Rs 3,000–5,000 according to their qualifications. The very low level of wages is advantageous to the transnational companies: they would have to pay much more for a Western worker doing the same job. For a Pakistani, however, this salary is six to ten times higher than what he could earn in Pakistan. Moreover, free food and accommodation are sometimes provided. The wage policy practised in the immigration countries is also influenced by the long tradition of alternative forms of remuneration, such as *bakshish*. All in all, the migrant may earn more than what is included in his work-contract.

Neither the receiving country nor the duration of migration has any influence on the size of the salary. It remains the same throughout the years. The rotating migration prevents the villagers from benefiting from long-service bonuses and there are no vocational courses in the receiving countries which could allow them to improve their skills.

Part of the salary covers the migrant's daily expenditures. He restricts his standard of living abroad so as to save as much as possible. The rest of the wages is either saved in cash or used to purchase numerous and costly presents, such as clothes, radios, cassette-recorders, watches, cameras, electric irons, juice-mixers and blankets, which he brings home during one of his leaves. It is difficult to calculate the value of these gifts because they are distributed between various households of the migrant's relatives. They expect him to be generous and some migrants complain about this practice which can postpone the establishment of a savings fund.

As a rule, between a third and a half of the wages is remitted home. The differences are due to the migrant's level of salary and to the cost of living in the receiving country. For example, very little money is sent from Iran because of the difficulty in saving from the salary which averages Rs 1,500 a month. The situation is similar for the migrants working in England and also because of the presence of the migrant's closest relatives who might have moved there as well. Unemployment could be a third reason.

Some receiving countries present another kind of problem for the Pakistani worker. It is very difficult (e.g. in Libya), if not impossible (e.g. in Iran), to send remittances out of these countries through official channels. The migrant has to smuggle the money out himself or through some trustworthy friends travelling to Pakistan. This method is not without risk since groups of bandits in the Irani Baluchistan have specialized in the robbery of Pakistani migrants travelling home. Moreover, the rates of exchange of the Iranian rial and the Libyan dinar are very low in Pakistan and all the migrants complained that they had nothing left once they had changed their money. Consequently the families could not regularly profit from the remittances and migration in this case entails an economic loss rather than a gain. The debts incurred for financing the departure could not be paid back and the sold buffaloes could not be replaced.

Usually the remittances are not sent every month but every six months, sometimes only once a year. In this way both the sender and the receiver do not have to go to the bank too often and deal with bureaucratic procedures. This means, however, that the receiver must establish a monthly budget so as not to spend all the money at once. This is not easy because the villagers are not used to handling so much money at once. They are tempted to purchase goods which they could not otherwise afford. It is not unusual for a wife to have to ask for more money for the children because of her poor budgeting of the large sums of money sent infrequently.

The head of the household is the receiver, especially in extended families. In most cases, it is the father or, if he is no longer living, his widow. An elder brother may also be the contact person in Pakistan. When the migrant is older and the head of a nuclear family, he usually sends the money to his father. He might also send it to his wife if he has allowed her to open a bank account. This procedure also requires that a woman feels at ease going to the city and being confronted with a male-dominated sphere.

Households try to avoid internal family feuds provoked by the arrival of remittances. Irrespective of the receiver's social position in the household, he or she has to redistribute them in a fair manner. In an extended family, the money is used by all the members because they cook together, but the ownership of any productive investments belongs solely to the migrant and/or his father, even if they are shared jointly with other members of the household. However, disputes may arise between the migrant's parents and his wife when she feels that she does not receive a proper share of the remittances. Both sides abuse each other and the migrant does not know whom to believe in the letters he receives explaining the disagreement.

The social hierarchy is respected when two migrants from the same household are abroad in the same country. The younger migrant transfers his share of remittances to his relatives' bank account (usually the elder brother). Expenditures are made jointly, but each brother knows precisely how much he has given and which items have been purchased with his money. They keep records of these expenditures for the sake of avoiding conflicts.

Use of Remittances

For most of the men abroad, their absence from the villages has been too brief to lead to a significant betterment of their economy. The use of the remittances underlines the economic needs as driving forces for leaving the village. They cover the consumption expenditures of the migrant household, such as food and clothes. Only two migrant households have debts with the local shopkeeper, however, with the guarantee that they will easily reimburse him. As a migrant's mother expressed it:

> Now we live in peace. We don't have to think about food and money. We eat better. We have passed from a state of undernourishment to an almost normal quantity of food for us but not according to Western standards.

Another villager said:

> We eat better food and wear better clothes than before. Sweets, rice, vegetables and meat are available daily.

The migrant households do not change their daily consumption habits even though they can afford to do so. For example, they continue to use kerosene lamps although they could easily pay for the installation and cost of electricity. However, they have the economic security of being able to purchase food when they need it. Consumer durable goods, such as radios and TV sets, sewing-machines, wristwatches and electric grinders are also brought by the migrant when he visits his family. These goods are considered a means of increasing prestige, particularly if the house does not have electricity.

Remittances also offer a better security against unexpected expenditures. Only part of the remitted money is used for daily needs. In fact, before leaving his village, the migrant has three main ideas in mind concerning the use of the first remittances.

First of all, he wants to pay back the money borrowed for financing his departure. Too much of his own honour as well as that of his family is at stake concerning the reimbursement of his debts and not behaving fairly and honestly with his creditors. The only case in which a migrant had paid nothing back of the borrowed Rs 25,000 after three years abroad, occurred in a *lambardar's* household of Baranpur. One may assume that his political position allowed a greater patience and tolerance on the part of the creditor, as well as a lack of means of pressure.

The time required for reimbursement obviously varies with the amount borrowed and the level of a migrant's wages. Usually it takes him from one to three years.

When the migration has been financed by a father or a brother, it is not considered as borrowed money but as an investment beneficial to the household. However, when debts are incurred with relatives who are not as close, such as the father's brother's level or the affinal parents, it is compulsory to pay them back as soon as possible. The solidarity between the two households will otherwise be severely eroded.

Simultaneously with this reimbursement, the migrant puts aside money to finance weddings, either his own and/or his brothers' and sisters' because of the solidarity he is expected to show towards the other members of his family. The amount of money put aside for this purpose does not depend on the length of the migration but on the desire of the household to increase its prestige through a costly wedding ceremony and an impressive dowry. In fact, parents worry about not being able to give their daughters a decent wedding and dowry, especially when they follow each other in a row. It also becomes easier to find a suitable partner when the bride's economy is sound. In other words, the more one spends, the more respect and prestige are accumulated. The family is proud if it can offer Rs 50,000 or more. It is not rare for children of the same household to be married at the same time. This has two advantages. First, it saves money through only having to pay for one ceremony; second, it gives an impression of ostentation with the display of many more gifts than if only one person had married.

This never-ending race for more prestige is well illustrated by the case of two barbers from Chahiwala who were sent to Dubai with their army corps in the middle of the 1960s when Pakistan began to have military advisers in several countries of the Gulf. These two brothers had a yearly income of Rs 240,000 from which they remitted Rs 85,000 home. They spent Rs 145,000 on the wedding of the eldest son of one of them in 1981 (Rs 95,000 for jewellery, Rs 25,000 for clothes and Rs 25,000 for the food and other expenses of the wedding ceremony itself).

Figure 21: Holding ostentatious wedding parties is one of the main uses of foreign remittances. Here a son from the barbers' family gets married, wearing necklaces of banknotes.

The international migration causes an inflation in the cost of weddings. The households without a migrant cannot spend the same amount of money on this social ceremony. Even if they resign themselves to more modest weddings, they still make some special economic arrangements, such as selling cattle or a landholding, in order not to lose their honour. A wedding, then, is a great economic burden for a family if it has to live up to the villagers' expectations. One might even say that the need to marry one's children properly is one of the main reasons for taking a job abroad.

The third priority for the use of remittances is a consumption-type investment, such as the reparation of the old house or the construction of additional rooms, or the building of a new house. This type of investment was carried out in half of the migrant households during the first years after the departure.

The need to improve the residence is in fact very real. Villagers live in crowded rooms – sometimes only one – with no comforts. Many houses are still made either of mud or of half-brick/half-mud and require reparation by the women of the household after the summer rains.

Figure 22: A traditional house of a family without a migrant (Chahiwala)

Figure 23: Migrants' houses are large, have several storeys, and are made of brick

All the houses with a migrant in Chahiwala are equipped with a handpump in the yard. In Baranpur, however, the installation of a handpump is not a top priority even though providing water is very strenuous work for the women and/or the daughters of the household as soon as they are old enough to carry 20 litre buckets on their head. An average time of one hour ten minutes is required for this daily domestic task, depending on the number of members in the household and the distance to the wells.

Faiza said:

> Women could help more in cultivation if they could save these three hours spent in fetching water. We cannot look after the children properly. The timing of meals would be more fixed if our daily routine was not always interrupted by the need for water.

Three migrant households from Chahiwala have bought residential land in Pasrur and Gujranwala. Some men find the village life too simple and too conflict-ridden after they have worked abroad.

To summarize, the majority of migrant households do not use their remittances for the financing of productive investments. Too many basic needs – material as well as ideological – have to be satisfied first. Only one migrant household in Chahiwala and five in Baranpur have begun to follow another economic pattern, but only because they have a large amount of resources at their disposal.

In the case of Baranpur, these migrant households belong to the group of the largest landowners of the village and their members have been abroad longer than the average time spent by the other migrants. They purchase agricultural land in the village from landowners who wish to return to their home area in Kashmir. In two cases agricultural implements – a tractor with a trolley and a wheat-grinder – have also been bought. Their owners gain new sources of income by renting them out.

As regards Chahiwala, some landowners think that there will be a change in the redistribution of land in the years to come. The sons of the landowners, who own very small holdings today, will not be able to sustain their family's livelihood from the inherited plots. They will have to move outside the village and might then sell their land. Therefore, the better-off landowners believe that they will have the chance to increase their landed property. So far, however, only the household with the two barbers working in Dubai have used their remittances for productive investments. They have bought 44 acres of cultivable land over three

Figure 24: Wheat-grinder purchased with migrant's remittances (Baranpur)

transactions (12 and 10 acres of middle quality for Rs 10,000 and Rs 6,000 in 1967 and 1968 respectively, and 22 acres of the best quality for Rs 400,000 in 1979). They have therefore become the biggest landowners of the village. In addition, they built a large modern stable for Rs 4,000 in 1979 and purchased three buffaloes. They also installed a tubewell worth Rs 8,000 in 1975 and bought a variety of agricultural implements: a Fiat 640 tractor with plow and harrow for Rs 75,000 as well as a trolley worth Rs 22,000 in 1978 and a Rs 20,000 wheat-thresher in 1979.

The other form of investment which this family has chosen is the provision of a good education for the children, especially the sons. They go to a boarding school in Abbotabad and also have private tutors at home. A minimum of Rs 2,500 is spent on their school fees monthly.

All the villagers have been impressed by the economic results achieved by the barbers' family, especially because it is a craftsman's family, and yet is now the wealthiest in the village. Landowners have always considered themselves superior to barbers and cannot accept this transformation of the social life in the village. This indicates that working abroad is the only way to become better off. Other migrant households would like to follow in their footsteps and mechanize the agricultural processes, mostly by the purchase of a tractor.

The Budget of Migrant Households

The economy of a household with a migrant is a sensitive subject. People are reluctant to answer some questions, especially those concerning the size of their savings in bank accounts. They fear that the obtained information could be used by the authorities to levy taxes on these savings. Nevertheless, it was possible to gain an idea of the importance of remittances through talking to a migrant's jealous neighbours who are always overestimating a migrant's wealth. Taking an average between what a migrant's family said and what their neighbours said was a means to arrive at an approximate realistic amount. External signs like material possessions and the condition of a house could also indicate the household's living standard.

The budget of the migrant households is formulated according to the same method as that used previously for the households of landowners and of craftsmen, so it can be compared with the budget of households without a migrant.

The average budgets for the O.C.T.1 in Chahiwala and the S.C.2 in Baranpur are a little biased because they are based on just one household. Nevertheless, Table 6.6 gives an indication of the role played by the remittances in the monthly income. If one discounts the craftsmen of Baranpur (because of unreliable data concerning the amount of remittances and the unusual budget of the barber's family in Chahiwala), the migrant households have a total income which is at least three times higher than those of the households without a migrant. This difference is exclusively due to the remitted money. The agricultural income and expenditures are approximately the same in both groups since the migrants have not started to buy land and/or livestock, or to cultivate more intensively. However, the purchase of agricultural implements by the S.C.2 and S.C.4 categories of landowners in Baranpur provides a substantial supplementary source of income by ploughing other cultivators' fields or by grinding their wheat.

Table 6.6: Average monthly budget of migrant households (in Rs) – *continued overleaf*

Social categories	Av. members in household	Agricultural income	Other income	Remittances	Total income	Consumption expenditure	Agric. + cattle expenditure	Total expenditure	Surplus/deficit
			Chahiwala:						
S.C.1	6	666		1,000	1,666	834	446	1,276	+ 390
	(6.8)	(702)	(657)		(1,359)	(515)	(256)	(1,286)	(+ 73)
O.C.T.1	3	916		250	1,166	520	150	670	+ 496
	(8)	(860)	(581)		(1,441)	(572)	(304)	(876)	(+ 565)
O.C.T.2	5	1,333		700	2,033	640	150	790	+ 1,243
	(9.2)	(1,500)	(437)		(1,937)	(582)	(364)	(946)	(+ 991)
Blacksmith/carpenter	5	54		1,333	1,387	995	paid by tenant	995	+392
	(4.5)				(1,076)	(514)		(514)	(+562)
Barber	24	10,000		7,000	17,000	4,300	5,500	9,800	+ 7,200

Table 6.6 cont.: Average monthly budget of migrant households (in Rs)

Social categories	Av. members in household	Agricultural income	Other income	Remittances	Total income	Consumption expenditure	Agric. + cattle expenditure	Total expenditure	Surplus/deficit
				Baranpur:					
S.C.1	6.6	271	563	1,413	2,247	1,162	135	1,297	+ 950
	(6.2)	(212)	(500)		(712)	(638)	(111)	(749)	(- 37)
S.C.2	18	1,316		5,166	6,,482	4,046	690	4,736	+ 1,746
	(8.7)	(285)	(441)		(726)	(1,176)	(198)	(1,374)	(- 648)
S.C.4	18	1,809	650	2,083	4,542	2,399	250	2,649	+ 1,893
Former landowner	7.7		521	1,635	2,156	1,219	38	1,257	+ 899
	(6.5)	(300)	(690)		(990)	(640)	(87)	(727)	(+ 263)
Village craftsmen	6.5			475	475	1036	200	1236	- 761
	(5.9)		(818)		(818)	(499)	(147)	(646)	(+ 172)

It is apparent that although consumption expenditures are slightly higher, the consumption patterns remain similar. A household does not spend the remittances on luxury goods. The main difference between the two categories of households is not in the amount of money at the disposal of the family for its daily consumption but in the security of the remittances as a source of income. A work-contract abroad offers the migrant a guaranteed salary every month. This is not the case for the villagers even when they have off-farm employment. Moreover, the employing companies in the Gulf States offer medical protection to their workers. It is an advantage which is very much appreciated by the migrant and by the villagers as a whole because of the non-existence of medical facilities in the Pakistani villages.

In contrast with the permanent economic deficit or reduction of consumption in the households without a migrant, the migrant households have the means to face sudden expenditures, such as medical treatment, and to establish saving funds which will be used for covering the other social needs mentioned above.

The Perception of the Economic Consequences of Migration by the Non-Migrant Households

The opinion that the migrants dispose of endless economic resources is commonly shared in the villages. Statements like the followings are commonly expressed:

> Migrants don't care about money. If something costs Rs 10, they will pay 20. In this way the price of commodities has increased.

> The households with a migrant are considered as households which do not have to count money. Their members change their food, their clothes, everything. They do not ask for the price of things. They just buy them. They buy land, jewels, buses, shops, etc. They build brick houses which they decorate nicely. They marry their children properly. They invite dancers and musicians to the wedding ceremonies.

It is as if migration allows for the realization of each and every wish. There is no more material limitation to having one's dreams come true. Non-migrant households also consider migration to be responsible for the high cost of living prevailing in the villages today. The prices of daily consumption goods and of durable goods, such as houses and land, are said to have increased because of these new sources of income. Similarly, the costly social expenditures prescribed by the ideological system in the villages are also affected by inflationary tendencies provoked by the migration. It is a common wish among all the villagers to display as much money as possible on social ceremonies but only migrant households are able to do this.

This new economic inequality is felt very much by the households without a migrant. They can only observe the new social situation which is being established in the village and are economically powerless in this competition unless a work-contract in a foreign country is obtained. Jealousy and anger are not necessarily expressed but the villagers object that the same possibilities of working abroad are not offered to everyone.

Economic disparities have always existed in the village but the foreign remittances have totally changed the rules of economic competition between the villagers. The non-migrant households compare their daily life with its constant material hardships to the apparent ease which seems to characterize the migrant households. Some of them try not to lose their prestige by taking great economic risks :

> The poor man or the non-migrant cannot compete with the migrant. Everything is getting expensive due to migrants' income. Migrants give many foreign-made items in the dowry. Non-migrants can't give such things. So sometimes people sell cattle or land in order to compete with the migrant households.
>
> Poor people sell land and cattle so as to give a dowry to their daughters. Migrants give sofas, chairs and many things in the dowry. Poor people give only *charpai* [ordinary beds].
>
> Migrants spend a lot of money and in order to compete with them the other villagers borrow money and sell land. If a migrant gives 10 *tola*s of gold and 10 pairs of suits in the dowry, the non-migrant will try to give the same quantity.

The feeling of dissatisfaction is more widespread among the landowners than among the village craftsmen. This is probably because competition for social mobility is fiercer between landowners than between craftsmen. Landowners have to cope with the anger of not being able to compete with the migrants, especially when these are from a lower social status, since traditionally the landowners consider themselves as being of a higher social rank than the rest of the villagers. Since they cannot stop the village craftsmen from becoming wealthier, the landowners remind them that money cannot change their social position in the village, and that as *kammi*s, they are at the service of landowners. For example, when the family of the two barbers in Dubai got the electric connection for the tubewell, the head of the most important *biraderi* of landowners objected.

His opinion was that *kammis* should not get the same facilities as the landowners. The barbers then had to pay Rs 2,500 to obtain the landowners' approval for this electric installation. In other words, a strong *biraderi* of landowners can force wealthier families of craftsmen to work for them without any form of remuneration, for example ploughing their fields with a tractor bought with remittances without paying for the petrol. The only way for the *kammis* to defend themselves and to be respected would be to organize themselves in different villages. Any action in one village alone would only be successful if they obtained the support of the other petty landowners who also feel frustrated because of the domination exercised by the strongest *biraderi*. Otherwise, such actions would be fruitless since the *kammis* always belong to the minority in the villages.

The migrants perceive their situation differently. Forty-eight per cent of them consider that their standard of living has not improved, either qualitatively or quantitatively, while 32 per cent hold the opposite view. This perception of no economic improvement is sincere and is sometimes also due to a feeling of uneasiness over being more wealthy among poor people. The better-off villagers always excuse their economic status by saying that there are people who are still richer than themselves and that one should not be jealous of others' property.

Migration and Social Changes

Migration is a new cause of quarrels in the village. More land is cultivated by tenants or by the migrant's relatives, and disputes over the division of the shares after harvest are more frequent. The jealousy and competition between families of the same *biraderi* and between members of the same family cast a shadow over the migrant's departure.

In general the migrant does not break off contact with his village and follows what happens in his home. The wife writes to inform her husband about the behaviour of his parents or brothers. Usually, the traditional disagreements between the wife and the in-laws become more acute because they try to control their daughter-in-law more than they would be allowed to do if her husband were at home. The migrant does not know how to handle these family quarrels when he is 5,000 km away, even if they had already occurred before his departure. He gives support alternately to both sides in his replies to them. He is irritated by the type of relationship based upon competition which the villagers have with each other and often starts to disapprove of some aspects of the village social life as his worldview becomes broader.

Since most of the women are illiterate, they have to find a suitable person to write their letters. It has to be someone in whom they can confide their family problems. Usually it is a man, preferably the head of the *biraderi*. However, a woman is then limited in the nature of information which can be sent to her husband. For example, she cannot mention any sexual problems, such as her fear of being pregnant again when her menstruation is delayed either because she is really expecting a child after her husband's holiday visit or because she is psychologically disturbed after her husband's departure. She then has to keep her worries to herself or confide in her female friends.

The use of remittances is another source of strife between household members. The traditional decision-making process delegates the last word to the head of the household. Sometimes the migrant does not agree with the choice of investment. Nevertheless, he has to accept it because of the social norms which demand respect for one's elders, although he feels frustrated.

Bashir says:

> I do not like to remain in the village, but my father forces me to build a house here. I will spend Rs 100,000 against my wishes. My father wants us to live as an extended family. I don't.

Being away from one's family and familiar socio-cultural environment provokes a variety of reactions, depending on the migrant's personality. Villagers, as a rule, are very discrete about everything concerning their emotional life. A migrant's standard answer is the longing for his children. However, he does not experience any problems of social readjustment to village life after two or three years of absence.

> I do not face any cultural problems when I am again in the village. I have not changed myself. I am the same man and the village has not changed.
>
> The first time I came back to the village after three years abroad, I did not feel anything special. I was neither happy, nor unhappy. Three years are nothing. All my family lives here. I have grown up here. I could not see any differences in the village. I left all my memories of my travels there [he works as a sailor] and I don't miss the things I have seen abroad.

As Mohammed Aslam said:

> As soon as I am landing in Karachi or Islamabad, I am very happy to be back in my country. I forget everything, all the problems from Libya.

In other words, from the migrant's point of view, a long absence does not change his relationship with his background. His cultural identity is deep-rooted enough not to be disturbed by the social environment of the receiving countries, especially when they are Arabic. The common Pakistani does not consider the Arabic society to be as intellectually and culturally developed as the Pakistani society and consequently does not have any desire at all to establish himself there. The transformation of a migrant's worldview may be greater if he works in Europe and he may lead a double life with family here and there.

What the migrant feels the most when he is in the village again is the state of poverty. Once he has been used to basic facilities abroad, he feels more acutely than before the lack of running water, electricity, medical care and proper educational arrangements for the children.

Although none of the migrant households has noticed any form of aggression or alteration in their relationships with the other villagers, almost half of the non-migrant population considers that migration leads to a change in the social behaviour of the individual. The migrant is criticized for his new arrogance and pride, sometimes in strong terms:

> If I give good fodder to my cattle, they will become fat and strong. They will try to push away the other cattle. The migrants behave in the same way. When they get money and the chance to work abroad, they think that their importance has increased.

A widow expressed her feelings in these words:

> Migrants and non-migrants cannot be equal. The women in migrant families do not allow us to sit near them because they wear foreign-made clothes. They consider us as foolish and stupid. The migrant deposits a lot of money in the bank. When their wives or other members of the family go to the bank to get the money, they say: we are going to the bank to cash a cheque. This way they show their superiority.

Complaints are made against the migrants for not helping the poor people (as is prescribed in the Qur'an), for not economically supporting their *biraderi* (the remittances are only used among the migrants' close kin and consequently some very poor people may co-exist alongside some better-off people within the same *biraderi*), for not sending work-contracts to their relatives from abroad, and for no longer following the customary social laws and precepts of the village because their new wealth allows them to become socially more independent. With their remittances they do not have to rely as heavily on the co-operation within the village as before.

This change of attitude proves to some villagers that money is turning people's heads and they feel uneasy about the transformations occurring in the social life of the village. They think that money is becoming more and more important in the villagers' relationships and it threatens the traditional solidarity between people, like the rituals of *vartan bhanji*.

However, some villagers express a more balanced opinion. They do not blame the migrants as a whole but only certain individuals among them. A migrant's behaviour depends on his personality and background.

> Those migrants who belong to good families don't change their behaviour, but those who don't become proud and try to show that they have money.
>
> There are different types of people. Some have a good nature, some have a bad one. It is the same in the case of migrants. Some behave in a good way, others don't.

To summarize, international migration is also considered responsible for negative economic and social changes. One of the main transformations it entails concerns the traditional position of women in the village, which is discussed in the next chapter.

Note

1 *Hadith* [Tradition] refers to the 'record of the sayings and doings of the Prophet Muhammad and his companions, and as such is regarded by Muslims as a source of Islamic law, dogma and ritual second only in importance to the Qur'an itself' (I.R. Netton 1992:90).

2 A type of contract where the share of the input and output is on a one-fifth/four-fifths basis.

7 INTERNATIONAL MIGRATION AND WOMEN'S ROLE IN THE VILLAGE

This chapter introduces the social and economic consequences of international labour migration upon the village women. It will investigate whether their participation in the process of income-generating production has increased or remained the same, whether women have begun to occupy a more important position in the decision-making process due to the absence of their husbands, and finally whether it has led to a greater number of female-headed households.

Role of Ideology for the Sexual Division of Labour in the Household

Gender relations in Pakistani villages are determined by a political economy of honour (*izzat*) which is the ideological legitimacy of patriarchy. It defines for each gender a set of perceptions and practices which place women in a position both subordinate to and dependent on men. These relations are logical in the villagers' conceptions of the individual and are shared by both genders across the economic divisions. Any transformation of the women's socio-economic position in the village due to the men's international labour migration cannot be analysed without relating them to this ideology.

Honour and gender relations are very closely intertwined. The honour of an individual is very fragile and must always be protected because it is extremely difficult to achieve or to regain once it is lost or damaged. In fact, the quantity of honour fluctuates. It can increase and decrease but it should not drop badly.

The reputation and status of the patrilineage, the family and the household are affected when a female member loses her *izzat*. This is because the honour of a woman is not her private property; it is intermingled with the honour of her consanguineous ties, and also after her marriage with the honour of her affinal ties. A woman's honour refers to her modest behaviour. This modesty is ensured by covering her body – the extreme form being the veiling of the face – and by her avoidance of any kind of contact with male strangers, including eye contact.

The main criterion for a respectable woman at the time of marriage is her virginity. A virgin bride is the proof that parents have been vigilant and that they have correctly socialized their daughter. It also means that she has understood her responsibilities towards her family and behaved accordingly. She might therefore become a good wife.

The consequences for the family's honour are less severe when it is a male villager who is involved in incorrect actions. In the patriarchal society, the dichotomy of honour/shame has been defined by the men and therefore illicit sexual relations are in most cases considered to be caused by the woman's provocative behaviour while the man is looked upon as a seduced and weak victim.

A means of protection is therefore essential for safeguarding the collective honour. In both villages, the definition of the ideal woman across the economic divisions stipulates her confinement (*purdah*), and a segregation between genders. Through *purdah*, women are prevented from meeting male non-relatives. *Purdah* is also considered to be correct behaviour due to its religious connotation. Respect is gained by following orthodox instructions.

The economic consequence of this ideology is the women's total exclusion from phases of the production process occurring outside the house. The patriarchal ideology specifies that female tasks are to be confined to the running of the household and to biological reproduction. However, the practice of *purdah* cannot be separated from the economic status of each family. In fact, the possibility of achieving this ideal behaviour depends on economic resources and on the position occupied by the household in the social divisions of the village.

In both villages, women are not secluded in their house. They walk freely in the streets of the village and do not veil their face. They are not even obliged to wear a *burqah*[1] when they go to the market towns. They are, however, accompanied by a male child or a female friend. The only restriction is that they do not leave their houses alone in the evening. The state of the economy in the two villages is directly responsible for this lack of orthodoxy. In both places the poverty of the villagers has slowly receded in the last 100 years, but not enough to allow them to follow what they consider to be proper and ideal Muslim behaviour. Villagers regret not being able to live up to their ideal and one aim behind their wish to improve the economy of the household is to provide the economic basis for a satisfactory practice of *purdah*.

A landowner belonging to the strongest fraction of the *biraderi* which controls the village Chahiwala, namely the fraction most likely to enforce the orthodox behaviour of its women, thus increasing its prestige and political power, describes the situation in these terms:

> The observance of *purdah* began to decline after the construction of the half-*pakka*/half-*katcha* road between Pasrur and Gujranwala in 1965. Men started to go more to the city; women did too and saw other women there who were moving more freely. Before, when male visitors came to a house, women used to sit in one corner of the room and to hide their face, since there was no special quarter for women in the house.

Nowadays in fact, the unsound economy still does not allow the separation of houses into the women's quarter (*zenana*) and the men's area (*merdana*). Some houses have only one room which is used for the diverse activities of eating, receiving guests and sleeping. Women cook outside under a shed in the yard and remain there when male non-relatives visit. However, the situation changes when migrants have saved enough money to build a new house or to enlarge the existing one.

If after many years of working abroad – at least 10 years – a migrant's household has become more prosperous by village standards, the tendency is then to observe *purdah* more strictly. The household then has the economic means to pay labourers to carry out the women's extra-domestic duties and can therefore afford the seclusion of the womenfolk. According to the villagers' way of thinking, observation of the orthodox rules regarding the women's behaviour is a means of increasing one's social status. Therefore the women's confinement is a logical consequence both for the class of landowners and for the class of craftsmen when it becomes economically viable. This trend occurs even more rapidly among the craftsmen because this behaviour is considered an adequate strategy for reducing their social differences with the landowners and therefore for increasing their social status. For example in the case of the barbers' family with two migrants, the beginning of a tendency to observe a more strict *purdah* was obvious. The oldest son of one of them married while I was there, and his young wife was not allowed to be seen by strangers. The wealth of this family has not allowed them the possibility of access to a recognized social status in the village. Rather, by adopting orthodox rules for the new bride, close to the ideal behaviour, the family hopes to become more respected. I noticed the same trend in a village of the Jhelum area in 1977, where the richest families with out-migrants in Western Europe could finally afford the seclusion of their women.

It is therefore not money itself which is the channel to reach a better social position among the villagers but rather its use according to the ideal norms. From this angle, the woman's seclusion is a practice which brings most respect. In other words, the expression of men's economic superiority is related to women's greater dependence on the male members of the household.

In the long run, out-migration thus seems to strengthen the observance of *purdah* among the wealthiest families of the village. However, in the short run, the migrant must ensure that his departure does not have an immediate adverse effect. An economic improvement through foreign remittances must not be accompanied by a loss of prestige, as will inevitably be the case if the women's role and authority in the village are radically transformed.

The migrant has to make arrangements so that his absence will not entail a shortage of labour in the household which has to be compensated for by an increase in female participation in the process of production. Neither should it lead to the woman's greater responsibility in decision-making. Furthermore, migration should not compel the women to have more contact with the male-dominated sphere of the society outside the village. To sum up, out-migration should not mean the diminution of the migrant's power of control and decision in the household.

Migration and the Role of Women in the Production Process

The specialization of tasks in the village defined by the *seypi* system also determines the relationships between women. Class and gender are interrelated. The level of engagement of female labour in the process of production is determined by differing levels of economic resources at the disposal of each household. At the same time, however, all women must submit to the same customary rules which define relations between genders. Their work has traditionally been an essential component of the household subsistence economy but nowadays is also related to the market economy through their processing of cash-crops.

Women's Participation in Agriculture

Women, besides their domestic work inside the house, participate in agricultural labour, especially during the harvest season when the different operations have to be executed rapidly because of the potential risk to the crops from bad weather.

The higher level of poverty in Baranpur is responsible for a greater female participation in agricultural tasks than in Chahiwala. In fact, as a rule, the women of Chahiwala do not cut the crops themselves, except in the poorest families, where all available manpower is recruited for harvesting the better-off cultivators' fields. For poor households, it is more important to ensure sufficiently large quantities of rice and wheat than to have their women observing *purdah*. However, a division of labour between females according to their age occurs: grown-up daughters are responsible for the purely domestic work while the elderly mother works in the fields. Sakeena Bibi, whose husband works in a steel-mill in Karachi, says:

> My father-in-law lives in our house. He is an old and sick man. He is not able to manage the affairs of the house. He only takes care of the buffaloes. My husband does not earn enough. Often he only comes home once a year so as to save the travel costs. I am responsible for all the things here. I work very hard. I cut grass in different fields everyday. I also cut rice and sugar cane during the harvest. I bring fodder to the cattle and I give sugar cane to the landowner. My daughters help me to get more money. They do embroidery and needle work. In this way, they can earn Rs 100 monthly. We also sell milk.

During the harvesting seasons, women have to work with hardly any breaks during the day. They spend 5–6 hours daily in the fields cutting

Figure 25: Landowner woman cleaning seeds from cotton (Chahiwala)

the crops. The hiring of casual and seasonal labourers is not practised in poor households. Instead they use the system of reciprocal help between *biraderi* members (*mangi hal*) to make up labour shortages. Friends help too. This co-operation means increased domestic work for the women since meals are served three times a day to the labourers.

Jasmeen, a landowner's 18-year-old daughter in Baranpur, says:

> During the time of harvest, one woman has to remain in the house to cook the food for the people cutting wheat. It does not matter who she is. She might be a young daughter of 13–14 years or an old woman. In the morning she prepares breakfast. Then, when the people have started the cutting, she makes tea which she brings to the fields in the middle of the morning. When she comes back to the house, she cooks the lunch. She brings it to the fields or the labourers come to the house to take it.

In the afternoon, she makes tea again. She brings it to the fields. Later on, she prepares the dinner. She also has to wash the dishes and fetch the water. The children help her in this task. Many of the women who cut have to do the same work once they are back home from the fields. They give fodder to the cattle and milk them. They bring water from the well. It means that the household eats the evening meal an hour later than usual. The men may remain longer in the fields than the women in the evening.

The agricultural tasks accomplished by the women are:

- *preparation of the threshing ground* by making a fresh layer of mud and cow dung in order to prevent dust and dirt being mixed with crop grains;
- *threshing of wheat and rice.* They help the men in this agricultural operation. The archaic method of threshing entails that a great quantity of crops is wasted. Women of the poorest households go to the threshing places to glean the remaining grains when the threshing is finished;
- *winnowing.* This is solely a female task. Women may winnow the same crops several times. In Chahiwala, for one harvested acre of paddy field, three women winnow 4–5 hours daily for 3–4 days;
- *picking and carding of cotton in Chahiwala.* The seeds are crushed so as to make oil which is used either as cooking oil or as a complement to the fodder for the buffaloes. The milk is then more consistent;
- *other tasks.* When the household has a vegetable garden, women are responsible for its maintenance. Caring for the poultry is also a female activity.

Tending cattle, which is the other main productive work of the household, is a task carried out by men, women and children, according to the following gender division of labour:

- Cutting fodder and feeding the cattle are done by men, women and children. Those from poor households do the strenuous work of cutting grass with a sickle from different fields. The fodder-cutter, like all other agricultural machines, is operated only by men.
- Milking is done by men and women.
- Cleaning the stable or cattleshed is the work of women and children. A few families in Chahiwala employ Christian women for this

specific task as an element of the *seypi* relationship. One or two *maunds* of rice and wheat are given as yearly payment.

The women prepare the dairy products – clarified butter (*ghee*) and buttermilk (*lassi*) – which are sold to hawkers coming to the village. Some households earn Rs 100 monthly from this trade.

Figure 26: Landowner woman threshing wheat (Baranpur)

On average, a little more than 3 hours per day are spent by women for cutting fodder, feeding, milking and cleaning the cattleshed. With regard to the cultivation of crops, work is divided on an approximately equal basis between genders, since the average number of working hours on these agricultural tasks is only slightly higher for the women, with 5 hours daily against 4 hours for the men. However, all in all the women's workload is much greater, since it is in addition to her participation in exclusively female chores.

To summarize, the village women's involvement in the extra-domestic work is never remunerated. None of them works in a factory or has any kind of unskilled job in the town. They are engaged only in the agricultural sector.

Their importance in the household productivity is related to the economic situation of the household and to the number of men who are themselves engaged in agricultural activities. The Green Revolution has not made their workload easier since only the production of crops has been improved while the techniques of crop harvesting and processing mastered by women have remained archaic.

The departure of a male member is not intended to bring about a change to the traditional division of labour between men and women. The female workload is identical in migrant households. It has neither increased (as would be the case if a shortage of manpower in the household leading to a greater participation by women in the process of production should occur) nor decreased (through the purchase of modern agricultural implements which could facilitate the women's tasks). Women still work according to the traditional labour-intensive and time-consuming techniques.

Shortage of labour due to out-migration is not a problem in the case of households with an extended family but it might matter in households constituted by nuclear families.

The economic improvement must not be accompanied by a loss of prestige. Increased involvement of the female workforce in agriculture would be evidence of such a loss of prestige. Instead, the migrant's land will be tilled by a very close relative (father or brother) on a tacit agreement. The cultivator will receive a share of the crops but not the rate customarily followed in the case of tenancy. If no male relatives are available, land is cultivated by a tenant. He receives one-third of the rice and one-quarter of the wheat production. In both cases, these arrangements mean that the migrant's wife does not have to work more in the fields. However, her importance in the decision-making process might increase in the event of problems with the tenant.

Women's Work in Households of Craftsmen

Not all the households of the craftsmen are engaged in traditional *seypi* relationships. This is due either to the absence of work demanded by the landowners or to the refusal of the landless people to work for landowners who treat them as their servants. In some cases, the *seypi* relationships are based on the complementary nature of the women's and men's work. The occupational *zat*s have traditionally been poor and there has been no economic possibility for their women to observe *purdah*. There is even more necessity for women in such landless households to become income earners than women in landowners' households. The existence of poverty means that all the available labour force, including women, has to be engaged in productive activities. The pooling of the diverse sources of revenue is more important than ever.

The *zat* of water-carrier (*machi*) in Chahiwala fulfils another function besides bringing water to the households, namely the selling of roasted wheat and rice. In six out of ten *machi* households, women roast wheat and rice on a large iron frying-pan outside the house. The roasted crops are sold by the husband in towns. The women do not usually go there because it entails permanent contact with strangers. They also roast the crops brought by the village women and children to the roasting place every day. The *machi* woman takes a handful of crops from each customer. On a monthly basis, it is equivalent to 15 kg of each crop.

Figure 27: Aisha of the water-carrier *zat* roasts wheat (Chahiwala)

When the man of a bard's or barber's household is engaged in *seypi* relations, the woman helps him at social ceremonies. Together they clean the house, the host's cooking utensils and china before and after the party. They cook and serve food for the guests. The woman's payment in wheat and rice is included in the share of crops given to the man on the basis of *seypi* relations. It is thus not possible to quantify exactly the amount earned by the woman.

In the weavers' households, the women's participation in the process of production was traditionally to make the patterns of the piece to weave on the horizontal loom.

Women of the other occupational *zat*s do not participate specifically in the *seypi* relationships. However, unlike the women of the landowners' households, they show a more entrepreneurial spirit. The craftsmen's households are more poverty-stricken and have to mobilize all their available man-power resources. Some women have opened a tiny shop in a room of their house; others take care of their husbands' shops when these are away in the town purchasing goods.

Figure 28: Shaheda in her shop (Chahiwala)

Another source of income for landless women is through the production of handicrafts which are sold either in the village or to hawkers from nearby markets. For example, some women of the shoemaker *zat* make straw-baskets, especially in the summer after harvest.

They dye the straw themselves into different colours and create geometric patterns. A woman can make one basket per day. They are sold for between Rs 5–10, according to the size. The weaving of multicoloured threads into a belt and embroidery works on shawls are also common in several households.

Figure 29: Woman of the craftsmen's class making a basket (Chahiwala)

Women of landless households are also engaged in agricultural activities when their menfolk take part in the harvest of landowners' fields. For instance, Christian women are recognized and appreciated for their competence in the winnowing of crops and seeds. They also clean the stables and cattlesheds for the landowners. They do not have to make dung-cakes but leave the dung in a heap for the landowners' women.

As mentioned above, the households of village craftsmen with a migrant belong to the blacksmith-carpenter *zat*, where women are not involved in *seypi* relations, and to the households which did not practise traditional skills in the village. Therefore, the women's economic role has not decreased because of the men's departure. On the contrary, some of the landless households have had to take great economic risks to finance the migration. It has meant that the women's role has become more important, given the possibility of unsuccessful migration. The overall economic situation of the household is, in fact, worsened by the migrant's return after a few months. At this stage he has not been able to save enough cash to cover his departure expenses. The only way for the household to deal with this new situation is to have more of its members involved in cash earning. For instance, children may have to work in a shop and women will do more embroidery work at home. In other words, emigration in this social category of villagers has either meant no change in the woman's role in the process of production whatever or it has led to a greater importance of her economic role because of a sudden economic crisis.

Women and Property

Another factor which defines the woman's economic position is her relationship to property, both movable and immovable (U. Sharma 1980). The woman's movable property consists of the dowry gifts brought by the new bride into the husband's family, and the immovable property refers to the share of her father's land.

The Movable Property

Marriage has always been the most costly social celebration amongst villagers and one of the reasons for their indebtedness before independence. In the collective ideology, a good marriage is traditionally associated with – apart from the agreement between two families for finding compatible partners – the abundance exhibited during the wedding ceremony. The honour of the family is then at stake.

The importance of this ostentation is illustrated by the role of the institution *vartan bhanji*, which enables the villagers to cope with the expense of social ceremonies by offering an institutionalized frame of economic assistance.

The dowry is not a property which produces wealth. It is composed, on the one hand, of all the domestic and extra-domestic implements which the women use in their daily chores, and, on the other hand, of gold jewellery, clothes and other personal belongings. The value of the dowry depends on the wealth of the woman's family, on the desire of her parents to treat their daughters equally, and on the expectations of the bridegroom's family. Whatever the value of these gifts, none of them allows a woman the possibility of becoming economically independent, even assuming that she wanted to be. These gifts are used for the maintenance and social reproduction of the household. The competition between villagers and the urge to accumulate honour leads to high expenses and explains the presence of items such as refrigerators and television sets in houses without electricity. It is not so much the use-value of the object that counts but its prestige-value. In fact, the display of the bride's dowry is the favourite opportunity to flaunt one's social status. Conversely, the gifts offered by the groom are not compulsory or used by the parents as a means of demonstrating their status.

The bride's family is also constantly obliged to offer gifts to any new daughters-in-law (the sisters of the groom) to ensure that their daughter will be treated fairly.

Figure 30: Display of the bride's dowry in a migrant's household (Chahiwala)

There is a direct relationship between the international migration and the increase in the value of the dowry. To be able to marry off one's children properly is one of the motives behind the villagers' departure. The international migration has changed the importance of *vartan bhanji*. Even with this institutionalized help, the non-migrant household cannot compete with the amounts spent by the migrant household and feels frustration over not being able to afford a decent wedding party for their children. In order to face this new situation without losing their honour, the poor villagers borrow money.

Amin, a landowner from Chahiwala, says:

> If I go abroad, I want to purchase a Russian tractor. But the first expenditures covered by the remittances will be the financing of my daughters' marriages. I have four daughters and it will cost at least Rs 50,000 to marry each of them. It is more important to get them married than to purchase a tractor. If I reduce the dowry, it will mean that nobody would like to marry them.

He could not go abroad before the marriage of his eldest daughter and had to sell one acre of land to cover the expenses.

A landowner's wife has her own story:

> We spent all the son's savings on his marriage. Before he went abroad, we could not find him a wife because of the poor economic status of our family. We will use the next savings for the marriage of our second son and for the marriage of our daughter. According to the Holy Qur'an and the Traditions, a family cannot eat the food prepared by a daughter when she begins to menstruate. Therefore she should marry soon.

Different ideological factors may explain this behaviour. First, the notions of honour and prestige are significant in understanding the social interaction between villagers. The expenses associated with marriages cannot be measured according to a Western rational economic approach. One might say that it is irrational for a household to spend many years' income, to sell cattle or even some land, in order to cover the cost of its children's marriages. However, the social life and the political organization in the village function according to other criteria. The household will gain prestige and respect if it spends more, especially if the household already belongs to the dominant *zat* and *biraderi* in the village, i.e. to the class of landowners.

We have seen the heterogeneity which characterizes the composition of each socio-economic class in the villages. In the political sphere, the village community is run by the landowners, while the craftsmen are subordinated to them. However, among the landowners too the political position of each individual depends on the size of his holding, on his personal charisma, on the strength of his *biraderi*, and on his ability to gather allies. Each factor influences the others reciprocally. It means that even if an expensive marriage increases one's social prestige, it does not lead to a stronger political position if one does not already belong to the dominating group in the village.

This is well illustrated by the barbers' household with two migrants in Dubai. It is the wealthiest family in Chahiwala but its prestige did not increase even after a fortune was spent on the marriage of one son. The influential landowners cannot stop the economic improvement of this family but they still have the power to control its social mobility. They always remind the barbers that their wealth cannot buy a higher social position. Therefore a migrant household which traditionally belongs to the subordinated lowest socio-economic strata of society faces opposition from the dominant landowner class if it tries to transform the power structure of the village. A social mobility which challenges the status quo of the social order is very difficult to achieve.

An illustration of the social role played by remittances is given by listing the expenditures on marriage in two households, one with a migrant and one without.

Table 7.1: Comparison of marriage expenditures between households (in Rs)

Items	Household with migrant	Household without migrant
Jewellery	95,000	10,000
Clothes and other domestic items	25,000	5,000
Food and other expenditures for the wedding ceremony	25,000	5,000
Total	145,000	20,000

The increase in wealth is often accompanied by jealousy, even within the same family. This occurred in the Chahiwala barbers' family mentioned above. The bridegroom's mother remarked after the wedding ceremony:

> After Yaseen's marriage, I have been fighting with my brother-in-law and his wife. My son's in-laws have given a beautiful and expensive dowry. So my brother-in-law's wife argued that when her son was married I did not care whether he and his in-laws should have a good wedding, and that I did not show concern about the quality and quantity of the dowry. She thinks that I treated her son unfairly. One day, we had a big fight on this

> matter. Before this dispute, we were all living and eating together, but now my brother-in-law's family has moved to another house and my husband sends all the remittances to this brother. Because of this conflict my daughter-in-law will be settled in our farm outside the village where she will be free from all these problems of jealousy.

Thus migration increases the value of the bride's dowry. But the dowry in itself does not change in nature. It is still comprised of items which do not generate income. New luxurious gifts are given but they do not allow the bride to become economically more independent from her husband. She has no access to the commodities which could break this dependency. The husband's remittances reinforce the traditional customs instead of changing them.

Other ideological factors may also explain why women do not yet express the desire to break away from this dependency. First, their socialization and lack of education have not prepared them to consider another form of division of labour – with the exception of the women who have opened small grocery shops in their house. Second, it is difficult to draw a precise demarcation line between individual property and common property. The dowry is not given by the parents to their daughter but to the bridegroom's family. The bride will, of course, have access to the gifts but no more than her in-laws will. She is expected to share with them. This is especially the case with extended families. A dowry made of income-generating items, which would only benefit the bride, would demand a transformation of the notion of property.

This notion of property is better perceived in the case of the other movable property possessed by women, namely gold in the form of jewels. Some of these are part of the dowry and intended to be redistributed between the in-laws. However, most of them are personal gifts from the parents to their daughter on her wedding day. These are the only personal belongings she possesses. They are often conveyed from mother to daughter, which gives them an extra sentimental value. However, during times of economic hardship she is supposed to put them at the disposal of her husband, if not of her in-laws. It is no longer her individual property but a commodity used as a saving device for the entire family. Consequently, a new use of the wife's jewellery has appeared in the last years, namely the partial financing of a man's emigration. She will have no objection to selling them for her own husband's departure, but if the migrant is her married son, discussions may occur. The woman then uses her power of control over such valuable goods. In fact, it is not even certain that she will benefit from the remittances. In most cases money is sent to the migrant's father if he lives in a nuclear family. The mother does not then see any reason to sell the only savings she can dispose of for the economic improvement of her daughter-in-law. Here the traditional opposition between mother-in-law and daughter-in-law takes on a new appearance.

The Immovable Property

The immovable property is synonymous with land. In the village, it is the only commodity apart from cattle which is income-generating. It is controlled by men, even though legislation gives the women the right to inherit a share of their father's land. Two sets of rules govern the relations of the women to the land: the statutory law of the Pakistani state and the customary law of the village.

According to the Muslim Family Laws Ordinance of 1961, sons inherit equal shares from their father's property while daughters get a share equal to one half of the sons' inheritance. In reality, however, daughters do not take their share but leave it to their brothers. They do not feel that their rights have been abused and the prevailing ideology explains their behaviour.

First, the virilocal residence after marriage means that the woman does necessarily live close to her natal land. This makes it inconvenient for her to control the tenant tilling it.

Second and more importantly, the woman needs the protection of her brothers after the death of their parents. In the case of conflict with her in-laws, her brothers are the only relatives who will defend her. She may take her inheritance but if she does so she knows that her brothers' reaction will be to reject her socially and economically. It is much more important for her to remain on good terms with them than to follow the Shariat law.

The following example illustrates what kind of hardship a single woman has to face when she owns land.

Sultana from Chahiwala was widowed in 1966. From that time she has been facing many problems because of her landed property. She says:

> I inherited 8 adjoining acres from my husband. I changed tenants many times during all these years. None of them cultivated the land properly and they did not give me the fixed share of crops. My children were too young to help me at that time. My brother-in-law did not defend me.

> He wanted to marry me because of my land but I refused. He beat me many times. When it became clear that I would not marry him, he said to my tenants that they should cheat me. Three or four years after the death of my husband, I did *patta* of water with Zarif for ten years. It is a tenancy contract stating that I get water from Zarif for a share of the yield. It went without problems for seven years. Then Jabir, the strongest landowner in the village, bought Zarif's tubewell. Jabir did not provide me with water but came to take his share – almost all the crops – at every harvest. According to the *patta* agreement, he had to continue to provide water until the period of 10 years was over.
>
> I put my land under *thekha* tenancy for a period of one year in 1981. At the time of harvest, the tenants did not give me the fixed share of crops. I reported them at the police station. One day the tenants asked me to put my thumb print on a white piece of paper and when I went to cut fodder in my fields they showed me that I had undersigned a five-year contract.

The tenants said:

> We have given her the share of crops. She gave us land for five years from 1981 to 1985 and now she tries to get it back. We won't give it back before 1985. We thought that if we cultivated for her, we could help her since she is a widow. But now she is against us.

Sultana answered:

> People think that I have a bad character but only God knows that my character is very good and that I am a very pious woman. I don't want to go to the city but people force me to go to the police station or to the court. I feel sorry and upset when I have to go there but this is the only way to protect myself from the villagers' cruelty. They want me to leave this village so they can take my land. I have been struggling for this land for many years because it is my only source of income. Nobody can take my land because it is the property of orphans. I face all these difficulties for the sake of my children. All my tenants have been very selfish. They did not take into account that it is the land of a widow.

As a last resort, Sultana asked for the help of the strongest faction of her *biraderi*, i.e. Jabir's faction, despite its members' previous bad behaviour towards her. However, she had no choice.

One should note that all the persons involved in this dispute belong to the same *biraderi* of landowners, namely the *Jat Virck*. Sultana is very much aware of all the double-dealings taking place:

> I feel very lonely because nobody really helps me. If Amir's[2] brothers help me, it is because they also want to get my land for cultivation. They

> won't give me my share or anything. I have been beaten many times because of this land. Only God will help me.

On the afternoon of 4 January 1982 I heard voices shouting loudly in the fields. Karrar and his brothers – Sultana's protectors – had a fight with her tenants. The dispute started when Sultana cut fodder from her fields where she is not allowed to enter according to the tenancy agreement. The tenants objected to this and tried to take some of the fodder from her bag to show it at the police station as proof of her non-respect of the tenancy contract. She resisted and they started to beat her. She called Karrar for help. He came with his brothers and a cousin armed with four rifles. The other party had two rifles. Men from both groups also had sticks and bricks in their hands. Ameen, the chairman of the Union Council, who was related to both parties, went there to reconcile them. Sultana went to the police station and reported her tenants.

This type of violent quarrel has occurred many times before. Once the police came to the village to arrest two tenants after Sultana had accused them of raping her. A doctor gave a medical report confirming rape. The tenants' family defended themselves by saying:

> Jabir's sons advised her to go the police station and to say that while she was cutting fodder the tenants came to beat her and to rape her. At that time she had menstruations. We knew it because we saw her washing her pad in the courtyard of her house.

On 5 January 1982, Sultana and the tenant women had a fight. The latter called upon all the women of their *biraderi* – or more precisely of their *biraderi* faction. The main reason for this dispute was that Sultana reported them at the police station. They accused her of lying. Sultana and her 15-year-old daughter blamed all the women for having sexual affairs with different men of the village. The tenants' women replied:

> We know about the character of your daughter. Once she got pregnant and you arranged for her abortion. You had affairs with all the men who came to help you yesterday. You had intercourse with them. You have intercourse with all the men in the police station and in the court.

Sultana answered:

> Meena had an affair with the *lambardar*'s son last year. I saw you. You were making love with him in the dark. You asked me not to tell your mother. I did not tell your mother. I know very well about your character. You should not blame me and my daughter…

Figure 31: Dispute between Sultana and women from her tenants' *biraderi* (Chahiwala)

In order better to understand the violence of the conflict between the two groups, other elements must be considered. The first cause of the conflict is the rivalry between the headman of *patti Kala* and the headman of *patti Dhedo*, a feud which has existed for many decades.

The father of Sultana's tenants said:

> Since my childhood, I have seen the two *pattis* fighting with each other. *Patti Dhedo* is strong and wants to have the people of *patti Kala* to be their servants. People of *patti Dhedo* do not want the people of patti *Kala* to become well-off and they will interfere to prevent them from becoming rich. At the beginning Jabir, the strongest man in the village, had no land and nowadays his sons own more than 10 acres. He took the land from different *kammis*, for example the land of Mohammed Ali.

His daughter added:

> Now Jabir's sons help Sultana but it is not a real help. They will write down all their expenditures for defending her. These are false expenditures. They will say: we have spent so and so with so many officials and you have to pay us back. Sultana won't be able to pay them back and she will be compelled to give them one or two acres of her land. This is the way this family gets land.

The other element is the dispute concerning a woman, Jabir's wife, Sahira. Sahira was first married to Raashid, a brother of Sultana's tenants. Jabir and Sahira ran away together to Multan (south Punjab) before independence. From that day the two groups never reconciled.

This rather commonplace dispute between a landowner and a tenant therefore takes on a dramatic dimension when it is placed in a wider context. Women, land and the struggle for power are the three intermingled elements behind the conflicts in the village.

The men's migration has not led to any change in the relationship of women to land. If a plot of cultivated or residential land is bought with migrant's remittances, it is still registered in the name of the male head of the household. The migrant's wife may express her opinion about the transaction, but she does not act for him. The household waits for one of the migrant's holiday visits to buy land.

The Role of Women in the Reproduction Process

The household cannot function smoothly without the women's involvement in the production process. But their presence is also irreplaceable in the social maintenance and reproduction of the household.

The Role of Women in Maintenance of the Household

Whatever the size and type of family – nuclear or extended – women play a key economic role in the daily maintenance and running of the household. Hard work and obedience to the husband and/or mother-in-law are qualities required for the social integration of the newly married woman into her in-laws' family. The ideological belief prevailing in the village supports a very strict sexual division of labour. Only women are involved with the cooking, the cleaning of the house, the child-rearing tasks and all kinds of activities which allow a household to live on very low economic resources. It is not considered proper for a man to spend too much of his time at home. He has more social interaction with the outside world than a woman. The difficulties mentioned in the following examples illustrate how the domestic labour carried out by the women is essential.

> When my wife died, I had two daughters aged 2 and 4 and two grown-up sons. We had to face many problems after her death. Nobody was able to look after the young children. Sometimes my brother's wife helped me with the domestic work. But this was not very easy because

> we did not live in the same house. I performed a father's role and a mother's role at the same time. I married off one of my sons at a young age only for the sake of having a daughter-in-law to take care of the house. But she wanted to live independently. Some members of my *biraderi* condemn my son and his wife for not living with me. They should have waited until the young daughters are married before starting to live separately.

A 18-year-old girl who is the only daughter in her household related the following:

> We were very poor because my mother had been ill throughout her life. She had TB. My father had to sell everything in the house for her treatment. He also had to borrow money. She died when I was 4 years old. After her death some relatives took care of me. When my brothers grew up they helped my father and our economic situation became much better. We installed a tubewell four years ago. After the marriage of my brothers, my sisters-in-law did not treat me properly. They started to live by themselves. Today nobody pays any attention to the fact that I am the only woman in the house.

This last example also shows how important it is to have daughters who are able to help their mothers. Already at the age of 6 or 7, girls take care of their younger brothers and sisters. This is a great help since it allows the mother to be engaged in other tasks. It is not unusual to see daughters aged 11 or 12 cooking for the entire household under the supervision of their mother, or at least cleaning the house, washing dishes and washing clothes. Women often feel physically tired because of repeated pregnancies and are very happy to leave a part of the workload to their daughters. Consequently, a woman who has no daughter to help her in her domestic chores is disappointed when her son establishes a nuclear family. She had been expecting that the arrival of a daughter-in-law in the household would relieve her housework burden.

Women's Daily Rhythm of Domestic Activities

A woman's usual day consists of the following sequences:

5.00–5.30 a.m.: The woman gets up before sunrise and goes to the fields which are used as latrines. She does not go far from the settled area because of her fear of being disturbed by someone, even if she is accompanied by a sister-in-law or a grown-up daughter. Moreover, it is difficult to find places where one cannot be seen because of the absence of trees. Consequently, she has to go while it is still dark.

5.30–6.00 a.m.: She washes herself. It is usually done rapidly unless she has had intercourse during the night. She then puts clean clothes on. Afterwards she recites her morning prayer.

6.00–7.30 a.m.: She lights the fire in the kitchen and prepares breakfast. Fresh *chapatis* are always made.

7.30–8.00 a.m.: She serves breakfast to the children and to the male members of the household. If some of them sleep in the stable near the fields, she takes food there. People do not eat together in the same room at the same time.

8.00–8.30 a.m.: She washes the children and dresses them.

8.30–9.30 a.m.: She cleans the house and washes up the plates and cooking utensils used for the dinner from the previous day and for the breakfast.

9.30–10.30 a.m.: She brings fodder to the cattle if no one else has done it before. She cleans the stable or the cattleshed and makes fresh dung-cakes which are left to dry in the sun on whichever surface of wall is available.

10.30–11.00 a.m.: She may wash herself thoroughly if she did not do it earlier in the morning. The outside temperature is now warmer and her hair can dry more rapidly. Otherwise, she may rest after she has sent a daughter to buy food in the local shops. Girls are generally more at home during the day than boys. This is due to the parents' traditional view on education. It is not considered necessary to send daughters to school more than the strict minimum. The type of investment represented by children's education is lost for the family when daughters are married off. It is also believed that too much education can have a bad influence on the girl's character and consequently make it difficult to marry her off.

11.00 am–12.00 p.m.: She prepares lunch.

12.00–13.00 p.m.: She brings food to the male members of the household working in the fields. It may take up to one hour to go back and forth.

13.00–13.30 p.m.: The boys have come back from school and eat their lunch. The mother eats too.

13.30–16.00 p.m.: She is busy with various chores according to the season or what is happening in the household. For example, she washes clothes at the washing-place with other women of her *biraderi* faction. She may visit a doctor if a child is ill. She goes to the fields to cut fodder for the cattle. In the winter she knits sweaters and caps for herself and her children. She does embroidery. She washes the beds, etc.

16.00–17.00 p.m.: She is back home and if she tends the cattle of the household, it is time for feeding and milking them.

17.00–18.00 p.m.: She prepares the dinner, which is the main meal of the day.

18.00–19.00 p.m.: The family eats dinner. The men have come back from the fields or from the stable to take it.

19.00–20.30 p.m.: She makes tea for her husband and any guests. She may sit with them if they are close relatives and take part in the conversation.

20.30 p.m.: People go to sleep at about this time in households without electricity and not more than an hour later if there is electricity. She recites her prayer before going to bed.

This is the daily rhythm for women the year round. They are busy approximately 12 hours a day while the men work 9–10 hours. The women agreed that making dung-cakes, bringing lunch to the men in the fields and cutting fodder for the cattle are tasks which each require one hour daily. The women of Baranpur also have the strenuous task of fetching water from the wells twice a day. This is usually done by the young daughters. The difference of activity between genders is also determined by the intensity of work. Men have more breaks and social gatherings than women during their day because, on the one hand, their control over the political life of the village demands frequent discussions, and on the other hand, their activities take place outside the household and therefore facilitate interrelationships. Villagers' values justify a man spending more of his time in talking than a woman.

Supplementary tasks during the agricultural peak seasons and the change in the weather affect the women's workload. After the monsoon, the women's duty is to repair the destroyed mud walls of the house, both outside and inside. After a fresh replastering, they also make wall-paintings around the doors and on the indoors granaries.

The daily routine is also interrupted by a woman's visit to her parents' house or by the visit of one of her relatives. Religious festivals and social events are also the occasions of diversion and increased work because of guests. In fact, not every landowner household can afford the help of the

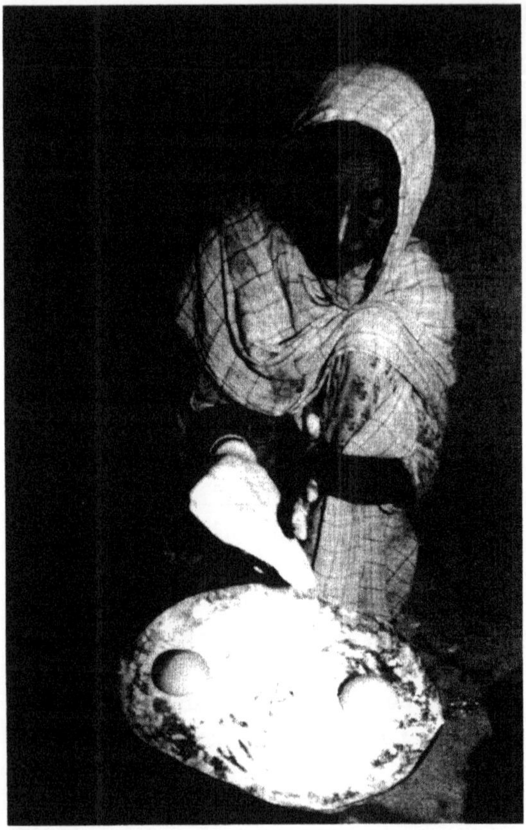

Figure 32: Fresh *chapatis* are a must at every meal (Baranpur)

kammi women on these occasions. The quality of the food served is also a means for the housewife to increase the respect of the household.

The above work schedule should be taken as an illustration. It varies, of course, with each household according to its size, its wealth and its members' personalities. For example the *lambardar* of *patti Kala* in Chahiwala, who lives in a gloomy house, says:

> There were many women whom I could marry at that time, but I liked most my present wife because she was beautiful, strong and belonged to a landowner's family. The area from where she came was not clean. That is why she does not keep the house tidy. It is my desire that she should keep the house clean and decorated but she is careless. I am a big landowner and my income is sufficient. So it is her duty to maintain the

house in such a way that it should radiate the economic condition of this family. She does not even take care of herself. When she came to the village after our marriage, people came to see her because of her beauty. I could not change my wife but I could change my behaviour. Now I am careless like her.

Migration can affect the domestic tasks in two ways. On the one hand, one might assume that the migrant would buy electrical items which could facilitate the woman's tasks. However, this only happens rarely. In Chahiwala, out of 20 households affected by international migration, only six have electricity. Besides being a facility, electricity is also a means to gain prestige. Important men of the village, like the *lambardars*, the headmen of *biraderis* and the chairman of Union Council have installed electricity in their house. Electricity and handpumps are used as indicators of the household status. In fact, foreign remittances have financed the sinking of a handpump which costs between Rs 500–1,000. Today all the migrant households in Chahiwala have a handpump in their yard. This is not the case in Baranpur because the installation of a handpump costs at least Rs 4,000 since one must drill on average to a depth of 15 m to find water. Only five of the 23 migrant households have so far used their remittances on this installation.

The other way migration can lead to a change in a woman's domestic tasks is in the reduction in the quantity of work necessary because of the migrant's absence. Whatever the type of family, the majority of women say that their workload has not changed. They have to fulfil the daily activities regardless of the other members of the household. In an extended family, the distribution of tasks between women is not modified. Only a few women from nuclear families mentioned that they felt they had more freedom with the organization of their work. However, this relative freedom depends on the relationships they have with their in-laws. The in-laws might think that their daughter-in-law lives an improper life with too many female friends if they do not see her working constantly. They will thus try to impose a stricter control on her.

The Food in the Village

The quality and quantity of food served depends on the economic situation of the household and on the desire of its members to spend money or not. Migration does not entail a change in food habits. Nevertheless the quantity and regularity of food do improve and migrant households do not have to worry where their money will come from. They feel secure. At the occasion of the *Idd-ul-Fitr* festival, migrant households enjoy the privilege of being able to slaughter a goat or a sheep by themselves instead of having to share this offering with a close relative, as was previously the case, or being dependent on a good harvest to afford the expense. They feel that it is best to make their own offering and their social prestige will increase accordingly.

Organization of Labour in the Household

As we have seen above, each member accomplishes a task in the household according to gender, age and ability. The children's participation in household work is also a socialization and apprenticeship process, since the learning of their future work is accomplished in close collaboration with their parents.

The structure of the family is another element which conditions the nature of the organization of labour. A woman who lives in a nuclear family is her own master in controlling domestic tasks. She has to make sure that everything runs smoothly so that her husband does not have to complain. Particularly in this type of family, daughters are a great help to their mother, especially during her pregnancies. The mother's role is one of supervision while the daughters divide the domestic tasks between them, according to their knowledge. For instance the division of labour in a household with seven children is organized on the following pattern in the morning:

- Rifat (9 years old) washes her two younger brothers aged $1^1/_2$ and $4^1/_2$.
- Ismat (11 years old) washes up the dishes from the evening.
- Musqad (12 years old) makes *chapati*s for the breakfast.

These tasks are not always performed with pleasure. The girls much prefer to stay longer in bed or play. However, their mother is present to watch and scold them.

In households with grown-up daughters, there is a preference for the mother to carry out the extra-domestic activities while the unmarried daughters are busy with cooking and cleaning or with tasks which do not require leaving the compound.

Similarly, sons are expected to help their father. The most common task is to tend cattle, i.e. to wash them and to bring them to grazing areas.

The situation is different in households where an extended family lives. Here the senior women have control over the labour of the younger

Figure 33: Fetching water is a daily duty for young girls (Baranpur)

women, and the unmarried daughters over the daughters-in-law. However, variations are found from family to family. The relationships between household members are determined not only by the social structure of the family but also by the personality and character of each individual. It may happen that this hierarchical allocation of tasks does not lead to conflicts within the household if its members have a good understanding with each other. Generally, however, conflicts between in-laws are more the rule than the exception. There seems to be greater collaboration and solidarity between daughters-in-law than between them and their sisters-in-law. They have the same social status until one of them bears a son. She then becomes the favourite daughter-in-law.

As mentioned above, some women living in nuclear families have a feeling of greater freedom in the organization of work when their husbands work abroad. They become the family head. However, they also complain that the absence of their husbands compels them to take over tasks which are usually only done by men. They refer here to the obligation where they have to go to the town for different reasons, such as the endorsement of remittances. If a male in-law or a man from their own family cannot accompany them, a son – whatever his age – chaperons them. He will also be sent to the market to do some shopping. The migrant's wife feels uneasy to have to move suddenly into a male-dominated sphere. Here again, the nature of the relationships with in-laws is decisive.

Safia says:

> After the departure of my husband, my in-laws do not behave properly towards me. I always have fights with them. I am not allowed to change clothes frequently. If I do, they rebuke me and say that I don't have a good character. Sometimes I feel upset but I cannot say it to my in-laws. It is my husband who should write to his parents and say that they should take good care of me. My husband is responsible for this situation because he alone decided to migrate. But he is a lenient man. Sometimes he supports me; other times he supports his parents. I am very lonely and I never leave my house. I visit my parents one night every year. I am allowed to go and see them more often but I do not want to leave my house empty. I do not trust my in-laws. If they watch my house, they might steal something or do something against me. One night some thieves came into the yard. I am very afraid during the night and I cannot sleep properly. Sometimes, a brother-in-law sleeps in the house to protect me. My brother helps me in every matter, however not in agriculture. He is not allowed by my in-laws to go to my husband's fields. They cheat me with the quantity of crops they give me and my brother would see what is the real production if he was present at harvest.

One episode of this strife was the arrest of two of her brothers-in-law by the police. As a retaliation against their behaviour towards her, she reported them to the police for having stolen a buffalo from a midwife in another village.

Another example is the case of Jamila. Here it is the father-in-law who keeps an eye on her in every matter after the departure of her husband:

> I always have fights with my father-in-law. He beat me last month. He thinks that I am very spendthrift and that I have too many female friends around me. I moved back to my parents' house. After one month, my father in-law came to take me back. Life without my husband is very hard. The happiness I found in my husband's presence cannot be replaced.

The extra control exercised by in-laws upon the migrant's wife is thus particularly felt in nuclear families. Even if the woman has become the family head, she has to fight more now than before her husband's departure. In extended families, her social status is not much altered because she occupies the same place in the organization of labour as before her husband's migration.

The Function of Biological Reproduction

The last words in Jamila's statement concern another problem caused by migration, namely the physical and emotional separation between spouses and between the migrant and his children.

Women face psychological strains when their husbands leave the village, especially when they are newly-weds. We saw that the migrant's marriage is one of the main uses of remittances. The wedding ceremony takes place during one of the bridegroom's holidays from his work abroad. Sexuality between spouses is under the husband's directive but within limits which are socially determined. Just after marriage, the young couple are left in peace for some days. Later on love-making is rapidly ended because of the proximity of the other members of the household. The couple must be ready to make love during the day when the house is empty of its inhabitants for a short time. They do not undress. The father, the mother and brothers might enter the room at any time and it is not appreciated if the couple locks the room. The household members will then think that the couple has nothing else to do during the day. As a rule, husband and wife do not sleep in the same room during the night but with the other members of the same sex in the household. A mother-in-law particularly objects when her son has a good sexual understanding with his wife which leads to his desire to sleep with her every night. She has a strong influence upon her son's emotional life.

Women discuss the sexual relations between husbands and wives. They often compare the virility of their respective husbands. In their opinion, a strong man should have a long, hard and stiff penis and a woman should feel pains when she is penetrated.

Bushra, Amir's 28-year-old wife, says:

> My husband is very strong. After our marriage, I did not want to have a strong husband because I felt pains more than three times every night. I talked about this with some other women. They recommended a good recipe to cool down my husband sexually. I should give him ground coriander seeds mixed with almond powder. I did so. One day my husband discovered what he was eating. He got angry and told me that he has more self-confidence when he feels strong sexually. He also said that it is better for me because I know about sex now and I have a sexual appetite to satisfy. He asked me what I would do if he could not fulfil my needs. I got the point and from that day I never used such recipes again. I believed that my health would be affected if I had intercourse every night. I got pregnant nine times and each time my health has been

> deteriorating during pregnancy. Nowadays, I feel old even though I am still a young woman. However, it will be very difficult when my husband works in Saudi Arabia. I think that we are very close to each other when we have intercourse. We then have no hindrance. We can feel each other. We are united and we can sacrifice so many things to get these feelings of satisfaction. But I will also be happy not to be pregnant again when my husband is abroad.

The sudden beginning of a sexual life entails far more psychological disturbances for the women than for the men. They are ill-prepared and it is difficult to tackle physical intimacy when they hardly know each other because of the practice of arranged marriage. When a migrant leaves only a few weeks after the marriage, his young wife feels lonely, frustrated and of course is not permitted to have affairs, although extra-marital sexual relationships are possible for the men.

A migrant does not have enough economic resources to pay for his wife and children to come with him. Moreover, it is not allowed under the type of work-contract and stay-permit which he has obtained.

It is not only newly-married women who experience emotional problems. When a disagreement has not been resolved at the time of her husband's departure, a wife may feel disturbed and unhappy until his next visit to the village.

Bilquees from Baranpur says:

> Razia's husband came back for a three-month holiday. He was very happy to find his wife in his house. There are some conflicts between the in-law families. He wrote before coming that if his wife was living with her parents when he arrived, there would be a big quarrel. They have intercourse every night but since Razia did not have sexual relations for one and a half years, she feels a lot of pain. She had to go and see the doctor. Her menstruations which had stopped for one and a half years have suddenly come back. She does not weep any longer.

In other words, many wives left behind are faced with new psychological problems provoked by a disturbance in their emotional life. Feelings are not discussed between spouses. In the Punjabi patriarchal ideology, the main expectation from a household towards the new daughter-in-law is not the love which she should have towards her husband but the bearing of children, especially sons. Descent is traced through the male line, and sons will support their aged parents, in contrast to daughters who are married off. Sons also strengthen the political power of the *biraderi*. They represent therefore the best means through which a bride can improve her social status. Infertility, which is always considered to be the woman's responsibility, is a great unhappiness for the newly married wife. It can lead to psychological distress, and the woman will try to solve this problem through different means, more particularly through her confidence in a religious *pir*. She then makes repeated visits to the *pir*'s holy place or shrine. But if amulets or other traditional medicines do not appear to be successful, her husband might decide to take a second wife. However, no cases of polygyny have been registered in the two villages.

The analysis of the women's biological role in the household is based on a sample of 44 and 99 women in Chahiwala and Baranpur respectively about whom I have recorded the age, the total number of living children and the total number of dead children. However, I do not have any data concerning cases of stillbirth, perinatal mortality, or spontaneous and provoked abortions. I only took women of the 16–40 age group into account: 16 years because it is the legal marriageable age in Pakistan and forty years because the information given by younger women was more reliable. They could name all their children who were either still living under the same roof or who were just married. Conversely, older women sometimes omitted to mention their children who were no longer living at home, like married-off daughters or sons who had gone to live in another town.

Frequency of Pregnancies

In order to calculate the frequency of pregnancies, the 24-year period of fertility (corresponding to the 16–40 age-group) is divided by the total number of declared pregnancies for each mother.

The average interval of time between two pregnancies is 2 years and 9 months, irrespective of the socio-economic class and the presence of a migrant in the household. As a rule, a migrant comes home on holiday every two years when his work-contract expires. Therefore migration has not so far meant a change in the number of conceptions.

Similarly, the number of living children per mother does not fluctuate very much according to the socio-economic categories of villagers. It oscillates between 2.5 and 4.5 children. The mean number is 3.8 children. Households with a migrant do not show any difference from the average. All in all, migration does not affect the number of children born in a family.

Abortion

Provoked abortions in the village occur, although it is difficult to know their frequency. Abortion is forbidden by religion since pregnancy is believed to be the will of God. Illegal abortions are generally practised on women who are pregnant before marriage. If the foetus is older than three months, the mother gives birth in the house of the abortionist and the baby is killed during delivery. It is then said that the child was stillborn. In 35 years of practice, the midwife of Chahiwala has heard of five or six cases of illegal abortion.

The case of abortion described below occurred in the household of my hosts in Chahiwala. I could therefore follow the case and no one tried to hide it from me.

An extended family lives in this household. The relationships between the in-laws are very tense and have always been so since the son's marriage. The finances rest in the hands of the mother-in-law and her eldest daughter. The only son, who cultivates jointly with his father, never has any money. His father, a greedy man, does not pay him and controls his expenditures. Consequently, the daughter-in-law never has any money either. This situation is a source of permanent conflict.

Munira was six weeks' pregnant and wanted to get an abortion. She already had three daughters (3, 4 and 5 years old) and one son of 2 years. She was on bad terms with her husband. During my stay in the village, he tried to kill her during a violent dispute. Her husband was against the abortion. However, her in-laws agreed with her, even though they thought that she alone was responsible for this pregnancy. A sum of Rs 50 had been demanded by a woman of a nearby village who practices abortion. In order to annoy her daughter-in law, the mother-in-law was only ready to give Rs 20. After lengthy discussions, which increased the psychological pressure upon Munira, the Rs 50 were finally given.

The day before the abortion Munira had prepared everything in her house for the next 2–3 days in case she felt ill afterwards. Due to her bad relationships with her in-laws, she knew that no one would come to help her. On the day of the abortion, she went to the other village with her youngest daughter, accompanied by a midwife of her village (the same one who had assisted her in her deliveries). Everything had to be kept confidential.

The abortion is achieved by the introduction of a thin stick of wood (*bahari* wood) into the vagina. To the stick is bound a piece of material soaked with medicines. This kind of wood is also used for making brooms. Munira returned home keeping the stick in her vagina and went to bed. In the evening she felt very bad and thought that she was going to die. Her female in-laws were around her and she asked them to pray for her. The midwife massaged her abdomen to reduce the pains. The atmosphere was very tense and Shahida (my counterpart) came to my room to ask for more cooking oil so that the midwife could give more massages. Munira's husband was in my room as he was on any other evening, talking and laughing with friends. He did not seem to worry. He remained there all night. The next morning the stick of wood came out of the vagina by itself and the bleeding started. After some time the abortion was over. Already in the afternoon Munira had a walk in the fields and started her domestic chores again. She washed the bed on which she had lain. Shahida told Munira's husband to be nice to his wife and the same evening he brought her a cup of hot milk. As she told us the next morning, she was very happy with this gesture.

Births

Deliveries take place at the mother's home in the presence of an older woman experienced in midwifery. The mother-in-law is also there but not the child's father. A more professional midwife is called if difficulties occur. The pregnant woman lies down on an old *charpai* in the main room of the house. Her feet rest on the wooden frame of the bed. She does not receive medicine of any kind during the delivery. The midwife massages the mother's abdomen so as to facilitate the birth and also massages her arms and legs. She bends the mother's head forwards. If the baby appears in a wrong position, the woman holds her arms around the bend of the knees. In 35 years of practice, the midwife of Chahiwala could only remember two such cases. But if she diagnoses that it will be a difficult delivery, she sends the mother to the hospitals in Pasrur or Sialkot. In fact, the midwife will be considered responsible if the baby dies right after birth and her reputation will suffer. Only a single case of a mother's death at delivery was recorded in this sample.

Only one midwife is registered in Chahiwala while six are active in Baranpur. The midwife in Chahiwala is about 70 years old and is very popular because of her experience. All the women in her family have been midwives. She belongs to the Fakir Joya *zat*. She also received training in the family planning centre in Pasrur. It was her duty to tell the village women about the use of different means of birth control and to take them to the family planning centre. Some of these had an intrauterine device fitted but became sick. The government paid her Rs 15 monthly. After two or three years she left this job as family planning adviser because her son was against it. He thought it was against Islamic rules. Consequently, the women in the village do not want to have anything to do with birth control today. The midwife's other children – two grown-up daughters who live in Lahore – also put pressure on their mother. They are ashamed of her profession. They think that midwifery is a degrading job and when they visit their mother, they scold her for looking like a servant. They did not want to become midwives themselves.

The midwife goes into almost every house at the time of delivery. When she started in 1947 she was paid Rs 5 for male babies and Rs 3 for female babies. Ten years later she got Rs 15 for boys and Rs 10 for girls. Today the payment is Rs 50 for boys and Rs 30 for girls. She is also paid with clothes, wheat, rice and sugar. She takes 12 kg of wheat and 12 kg of rice for doing massages at the time of delivery and twice a day for the two following weeks. Altogether her income is about Rs 400 monthly. She does not make any reductions in the rate of payment which may lead to the protest of the poorest mothers.

Women are aware that the expectant mother should have a special and appropriate diet if the economy of the household can afford it. In the last month before delivery, she should drink milk twice a day, in the morning and the evening. It is believed that the mother's lactation will then be facilitated and become more abundant. If she is unable to produce milk, cow's-milk or goat's-milk is given to the baby, but not buffalo's-milk: it is not easily digested because of its high fat content. Straight after the birth, the baby gets sugared water or rosewater and the mother a special dish. The mother is considered impure during the 40 days after delivery and consequently does not engage in household activities. However, this limitation can only be observed in extended families. In nuclear families, the mother is already active 10 days after delivery if no female friends or relatives come to help her.

Child Mortality

Among the 44 women of Chahiwala who were asked whether they had had an experience of child mortality, 22 gave a positive answer. If one takes the women's total period of fertility, the sample is then of 75 women with 51 positive answers or 68 per cent. The figures in Baranpur are respectively 43 per cent and 47 per cent. Child mortality was thus higher in the villages some 20 years ago and this decrease is probably due to the improvement in agricultural production. The less self-centred economy of Baranpur might also be responsible for its lower infant mortality. People there were more informed and open-minded. There was more food available. The average number of infant mortalities per mother is 1.3.

Sixty-eight per cent in Chahiwala and 63 per cent in Baranpur of the women sampled have experienced child mortality more than once. Three infant mortalities per woman is not uncommon. A majority of male children have died in Chahiwala: 97 boys (58 per cent) for 70 girls (42 per cent), while in Baranpur the proportions are equal: infant mortalities there have occurred for 48 children of each sex. One may explain the difference between the sexes in Chahiwala either by the greater weakness of male babies and/or by the greater sorrow which the parents feel at the death of a male child. Its death is therefore better remembered.

Neonatal deaths have been subdivided into early neonatal (first week) and late neonatal (second week). The age of the child at its death was recorded in 128 cases; 55.5 per cent and 74 per cent of them died within the first year in Chahiwala and Baranpur respectively. In other words, death does not occur, as it does in many countries of the South, when the child is around 2 years old, i.e. at the time when breast feeding is discontinued and the child becomes dependent upon the often inadequate nourishment from a new type of food.

The exact reason for a child's death is in most cases unknown to the parents. The most usual answer given is that the child developed fever overnight and died very rapidly, and the most common explanation is that it is the will of God. However, the suddenness of death is also attributed to supernatural causes.

A woman of the Fakir *zat* related the following:

> My first two sons died a few months after their birth. They were very healthy. In the morning they were drinking my milk and in the evening they were dead. I think that *djins* are responsible for their death. The same day that my second son died, I heard a woman's voice calling me from the roof of my house. I went up but I saw nobody. *Djins* can take the shape of women. A friend advised me to go and see a *pir* regularly

Table 7.2: Infant and child mortality by age

	At birth	**1st week**	**2nd week**	**2–4 wks**	**1–3 mths**	**3–6 mths**	**6–12 mths**	**1–2 years**	**2–3 years**	**3–4 years**	**Over 4 yrs**	**Total**
						Chahiwala:						
Boys	2	5	3	1	5	2	1	2	4	1	5	31
Girls	1	4	1	–	1	1	2	2	–	2	7	21
Total	3	9	4	1	6	3	3	4	4	3	12	52
% of total	5.7	17.3	7.7	1.9	11.5	5.7	5.7	7.7	7.7	5.7	23	100
						Baranpur:						
Boys	7	7	–	1	6	7	5	2	2	1	–	38
Girls	4	9	–	–	–	4	6	9	3	3	–	38
Total	11	16	–	1	6	11	11	11	5	4	–	76
% of total	14.5	21		1.3	8	14.5	14.5	14.5	6.5	5.2	–	100

and to ask for his protection. But I preferred to pray to God and since then none of my children has died. But I shifted to another house and my third child was taken to my parents' house in Gujranwala. I was too worried.

The Effect of Migration on Women's Economic Control in the Household

As previously mentioned, the international labour migration has not affected the amount of women's work. One should instead look at the woman's social influence in the households in order to find a change. Daily decisions have to be taken in the household. Some of them concern the process of production, others concern the social life of the family.

Women's Decision-Making in Social Affairs

The gender segregation of the society means that each sex possesses a complementary knowledge about the affairs of the village. In fact, even though women are limited in their physical mobility, they are well informed through their daily interrelationships about events which happen in each household. This information is communicated to the men of their own households, who can then intervene more appropriately in the worldly affairs of the village, for instance in the case of disputes. Women's gossip also plays an important role in disputes through its psychological effect.

Women are also involved in all matters regarding matrimonial alliances and the practice of *vartan bhanji*. They play an essential role in the choice of a daughter-in-law due to their contacts with young women. In this matter, men rely upon women's guidance. Similarly, the household's participation in the *vartan bhanji* relations also relies upon the women's record of the previous ritual. They know as well as the record register what kind of gifts or favours should be given to whom and when. But they can do something which the record book cannot, namely the readjustment of the household's external relationships according to conflicts or provisory disagreements between people. They can then advise the men in dealings within their social network.

Villagers' relationships seem to be exclusively run by men but they are dependent on the women's package of information. The female role in the maintenance of *biraderi* cohesion takes place behind the scenes and its importance is not recognized by men but it is primordial for continuing the household's reciprocal relationships. Obviously, this dependency increases in migrant households inhabited by a nuclear family. After two years of absence, the male head of the household will want to be informed of all the events which have occurred during his absence in order to re-establish himself in his social environment; his wife partly fulfils this function.

Women's Decision-Making in Agriculture

The male head of the household supervises the crops and the agricultural production. Women are dependent on the men's control over productive resources and fulfil this role only in exceptional cases. For instance, Qaisara blamed her husband for being careless in cultivation:

> We have plenty of land – 19 acres – but my husband is not interested in cultivation. We have given our land on *hissa* tenancy but even at the time of harvest he does not like to go to the fields to check the production. After my marriage, I was not allowed to go to the fields but when I saw

my husband's carelessness, I started to look after the crops. Now I supervise the crop production. My husband has worked as a bus conductor for many years. He does not want to go abroad because he has money and land. If he himself were cultivating, he would be rich and easily able to compete with the migrants' families.

It is different when the discussion concerns a transaction of land (either by sale, tenancy or mortgage) or the purchase of modern agricultural equipment (for example, the sinking of a tubewell or the buying of a tractor). Women take part in these talks. They feel concerned because these expensive investments directly affect the household's budget. The male members of the family listen to them and more particularly to the eldest women, since the same hierarchical division, based on age and social prestige, also exists between women. However, the final decision is taken by the men.

The migrant is not, as a rule, the head of the household in extended families. If he were, the senior woman would assume control over everything, although agricultural production would be a son's responsibility. Whatever the case, the migrant's wife does not assume a greater importance in the decision-making process in matters related to agriculture. This is due to the arrangement made by the migrant before his departure, which prevents women from interfering in male-dominated sectors of the economy.

In nuclear families, the same arrangement is reached. But in practice it depends again on the nature of the relationship between the migrant's wife and her in-laws. When it is bad, she may have to supervise the production during the harvest season, so as not to be cheated. But all other tasks of production remain the responsibility of the cultivator, who is either an in-law or a tenant.

In the households of craftsmen with a migrant, women do not experience any change in their influence over the process of production. This is due to the absence of land ownership and to the nature of the men's work.

Women's Decision-Making in the Household's Economy

The distinction between extended and nuclear families is again relevant when one considers who controls the household's economy. In extended families, the control of consumption expenditure is exercised by the senior member, either male or female, who is the head of the household. The consumption expenditure of a son's own family is included in the joint economy of the extended family. This arrangement is often a source of conflict. The daughter-in-law may feel that she and her children are treated unfairly regarding the quality and quantity of food and clothes they may enjoy.

The situation may vary from household to household but, as a rule, wage-earning sons give their salaries to their parents. In the case of joint cultivation between father and sons, it is up to the father to give them some pocket-money. No remuneration is given to the women for their part in the agricultural tasks and for their domestic work. The money earned from the crops is divided between the male joint cultivators. Women's own earnings – through embroidery work or other handicrafts – are under their control. But they rarely use this money on themselves. Instead, they buy something for the children (for example a small gift) or for the entire household. Unmarried women may, however, buy items for their dowry.

For costly expenditures, the members of the household discuss the matter together, but the eldest person's decision has to be respected.

When a son is a migrant or lives in another town in Pakistan, the remittances are not sent directly to his wife but to the head of the household. His wife does not benefit more from them or have more control over them than the other members. Disputes may arise but her social status as a daughter-in-law demands that she accept this situation. The migrant may also feel frustrated when his parents use the money without taking his own wishes into account. As a result he might then consider starting a nuclear family.

The responsibility of the economy in a nuclear family is shared by husband and wife. The male head of the household gives a portion of his income to cover the daily expenditures of the household to his wife and keeps the greatest part of it. She is fully responsible for the budgeting of this money and instructs her husband about what goods have to be purchased in the marketplace.

In households without an off-farm source of revenue, the women have total control over the quantity of stored food grains and plan their consumption accordingly. Without their very careful consumption strategy, the household would not be able to manage. It may even happen that a woman handles economic matters independently, as the following example illustrates.

Amir suddenly had the possibility of obtaining a visa for Saudi Arabia. Everything had to move very fast otherwise the labour recruiting agent would not reserve the visa for him. Amir told his wife, Zeena, to go to the bank to get Rs 4,000 from their account to pay the agent. However, she could not reach the bank before it closed. Moreover, there was not enough money in their account since Zeena had lent Rs 9,000 from their savings to one of her father-in-law's friends to buy rice and to speculate on it, without informing her husband. She worried about not being able to find the Rs 4,000 through other means. She did not ask her in-laws because she knew that they would refuse to help her. She went to several female friends and in a few hours had collected the money from three different people. These three women lent the money out without asking their husbands, who were not at home, but also without hiding it from them.

This form of economic help is usually practised between women on a reciprocal basis and is considered a part of their domestic duties. They lend small amounts of money to each other since the resources of the household make it difficult to face sudden expenditures. Rs 4,000 is, however, an exceptionally high amount.

To summarize, many women may feel that their husbands behave fairly towards them in economic matters. The mother-in-law, especially, does not like this mutual understanding between spouses, and may interfere with her daughter-in-law's private business when her son has gone abroad. We have seen that a migrant puts his family under the protection of his father and/or brothers. His wife becomes the head of the household and decides for herself, however within the restrictions imposed on her by her in-laws. Therefore, a majority of migrants' wives believe that their influence in the household has not increased. Remittances are sent either directly to the wife or to her father-in-law, who then has to give her a share. In either case, it often leads to conflicts, either because of the mother-in-law's jealousy or because the migrant's wife thinks that her in-laws do not give her enough money.

The new money in circulation in the village economy may hence entail dramatic changes in the social relationships between people, as evidenced by Ameen's story:

> I know a blacksmith family where the husband used to send remittances to his father. One day he began to send them only to his wife, asking her to keep the money or to give it to his parents. He asked for the money when he came back. His wife told him that she had given it to his parents. He went to see them and they said that they had not received any money. The husband then had a violent quarrel with his wife. She was so upset that she drowned herself in the canal.

Women's Decision-Making in Other Economic Activities

Some women of the poorest households have taken the initiative to open tiny shops in their houses. This new activity does not mean that they try to become more independent. It is only a new means to earn some more money for the household, as in Nazima's case:

> I opened a little shop in my house 20 days ago. This is not really a shop but a large store for the family. It was always difficult for me to get goods from the market. I thought it was better to buy all the items in a large quantity so I might also sell some of them.

A migrant's wife in a nuclear family cannot use the remittances for investment or for independently starting a project profitable for the household. The savings will be used for costly investments which are decided jointly. The husband remains the real decision-maker. The main change is the wife's freedom to run the daily expenditures of the household, and sometimes it is difficult for her to budget large amounts of money when the remittances are sent irregularly.

Women, Customary Rules and Migration

Out-migration has differing effects on the women's position in the village. Besides the migrant's economic situation before his departure, other factors play an important role in the changes experienced by women; namely, the structure of the family (extended or nuclear), the nature of the relationships between the in-laws, and the values of honour and shame which define the overall frame wherein the woman's social mobility can occur.

If a migrant household becomes well-off, it is then possible to follow what is considered proper Muslim behaviour for women; it means a stricter observance of *purdah*.

The migrant's wife must not make a greater contribution to agricultural production when there is a shortage of manpower. It would be considered shameful and reduce the status of the household. Good relationships with the in-laws are essential when they cultivate the husband's fields, or when she needs their help, as in the case of a conflict with her tenant.

The migrant's wife is always left under the protection of some male villagers, who are normally the migrant's relatives. They go beyond their role and in reality exercise a strict control upon her, especially when she lives within a nuclear family.

When remittances are sent to her, she has to face the jealousy of her in-laws. She is not allowed to take the initiative to make investments. Her role and authority are not increased in the decision-making process.

To sum up, customary rules which are believed to be Islamic determine the changes in the women's role and status in the household. Migration has not altered women's subordination to men. The majority of women said that they had not experienced any changes in their position in the household since their husband's departure. In reality, he is still the head of the family and gives his instructions through letters – which are read by a literate close relative – about affairs regarding the education of children, the decisions to take in agriculture, the strategy to follow in the marriage of a relative, and so on. They often mentioned that their authority over the children is inadequate since the male is the expression of authority in this patriarchal society. The migrant's wife might feel more free to dispose of her time but she may also feel more limited in her individual freedom when her in-laws keep a very close eye on her. Nevertheless, it is inevitable that women from nuclear families have more decisions to take in the daily routine when the head of the household is absent. In a patriarchal society, this phenomenon might appear to the women of non-migrant households to be an increase in female independence.

Note

1 *Burqah* is a garment which envelops the woman's body and covers the face. It has various forms of openings for the eyes.

2 Amir is one of Jabir's sons and head of the *biraderi* after Jabir's death.

CONCLUSIONS

The aim of this study was to analyse the international labour migration from two Punjabi villages in Pakistan with different forms of agriculture, in order, on the one hand, to determine the relations between the levels of their economic development and the necessity to take a job abroad, and, on the other hand, to determine the nature of the changes brought about by foreign remittances.

The economic situation of both villages is such that it is very difficult for the majority of the villagers to reach a satisfactory minimum standard of living through their traditional activities. Even though agriculture has seen some progress, thanks to the Green Revolution, it is still mainly at an insufficient subsistence level. Many villagers need external sources of income but the possibilities of finding jobs outside the village are very limited. The labour market policy followed in Pakistan also means that income from wage-labour is not sufficient to meet the expenditures of a household. Under these conditions, working in a foreign country is considered to be the most appropriate way to overcome unemployment, underemployment and poverty, especially when poor villagers are confronted daily with the relatively well-off appearance of the migrants' households. They believe that the migrants dispose of endless economic resources, that their consumption of material goods is unlimited, and that they can live up to the ideal values of society.

Although this perception of migration as a solution to economic difficulties is shared in both villages, the need for departure is more acute in the village with rainfed agriculture. The amplitude of migration is in reality directly related to the level of development of the agriculture found in the village. The economic improvements brought about by the Green Revolution are more limited in rainfed agricultural areas since a sufficient quantity of water at the appropriate time is a pre-condition for a maximum output from the new cultivating techniques. Cultivators, irrespective of their form of relationship to land, have more difficulties in making ends meet in Baranpur than in Chahiwala, and consequently in honouring their obligations towards the landless people of the village. Therefore international migration is more intense in these areas than in those with irrigated agriculture. To be employed abroad is just a renewed form of an economic practice which has existed in this part of the Indian subcontinent for decades, i.e. having a male member of the household working outside the village and coming back during agricultural peak periods.

For labour-exporting countries like Pakistan, the boom in oil prices in the Middle East has provided an opportunity for development. But the gains from migration depend on the economic policy pursued by the state. In other words, it depends on the nature of the state. In Pakistan, as in other post-colonial countries of the South, the colonial period and the neo-colonial relationships determine the structure of the state and the form of political life. At Partition, Pakistan inherited an important military-bureaucratic class allied to a strong landed class. The industrial and commercial bourgeoisie was either non-existent or very weak. The colonial policy served to increase the power of the landed gentry and to sharpen the differentiation between the rural classes. The role of a class of big landlords as a dominant group in the state apparatus led to a Green Revolution based on an elite farmer strategy.

Almost immediately after Partition, Pakistan started to be dependent on foreign aid. Economic assistance was provided mainly by the United States and by the World Bank. This aid was accompanied by the imposition of certain conditions, and Pakistan had to enter into the USA's military alliances from 1953 onwards. This relationship strengthened the power of the military officers in the socio-economic structure of the state.

The state has never been a body concerned with the general interest of the country but rather an instrument in the hands of social classes which use it to defend their socio-economic privileges. It is not surprising, then, that no long-term policy has been established for the transformation of foreign remittances into productive investments. The export of workers has just been considered as a source of foreign valuta like the export of any other commodities. However, out-migration has placed Pakistan in a dependence upon the fluctuating and external sources of finance from the oil states. Its balance of payment requires the income earned by its citizens working abroad. More and more people depend socially and economically on foreign remittances. They have become consumers rather than producers. The increase in local expenditures has entailed an augmentation of imports instead of an expansion of local production. Preference is given to the purchase of foreign goods because of their better quality and of their prestigious value. The remittances provoke inflationary trends since they lead to a rapid increase in the quantity of money in circulation which is unaccompanied by a concomitant rise in the national production of goods and services. Due to the economic changes it brought about, international migration has created new difficulties for the lower income classes.

The Pakistani rulers believe that labour migration is beneficial for the development of a country, even though the migration of workers from south European and north African countries to north-western European countries since 1945 has shown that this is not always the case. At village level, out-migration is supposed to bring the following advantages:

- foreign remittances are invested productively;
- the migrant worker acquires a skilled qualification which is used once he returns to his country – he is considered as a potential entrepreneur;
- the pressure on available jobs is reduced and unemployment diminishes.

However, the study of the two villages has not borne out these trends. Many situations experienced by migrant labourers in Western Europe reappear in this new context. Most of the villagers are engaged abroad either in unskilled tasks or in their traditional occupation. They do not increase their technical knowledge. They are paid the least and hired on a temporary basis. They also face all the social problems which are typically related to immigration: illegal entry, improper housing, unequal pay, and denial of rights.

Quantitatively, only a small percentage of the villages' male population goes abroad. The pressure on land and on jobs available in the neighbouring cities is therefore still very strong. The departure to foreign countries of able-bodied men has not, so far, helped in the creation of new employment possibilities. Instead, Pakistan experiences a shortage of skilled personnel. The best and the most productive part of its manpower is abroad; this certainly retards the development of the country.

The existence of supplementary economic resources in the form of foreign remittances does not lead to productive investment in agriculture or other economic sectors of the village, although the consumption of local goods has stimulated some domestic sectors of the economy, especially the construction sector. In fact, as long as some of the basic needs of the migrant's family are not met (better nutrition, improved housing facilities, medical assistance, and the like), it is unrealistic to think that the hard-earned currencies will be directly invested in income-generating projects, except in the case of a few individual entrepreneurs.

Only part of the foreign remittances is used on consumer goods. The villager does not increase his daily consumption beyond a maximum limit, even if he can afford it. He chooses a modest life-style so as to establish a ceremonial fund which is used for celebrating with pomp the rituals of the life-cycle and the religious festivals. In analysing the budget of the landowners' households with a migrant, it was noticed that the wealthiest among them only spend twice as much in monthly expenditure than the poorest households without a migrant, although their income is 4.5 times higher.

Even though some changes are in progress, the social life of the villages is still based upon traditional notions of social prestige, religious knowledge, generosity towards fellow men and upon the concept of hierarchy between individuals. Money in itself is not the key to becoming a predominant figure among the villagers; it has to be associated with at least one of the criteria traditionally required for the achievement of respect and recognition. International migration has not modified the traditional values at the base of the social relations, although one might have expected contact with the outside world to alter the migrant's worldview. On the contrary, migration has entailed an inflationary race between households with migrants, which compete with each other over the amounts of money involved in ceremonies. These are the occasions to display one's economic and social status by, for example, showing off the content of the dowry and by distributing cooked meals, sweets and offerings to relatives, friends and poor people. Generosity is the commonly expected mode of behaviour and must be proportional to the household's economic resources. Therefore, the village community anticipates ceremonies with a lavish style when they are organized by households with a migrant.

Ideology and Economic Development

The villagers' economic behaviour shows that an analysis of international labour migration that is confined to economic aspects does not give a complete picture of the phenomenon. Using this economist reductionism, migration is considered to have either positive or negative effects according to whether the migrant worker makes productive investments or not. His economic behaviour is expected to follow a logic similar to Western capitalist rationality.

Superficially the villagers' economic behaviour appears to fit the Western pattern of economic rationality[1] and it seems logical that the migrants' households would give first priority to the improved satisfaction of their basic needs. This apparent similarity with Western economic behaviour leads to the belief that the villagers would be interested in making productive investments when the general economy of their households has improved. According to this study, however, this is not the case because of the dominant ideology which exists in the villages.

The villagers' economic choice and priorities can be fully explained by placing them in their cultural context with its specific rationality. They behave according to the rationality of their ideological system. The significance of labour migration for an economic improvement of the village is achieved through an insight into the interrelationship between the villagers' meaning system and economic resources.

The mode of thinking in a non-capitalist and non-industrialized social formation such as the Pakistani rural society is characterized by another type of logic. The people have an ideal conception of their social life and of their selfhood which they try to live up to. Ideological values draw the frame of reference within which thoughts and actions operate, including their economic behaviour.

The villagers' economic behaviour is structured by a combination of several types of motivations. Precisely because their ritual life is greatly dependent on a wealthy economy, one may be easily misled and think that the villagers' behaviour is solely materialistic. However, their actions are primarily determined by the wish to increase their social status through respecting the cultural norms and the symbolic life of the community.

Honour and Money

Pakistani society is a society of honour (*izzat*) and shame (*sharam*). Honour is a dominant value in the villagers' perception of selfhood and reality. Without *izzat*, the individual is nothing. He/she has no identity and no place in society. He/she is regarded as no better than an animal. *Izzat* is the most precious property to own. It is both collective and individual. The collective *izzat* is the sum of the individual *izzat* of the members of the patrilineage. It is not an inherited entity but is achieved by one's deeds during life. Honour is obtained through a respectable behaviour in everyday life and through generosity expressed during rituals.

The individual constantly aims to accumulate and maintain his/her honour, and the international labour migration has not transformed this ideology which lies at the heart of the villagers' social relations – at the levels of the household, the family, the lineage and the social classes. Quite the opposite is true since the remitted money is considered as a new economic means which can be used by individuals, households and lineages in their competition for achieving more honour.

The villagers have succeeded in adjusting the channels for increasing their symbolic capital in the possession of more material consumer goods. The search for honour and its preservation demands that more and more money should be used during the ritual celebrations. Otherwise criticism from the patrilineage and from the other villagers is rapidly forthcoming. However, honour and money cannot substitute for each other. The villagers are well aware that wealth can be acquired through dishonest means and a great amount of money can be tarnished through its disreputable origins, while a lot of prestige is always appreciated. In essence it cannot be criticized: only the misuse of the advantages it procures may be questioned. It is still better for one's reputation to be poor with prestige than to be rich without.

Why Is Honour So Important?

The importance of honour is also found in the migrant's behaviour towards the women of his household. Migration must not entail a new division of labour within the household with the women becoming more engaged in the production sphere because of a lack of manpower. Apart from all the practical aspects to be solved before departure (the gathering of money to pay for travel and the procurement of the required official documents), the preservation of one's honour through the maintenance of the traditional woman's place within society is the migrant's other main concern before leaving the country. His absence must not entail social difficulties within his household which the improvement of the economy could in no way counterbalance. In the cases where migration leads to female-headed households, this change was unforeseen and deeply opposed by the migrant. It is a de facto situation which has great social and psychological consequences for the women as well as for the migrant because it could radically transform a fundamental aspect of society. To preserve the ideal values regarding gender relations, the migrant asks his parents and close male relatives to chaperone the women of his household. In both villages migration has meant a greater control over women during a man's absence and a stricter respect of *purdah* in the wealthiest migrant household.

This adaptation of a traditional ideological value to an economic transformation has been possible because the reference to honour is a permanent means to assure the maintenance and reproduction of the patrilineage which is the villagers' primordial frame of reference. It fulfils material, social and psychological functions for the continuity of the group and for the integrity of the individual. Individualism has a very limited meaning in this cultural setting. A person is not defined as an isolated being whose actions only have significance for himself/herself.

A very strong feeling of solidarity and accountability towards near and distant relatives is transmitted into the young generation. The child's socialization very early in life underlines the responsibility towards the group. Not to convey these obligations could threaten the integrity of the *biraderi*. It could bring disrespect for the past and the forefathers.

The villagers accept an absence of autonomy in their life-style and a lack of individualism in their mode of thinking because of the many advantages which are offered by the *biraderi* network in their everyday experience, and especially during periods of crises. Rivalries between individuals, families and *biraderi*s are frequent. In this social context, it is very difficult for a person to manage without relying upon somebody who is a sure ally in the case of conflict or dispute. People trust their own *biraderi* members and not strangers from other lineages or villages. They have no desire to leave this kinship network because their inter-dependence means security.

A central element of the villagers' rationality is thus the importance given to the maintenance of kinship ties. These are strengthened again and again by the celebrations of the life-cycle ceremonies because they are the occasion to display respect for the ancestors' traditions and consequently for the ancestors themselves. The more respect somebody has for the patrilineage and its customs, the more honour is obtained in return from the villagers. The grade of respect for the forefathers is measured by the ostentations of these celebrations and by the value of the exhibited items.

Not to celebrate the ceremonies according to tradition is considered a shameful attitude towards what the forefathers did and thought. In a face-to-face community, people are very worried about their reputation. Their families have lived there for several generations and will continue to do so for many generations to come. They cannot be indifferent to public opinion.

It has no meaning for the villagers to question the origin and reason of these traditions. These are the things to do because they have always had to be done. Furthermore, it is unthinkable for the majority of the villagers that the social organization and ritual life could be modified. This is a totally alien consideration. Change is considered as a threat to a status quo which is believed to satisfy everyone. This does not mean that the villagers are conservative by nature. They are just following the most adequate strategy within a society where the state does not provide any form of social security. There are no alternatives to the use of kinship ties in the case of hardship. Very few individuals have enough economic independence to allow them social independence. Furthermore, the potential entrepreneurs do not have the power to transform the ideological values of the society. Consequently, their economic improvement involuntarily strengthens an ideology which is related to former objective conditions of the society. Honour is now associated with money.

Usually development planners believe that the economic improvement of a rural community automatically occurs when its economic resources increase. But like any other behaviour, the use of money is a cultural phenomenon which varies according to the dominant values through which people define their identity. In other words, the understanding of an economic rationality requires an analysis of its interrelations with the ideological framework of the society.

In Pakistani villages, the economic conduct of the people aims not only at the satisfaction of their basic needs but also at the establishment of a ceremonial fund, the display of which is perceived as a sign of respect towards the community and the forefathers. The motivation sustaining this behaviour is the accumulation and the preservation of a symbolic capital, namely honour. Substantial economic resources – like foreign remittances – have not changed its importance. Honour is still the main criterion which defines the individual's status, and the functioning of the society remains based upon an ideology where the individual's reputation is evaluated through generosity. Therefore, the people do not invest productively and do not show more entrepreneurial initiatives because these actions have no significance in their meaning system.

The remittances strengthen the customs instead of transforming them. It is more important for the villagers to adapt traditions, which are elements of their cultural identity, to economic changes than to drop them and become alienated.

Note

1 For the sake of clarity, I have reduced the Western economic rationality to the technocrat's rationality. This means a rationality which is characterized by the assertion of the Western world's superiority and its right to dominate other rational systems. The course of history is perceived as being exclusively linear and its direction as going forwards. Non-Western rationality is a rationality which is based on the spiritual, ethical and social values of the local society.

APPENDICES

Appendix 1: List of Consulted Organizations

The institutions visited were divided into five categories.

1) History of the Punjab:

- Archives and Archaeology Section, Rawalpindi
- Department of History, Quaid-i-Azam University, Islamabad
- Islamic Research Institute, Islamabad
- National Commission on Historical and Cultural Research, Islamabad

2) Migration:

- Bureau of Emigration, Overseas Employment (Manpower Division), Islamabad
- Labour, Manpower and Overseas Pakistanis, Ministry of Labour Division, Islamabad
- Overseas Pakistanis Foundation, Islamabad

3) Industry:

- Ministry of Industry, Islamabad

4) Agriculture:

- Directorate for Agricultural Information and Publication, Lahore

- Ministry of Food, Agriculture and Co-operatives, Islamabad
- Ministry of Food and Agriculture for the Punjab, Lahore
- Ministry of Local Government and Rural Development, Islamabad

5) Diverse:

- Bureau of Census, Islamabad
- Department of Anthropology, Quaid-i-Azam University, Islamabad
- Department of Economics, Quaid-i-Azam University, Islamabad
- Department of History, Quaid-i-Azam University, Islamabad
- Department of Sociology, University of the Punjab, Lahore
- Economic Research Institute, Lahore
- Pakistan Institute of Development Economics, Islamabad
- Social Studies Research Centre, University of the Punjab, Lahore
- State Bank of Pakistan, Islamabad
- Survey of Pakistan, Islamabad

Appendix 2: Castes of Landowners According to Religion in Chahiwala

Date	Hindu	Sikh	Muslim
1860	Katri Lamba	Katri Talvar	Dihmal
	Katri Kassi	Katri Mokha	Bakral
	Katri Sacher	Sultan Singh	
	Brahman		
1886	Katri Niabok	Bet	Dihmal
	Kertre	Katar Beulwar	Kashmiri
	Nehet	Saharel	Gujjar
	Brahman	Nabar	Nigial Bahawar
		Gangri Sajjar	Darzi
1905	Katri Sacher	Katri Talvar	Dihmal
	Katri Kehana	Katri Mokha	Kashmiri
	Brahman Kalah	Katri Lamba	Gujjar
	Brahman Bet	Katri Govara	Mochi
	Brahman Sem	Katri Bassor	
	Brahman Ehser	Katri Med	
		Katri Chatowal	
		Soonara	
		Vangotra	
1947	Brahman Kalah	Katri Talwar	Dihmal
	Brahman Bet	Katri Mokha	Kashmiri
	Brahman Sem	Katri Lamba	Mora
		Katri Sacher	Mochi
		Katri Kehana	Nangial
		Katri Gawara	Dar Rajput
		Brahman Singh	
		Brahman Ehser	
		Zarger	

GLOSSARY

aal	unilineal descent group which is a subdivision of the patrilineal descent group (*zat*).
barani land	rainfed fields.
batai	a share-cropping payment.
behi	book found in almost every household, in which gifts are registered at the occasion of the *vartan bhanji* rituals according to the type of item, its value and the donor's name.
biraderi	patrilineage in which non-blood kin also is assimilated, since the kinship system in Punjabi villages is of a classificatory type.
bunjar jadid	new fallow land.
bunjar qadim	old fallow land.
chahi land	well-irrigated fields.
chapati	a flat, thin bread made of wheat flour.
chowkidar	watchman.
dhobi	villager who belongs to the hereditary and endogamous occupational caste of washermen.
dira	meeting-place of the landowner in each subdivision of the patrilineage (*patti*).
dofasli dosala	crop rotation pattern in which two different crops are grown on the same plot of land in two successive years.
gardawar	revenue officer.

ghair mumkin	uncultivable land used for residential purposes.
ghee	clarified butter.
ghur	raw sugar.
hissa tenancy	a form of tenancy in which agricultural input and yield are divided equally between the landowner and the tenant.
izzat	honour.
kachi vartan	ritual of exchange between people who have non-hereditary relationships.
kammi	one of the two main social divisions found in the village community. It refers to the groups of villagers who perform all kinds of services for the landowners, each according to its traditional profession.
kharif season	summer season, from April to September.
laag	small amount of money paid by the landowners to the craftsmen of the village for their labour.
Lambardar	administration officer established during colonial rule in the rural areas. He was responsible for the levy of land tax and handling of matters regarding law and order in the villages.
lassi	buttermilk.
lohar	villager who belongs to the hereditary and endogamous occupational caste of blacksmiths.
mangi labour	system of reciprocal service practised between landowners.
mehr	wedding compensation paid by the bridegroom's family to the bride's family in case of divorce.
merdana	men's quarter where male visitors are received without the risk of disturbing the women of the household.
nak	prestige.
nal chahi land	fields irrigated by tubewell.
neandra	gifts exchanged during the *vartan bhanji* ritual.
nehri land	canal-irrigated fields.
pachara	a type of partnership in trade under which expenditures and gains are shared on a one-fifth/four-fifths basis.
pakki vartan	ritual of exchange between members of the patrilineage who have strong and permanent ties.

patti subdivision of the patrilineage which was originally an administrative unit created by the colonial rulers for the purpose of levying land revenue.

patwari land registrar.

prali mats made of wheat- or rice-stalks.

purdah women's confinement practised in relation to gender apartheid.

querao to take land on *querao* is a transfer of property practised before Partition by Hindu usurers who took land as a form of reimbursement from their debitors.

quom socio-economic divisions constituted by people who trace their descent from a common male ancestor.

rabi season winter season from October to March.

sahookar a type of shop-keeper who officially registers his commercial transactions.

seypi system institutionalized relations of labour between landowners and craftsmen (*kammis*) in the village.

shamlat common land in the village.

sharam shame.

taccavi a loan system introduced in the villages by the colonial administration after World War I.

terkhan villager who belongs to the hereditary and endogamous occupational caste of carpenters.

theka tenancy a form of tenancy under which the landowner and the tenant fix the amount of the production yields (in crops or in cash) which is to be paid by the tenant after each harvest.

vartan bhanji ritual of prestations and counter-prestations which reaffirms the cohesion of the patrilineage.

zamindar one of the two main social divisions found in the village community. It refers to the groups of villagers who are landowners.

zat patrilineal descent group.

zenana quarters in the house strictly reserved for women and the closest male relatives.

BIBLIOGRAPHY

Aase, T.H., 1979. *Arbeidsvandring og vedlikehold av landsbyøkonomi i Pakistansk Punjab* [Labour migration and maintenance of village economy in Pakistani Punjab]. Skriftserie no. 17. Sosialantropologisk Institutt, Bergen: University of Bergen.

—— 1992. *Punjabi Practices of Migration: Punjabi Life Projects in Pakistan and Norway.* Bergen: University of Bergen.

Abbasi, N. and M. Irfan, n.d. 'Socio-economic effects of international migration on the families left behind. Islamabad: Pakistan Institute of Development Economics.' *Studies in Population, Labour Force and Migration,* Project Report no. 7.

Abdullah, T.A. and S.Z. Zeidenstein, 1982. *Village Women of Bangladesh. Prospects for Change.* Oxford: Pergamon Press.

Adams, R., Jr. and J. He, 1995. *Sources of Income Inequality in Rural Pakistan.* Research report 102. Washington, D.C.: International Food Policy Research Institute.

Adams, R.H., Jr., 1998. 'Remittances, investment and rural asset accumulation in Pakistan'. *Economic Development and Cultural Change*, vol. 46, no. 1, pp. 155–73.

Addleton, J.S., 1984. 'The impact of international migration on economic development in Pakistan'. *Asian Survey,* vol. 24, no. 5, pp. 574–596.

—— 1991. 'The impact of the Gulf War on migration and remittances in Asia and the Middle East'. *International Migration,* vol. 29, no. 4, pp. 509–525.

—— 1992. *Undermining the Centre: the Gulf Migration and Pakistan.* Karachi: Oxford University Press.

Agarwal, B., 1988. 'Patriarchy and the "modernising" state. An introduction', in B. Agarwal (ed.): *Structures of Patriarchy. State, Community and Household in Modernising Asia.* London: Zed Books.

Ahmad, E., 1973. 'Pakistan: Its role in US world strategy'. *Merip Reports*, no. 16, pp. 12–17.

Ahmad, I. (ed.), 1976. *Kinship and Marriage among Muslims in India.* New Delhi: Manohar Publications.

—— 1981. 'Pakistan: class and state formation'. *Race and Class,* vol. 22, no. 3, pp. 239–256.

Ahmad, J. (ed.), 1978. *Caste and Social Stratification among Muslims in India.* New Delhi: Manohar Publications.

—— 1985. *Ritual and Religion among Muslims of the Subcontinent.* Lahore: Vanguard.

Ahmad, S., 1970. 'Social stratification in a Punjabi village'. *Contributions to Indian Sociology,* no. 4, pp. 105–125.

—— 1977. *Class and Power in a Punjabi Village.* Lahore: Punjab Abdi Markaz.

—— (with sections by H. Alavi), 1974. 'A village in Pakistani Punjab: Jalpana', in C. Maloney (ed.): *South Asia. Seven Community Profiles.* New York: Holt, Rinehart and Winston, pp. 131–172.

Ahmed, A.S., 1976. *Millennium and Charisma among Pathans: A Critical Essay in Social Anthropology.* London: Routledge and Kegan Paul.

—— 1980. *Pakhtun Economy and Society: Traditional Structure and Economic Development in a Tribal Society.* London: Routledge and Kegan Paul.

—— 1984. '"Dubai Chalo": Problems in the ethnic encounter between Middle Eastern and South Asian Muslim societies'. *Asian Affairs*, 15, pp. 262–76.

—— [1988] 1990a. *Discovering Islam. Making Sense of Muslim History and Society.* New Delhi: Vistaar Publications.

—— (ed.), 1990b. *Pakistan: The Social Sciences Perspective.* Karachi: Oxford University Press.

Ahmed, F., 1975. 'Aiding underdevelopment in Pakistan'. *Merip Reports,* no. 42, pp. 19–22.

—— 1976. 'Pakistan: the new dependence'. *Race and Class,* vol. 18, no. 1, pp. 3–22.

Akhmed, R., 1978. 'Modern management and Pakistani business'. *Labour and Society,* vol. 3, no. 1, pp. 91–105.

Akbar, M., n.d. *Emigration from Pakistan.* Islamabad: Bureau of Emigration and Overseas Employment.

Akhtar, R. 1980. *Pakistan Year Book.* Karachi: East and West Publishing Company.

Akhtar, S.M. and A.R. Arshad, n.d. *Village Life in Lahore District.* (A study of selected economic aspects). Lahore: Social Sciences Research Centre, University of the Panjab.

Alam, S., 1974. 'Economics of the landed interests: a case study of Pakistan'. *Pakistan Economic and Social Review,* vol. 12, no. 1, pp. 12–26.

Alavi, H.A., 1971. 'The politics of dependence: a village in West Punjab'. *South Asian Review,* vol. 4, no. 2, pp. 111–128.

—— 1972. 'Kinship in West Punjab villages'. *Contributions to Indian Sociology,* no. 6, pp. 1–27.

—— 1973. 'Peasant classes and primordial loyalties'. *The Journal of Peasant Studies,* vol. 1, no. 1, pp. 23–62.

—— 1980. 'India: transition from feudalism to colonial capitalism'. *Journal of Contemporary Asia,* vol. 10, no. 4, pp. 359–399.

—— 1982. *Class and State in Pakistan.* Manchester: Faculty of Economic and Social Studies, University of Manchester.

—— 1988. 'Pakistan and Islam: Ethnicity and ideology', in H. Alavi and F. Halliday (eds): *State and Ideology in the Middle East and Pakistan.* London: Macmillan, pp. 64–111.

—— (ed.) 1989. *South Asia and Migration.* London: Macmillan Publisher.

Albrecht, H., 1974. *Living Conditions of Rural Families in Pakistan.* Islamabad: Embassy of the Federal Republic of Germany.

Alderman, H., 1996. 'Savings and economic shocks in rural Pakistan'. *Journal of Development Economics,* vol. 51, pp. 343–65.

Alderman, H. and M. Garcia, 1993. *Poverty, Household Food Security and Nutrition in Rural Pakistan.* Research Report no. 96. Washington, D.C.: International Food Policy Research Institute.

Ali, K. (ed.), 1982. *Pakistan: the Political Economy of Rural Development.* Lahore: Vanguard.

Ali, M.M. and A. Rehman, 1979. *Farm Accounts, Family Budgets of Selected Rural Families and Cost of Production of Major Crops in the Punjab, 1976–77.* Lahore: Economic Research Institute, publication no. 177.

Ali, M.M., M.A. Cheema and A. Ahmad, 1979. *Marketing of Farm Products and Farm Inputs in 'Barani' Punjab and NWFP.* Lahore: Economic Research Institute, publication no. 176.

Ali, T., 1971. *Pakistan: Dictature militaire ou pouvoir populaire?* Paris: F. Maspéro.

—— 1983. *Can Pakistan Survive? The Death of a State.* Harmondsworth: Penguin Books.

Ambirajan, S., 1978. *Classical Political Economy and British Policy in India.* Cambridge: Cambridge University Press.

Amjad, R., 1972. 'A critique of the Green Revolution in West Pakistan'. *Pakistan Economic and Social Review,* vol. 10, no. 1, pp. 17–41.

—— 1986. 'Impact of workers' remittances from the Middle East on Pakistan's economy'. *Pakistan Development Review,* vol. 25, no. 4, pp. 757–82.

—— 1989. 'Economic impact of migration to the Middle East on the major Asian labour-sending countries: An overview', in R. Amjad, (ed.): *To the Gulf and Back: Studies on the Economic Impact of Asian Labour Migration.* New Delhi: UNDP–ILO/ARTEP.

Anwar, M., 1985. *Pakistanis in Britain. A Sociological Study.* London: New Century Publishers.

Arif, M., B. Ahmed and M. Jannisar, 1984. *Expansion of Employment and Income through Local Resource Mobilisation. A Study of Three Villages in Pakistan.* Bangkok: Asian Employment Programme, Asian Regional Team for Employment Promotion (ARTEP).

Arnold, F. and N. Shah, 1984. 'Asian labour migration to the Middle East'. *International Migration Review,* vol. 18, no. 2, pp. 294–318.

Bajaj, S.K., 1972. 'British policy towards the Punjab peasantry with special reference to the Punjab Tenancy Act, 1868'. *The Punjab Past and Present*, vol. 6, no. 1, pp. 212–226.

Ballard, R., 1987. 'The political economy of migration: Pakistan, Britain and the Middle East', in J. Eades (ed.): *Migrants, Workers and the Social Order.* London: Tavistock, pp. 17–41.

—— 1989. 'Effects of labour migration from Pakistan', in H. Alavi and J. Harriss (eds): *Sociology of Developing Societies: South Asia.* London: Macmillan, pp. 112–22.

Banerjee, H., 1977. 'Agricultural labourers of the Punjab during the second half of the nineteenth century'. *The Punjab Past and Present,* vol. 11, no. 1, pp. 96–116.

—— 1978. 'Growth of commercial agriculture in the Punjab during the second half of the 19th century'. *The Punjab Past and Present,* vol. 12, no. 1, pp. 221–256.

—— 1979. '*Zamindar* cultivator relations and the struggle over rent in the Punjab (1849–1901)'. *The Punjab Past and Present,* vol. 13, no. 1, pp. 132–163.

Barth, F., 1959. *Political Leadership among Swat Pathans.* London School of Economics Monograph. London: Athlone Press.

—— 1960. 'The system of social stratification in Swat, North Pakistan', in E.R. Leach (ed.): *Aspects of Caste in South India, Ceylon and North-West Pakistan.* Cambridge: Cambridge University Press.

Bashir, F., 1981. 'Impact of Male Migration on the Joint Family Structure: A Case Study of an Agricultural Village'. Unpublished MSc thesis, Department of Anthropology, Quaid-i-Azam University, Islamabad.

Berland, J., 1982. *No Five Fingers Are Alike: Cognitive Amplifiers in Social Context.* Cambridge, Mass.: Harvard University Press.

Berreman, G.D., 1963. *Hindus of the Himalayas.* Berkeley: University of California Press.

Bilquees, F. and S. Hamid, 1981. *Impact of International Migration on Women and Children Left Behind: A Case Study of a Punjabi Village.* Islamabad: Pakistan Institute of Development Economics, Research Report Series no. 115.

Birks, J.S. and C.A. Sinclair, 1979. 'International labour migration in the Arab Middle East'. *Third World Quarterly,* vol. 1, no. 2, pp. 87–99.

—— 1980. *International Labour Migration and Development in the Arab Region.* Geneva: ILO.

Bourdieu, P., 1980. *Le Sens pratique.* Paris: Editions de Minuit.

Burki, S.J., 1980. 'What migration to the Middle East may mean for Pakistan'. *Journal of South Asian and Middle Eastern Studies.* vol. 3, no. 3, pp.47–66.

—— 1988. 'Pakistan under Zia'. *Asian Survey,* vol. 28, no. 10, pp. 1082–1100.

Burney, N.A., 1987. *Workers' Remittances from the Middle East and Their Effect on Pakistan's Economy.* Islamabad: Pakistan Institute of Development Economics.

Carchedi, G., 1979. 'Authority and foreign labour: some notes on a late capitalist form of capital accumulation and state intervention'. *Studies in Political Economy – A Socialist Review,* no. 2, pp. 37–74.

Chaudhary, M.A., 1978. 'Land concentration and agricultural taxation in Pakistan.' *Scrutiny. A Journal of the Department of Pakistan Studies.* Islamabad: Quaid-i-Azam University, vol. 4, no. 3, pp. 44–62.

—— 1979. 'Socio-economic implications of manpower emigration from Pakistan.' *Scrutiny. A Journal of the Department of Pakistan Studies.* Islamabad: Quaid-i-Azam University, vol. 5, no. 4–5, pp. 38–52.

Chaudhry, M.H., 1982. 'Migration and Social Change in Humak Village'. Unpublished MSc thesis. Department of Anthropology, Quaid-i-Azam University, Islamabad.

Clarke, C., C. Peach and S. Vertovec (eds), 1990. *South Asians Overseas: Migration and Ethnicity.* Cambridge: Cambridge University Press.

Clifford, J. and G.E. Marcus (eds), 1986. *Writing Culture. The Poetics and Politics of Ethnography.* Berkeley: University of California Press.

Cohen, S.P. and M.G. Weinbaum, 1982. 'Pakistan in 1981: Staying on'. *Asian Survey,* vol. 22, no. 2, pp. 136–146.

—— 1983. 'Pakistan in 1982: Holding on'. *Asian Survey,* vol. 23, no. 2, pp. 123–132.

Crooke, W., [1906] 1977. *The Native Races of the Northern India.* Lahore: Sh. Mubarak Ali.

—— [1879] 1989. *A Glossary of North Indian Peasant Life. Edited with an Introduction, Notes and Appendices by Shahid Amin.* Delhi: Oxford University Press.

Czichowski, F., 1986. 'Migration pakistanischer Arbeitskräfte in die arabischen Erdölstaaten und ihre sozioökonomischen Implikationen für Pakistan'. *Internationales Asienforum,* vol. 17, no. 1/2.

Daniel, V.E., [1984] 1987. *Fluid Signs. Being a Person the Tamil Way.* Berkeley: University of California Press.

Darling, M., Sir, [1925] 1947. *The Punjab Peasant in Prosperity and Debt.* Lahore: Vanguard Historical Reprints no. 1.

Das, V., 1973. 'The structure of marriage preferences: an account from Pakistani fiction'. *Man,* vol. 8, no. 1, pp. 30–45.

—— 1976. 'Masks and faces: an essay on Punjabi kinship'. *Contribution to Indian Sociology* (NS), vol. 10, no. 1, pp. 1–30.

Domin, D., 1974. 'Some aspects of British land policy in Punjab after its annexation in 1849'. *The Punjab Past and Present,* vol. 8, no. 1, pp. 12–31.

Donnan, H. and P. Werbner (eds), 1991. *Economy and Culture in Pakistan: Migrants and Cities in Muslim Society.* London: Macmillan Academic and Professional Ltd.

Douie, J.M., [1930] 1981. *The Settlement Manual with Notes.* Lahore: Mansoor Book House.

Dumont, L., 1972. *Homo Hierarchicus.* London: Paladin.

Eades, J., 1987. 'Anthropologists and migrants: Changing models and realities", in J. Eades (ed.): *Migrants, Workers and the Social Order.* London: Tavistock, pp. 1–16.

ECWA, 1982. 'Socio-economic characteristics of international migrants in the Gulf states', in United Nations Economic Commission for Western Asia: *International Migration in the Arab World.* Proceedings of ECWA population conference 1981. Beirut: ECWA , vol. 2, pp. 685–731.

Eglar, Z., 1960. *A Punjabi Village in Pakistan.* New York: Columbia University Press.

Ercelawn, A.A., 1979. *Rural Poverty, Agricultural Productivity and Adaption of Technology.* ESCAP/QAU Project on Social Participation in Rural Development. Islamabad: Quaid-i-Azam University, Department of Economics.

Esposito, B.J., 1974. 'The politics of land reform in Pakistan'. *Asian Survey,* vol. 14, no. 5, pp. 429–38.

Etienne, G., 1967. *Progrès agricole et maîtrise de l'eau. Le cas du Pakistan.* Paris: Presses Universitaires de France.

Farooq-I-Azam, 1993. 'The Gulf War and Pakistani migrants: Profile of returnees and resettlement experience,' in P. Wickramasekara (ed.): *The Gulf Crisis and South Asia: Studies on the Economic Impact.* New Delhi: UNDP–ILO/ARTEP.

Friedmann, H., 1980. 'Household production and the national economy: Concepts for the analysis of agrarian formations'. *The Journal of Peasant Studies* vol. 7, no. 2, pp. 158–184.

Fürer-Haimendorf, C. von, 1969. *Morals and Merit: A Study of Values and Social Controls in South-Asian Societies.* London: Weidenfeld and Nicholson.

Gardezi, H.N., 1985. 'The post-colonial state in South Asia: The case of Pakistan'. *South Asia Bulletin* vol. 5, no. 2, pp. 1–7.

—— 1991. 'Asian workers in the Gulf states of the Middle East'. *Journal of Contemporary Asia*, vol. 21, no. 2, pp. 179–194.

Gardezi, H.N. and J. Rashid (eds), 1983. Pakistan. *The Roots of Dictatorship. The Political Economy of a Pretorian State.* London: Zed Press.

Geertz, C., 1973. *The Interpretation of Cultures.* New York: Basic Books.

Gilani, I., 1983. *Left Behind or Left Out: A Study of the Left Behind Families of Overseas Pakistanis.* Islamabad: Pakistan Institute of Public Opinion, Migration Report No. 1.

—— 1985. *Citizens, Slaves, Guest-workers. The Dynamics of Labour Migration from South-Asia.* Islamabad: Institute of Policy Studies.

Gilani, I., M.F. Khan and M. Iqbal, 1981. *Labour Migration from Pakistan to the Middle East and Its Impact on the Domestic Economy* (parts 1, 2, 3). Islamabad: Pakistan Institute of Development Economics, Research Reports no. 126, 127, 128.

Gill, M.S. and S.A.A. Naqvi, 1966. *Cost of Production of Major Crops.* 1961–62 to 1963–64. Lahore: The Board of Economy Inquiry, West Pakistan, Publication no. 138.

Gopal, J., 1976. 'The tenancy policy of the British Punjab government and social development 1849–1900'. *Proceedings of the Punjab History Conference*, Feb. 28–29, 1976, pp. 269–276.

Government of Pakistan, 1972. *District Census Report Rawalpindi.* Islamabad: Census Organization Ministry of Interior, States and Frontier Regions.

—— 1972. *District Census Report*, Sialkot. Islamabad: Census Organization Ministry of Interior, States and Frontier Regions.

—— 1977. *Pakistan Economic Survey 1976–77.* Islamabad: Finance Division Economic Adviser's Wing.

Government of Punjab, 1976. *Report of the Punjab Barani Commission* (main report). Lahore.

—— 1977. *Punjab Agricultural Statistics, 1975–76.* Lahore: Department of Agriculture, Punjab.

—— 1978. *Punjab Agricultural Statistics, 1976–77.* Lahore: Department of Agriculture, Punjab.

Gray, J.N. and D.J. Mearns, 1989. 'Introduction. Household and domestic group – society from the inside out', in J.N. Gray and D.J. Mearns (eds): *Society from the Inside Out. Anthropological Perspectives on the South Asian Household.* New Delhi: Sage Publications, pp. 13–34.

Guisinger, S.E., 1986. 'The impact of temporary worker migration on Pakistan', in S.J. Burki and R. Laporte (eds): *Pakistan's Development Priorities.* Karachi: Oxford University Press, pp. 201–23.

Gustafson, W.E., 1976. 'Economic problems of Pakistan under Bhutto'. *Asian Survey*, vol. 16, no. 4, pp. 364–80.

—— and W.L. Richter, 1981. 'Pakistan in 1980: Weathering the storm'. *Asian Survey*, vol. 21, no. 2, pp. 162–171.

Haider, A.S., 1960. *Village in an Urban Orbit. Shah-di-Khui, a Village in Lahore Urban Area.* Lahore: Social Sciences Research Centre, University of the Panjab.

Halliday, F., 1977. 'Migration and the labour force in the oil producing states of the Middle East'. *Development and Change,* no. 8, pp. 263–291.

—— 1982. 'Labour migration in the Arab world: The ugly face of the new economic order'. *Labour, Capital and Society,* vol. 15, no. 1, pp. 8–22.

Hamid, N., 1974. 'The burden of capitalist growth – a study of real wages and consumption in Pakistan'. *Pakistan Economic and Social Review* vol. 12, no. 1, pp. 45–70.

—— 1982. 'Dispossession and differentiation of the peasantry in the Punjab during colonial rule'. *The Journal of Peasant Studies,* vol. 10, no. 1, pp. 52–72.

Hamman, M., 1986. 'Capitalist development, family division of labor, and migration in the Middle East', in E. Leacock, H.I. Safa and contributors: *Women's Work. Development and the Division of Labour by Gender.* Massachussets: Bergin and Garvey Publishers, pp. 158–173.

Haque, Z., 1990. 'Religion and economics: Islamization of economy in Pakistan (1977–88)'. *South Asia Bulletin,* vol. 10, no. 2, pp.25–31.

Hartmann, B. and J. Boyce, 1983. *A Quiet Violence. View from a Bangladesh Village.* London: Zed Press.

Hill, A.G., 1977. 'Les travailleurs étrangers dans les pays du Golfe'. *Revue Tiers Monde,* vol. 18, no. 69, pp. 115–130.

Hussain, A., 1984. 'Land reforms in Pakistan: A reconsideration'. *Bulletin of Concerned Asian Scholars,* vol. 16, no. 1, pp. 46–52.

Hussain, Z., 1986. 'Socio-economic Contraints on Overseas Returnees'. Unpublished MSc thesis. Department of Anthropology, Quaid-i-Azam University, Islamabad.

Ibbetson, Sir Denzil, [1882 and 1916] 1974. *Punjab Castes.* Lahore: Sh. Mubarak Ali Publishers and Booksellers.

—— 1883. *Outlines of Punjab Ethnography. Being Extracts from the Punjab Census Reports of 1887. Treating of Religion, Language and Caste.* Calcutta: Government Printing.

ILO/ARTEP, 1987. *Impact of Out and Return Migration on Domestic Employment in Pakistan.* New Delhi: ILO/ARTEP.

ILO-UNDP, 1993. *International Labour Migration from Asia; an Annotated Bibliography.* New Delhi: ILO-UNDP.

Imdad, N., 1978. 'Emigration and Social Change. A Case Study of Muree Hill Village'. Unpublished MA Thesis. Department of Anthropology, Quaid-i-Azam University, Islamabad.

Inayatullah, I., 1958. 'Caste, *patti* and faction in the life of a Punjab village'. *Sociologus,* no. 8, pp. 170–86.

Iqbal, M. and M.F. Khan, 1981. *Economic Implications of the Return Flow of Immigrants from the Middle East: a Preliminary Study.* Islamabad: Pakistan Institute of Development Economics, Research Report Series no. 132.

Irfan, M., 1981a. *Pakistan's Labour Force, Its Size and Structure. A View of Evidence.* Islamabad: Pakistan Institute of Development Economics, Research Reports Series no. 116.

—— 1981b. *An Introduction to 'Studies in Population, Labour Force and Migration'.* A PIDE/ILO-UNFPA Project. Islamabad: Pakistan Institute of Development Economics, Research Reports Series no. 118.

Irfan, M., L. Demery and G.M. Arif, 1979. *Migration Patterns in Pakistan: Preliminary Results from the PLM Survey, 1979.* Islamabad: Pakistan Institute of Development Economics.

Islam, M., 1983. 'Impact of male migration on rural housewives', in J. Huq, K. Salahuddin, H.A. Begum and S.R. Qadir (eds): *Women in Bangladesh: Some Socio-economic Issues.* Dhaka: Seminar Papers, vol. 1, pp. 46–53.

Jeffery, P., 1979. *Frogs in a Well. Indian Women in Purdah.* London: Zed Press.

Jeffery, P., R. Jeffery and A. Lyon, 1987. 'Contaminating states: midwifery, childbearing and the state in North India', in H. Afshar (ed.): *Women, State and Ideology.* London: Macmillan Press, pp. 152–169.

Johnson, B.L.C., 1979. *Pakistan.* London: Heinemann.

Joshi, P.C., 1973. 'Land reform and agrarian change in India and Pakistan since 1947, parts 1 and 2'. *The Journal of Peasant Studies,* vol. 1, pp. 164–185 and 325–362.

Karim, M.S. and W.C. Robinson, 1986. 'The migration situation in Pakistan: An analytical review', in F. Selier and M.S. Karim (eds): *Migration in Pakistan: Theories and Facts.* Lahore: Vanguard Books, pp. 21–39.

Kayser, B. (ed.), 1977. 'Migrations et développement'. *Revue Tiers-Monde,* vol. 18, no. 69.

Kazi, S., 1989. 'Domestic impact of overseas migration: Pakistan', in R. Amjad, (ed.): *To the Gulf and Back: Studies on the Economic Impact of Asian Labour Migration.* New Delhi: ILO-ARTEP.

—— 1993. 'The economic impact of the Gulf crisis on Pakistan', in P. Wickramasekara (ed.): *The Gulf Crisis and South Asia: Studies on the Economic Impact.* New Delhi: ILO, Asian Regional Team for Employment Promotion (ARTEP): United Nations Development Programme.

Kazi, S. and B. Raza, 1990. 'The duality in female employment in Pakistan'. *South Asia Bulletin,* vol. 10, no. 2, pp. 1–8.

Keely, C.B., 1983. *Research on Asian Labor Migration to the Middle East.* Summary discussion, East–West Population Institute Conference on Asian Labor Migration to the Middle East, September 19–23, 1983. Honolulu, Hawaii: East–West Center.

Keyes, C.F., 1983. 'Peasant strategies in Asian societies: moral and rational economic approaches – a symposium'. *Journal of Asian Studies,* vol. 42, no. 4, pp. 753–68.

Khan, A. (ed.), 1985. *Islam, Politics and the State. The Pakistan Experience.* London: Zed Books.

Khan, D.A., 1978. *New Technology and Rural Transformation. A Case Study of Pakistan's Punjab.* Lahore: The Economic Research Institute.

Khan, M.H., 1983. 'Class and agrarian transition in Pakistan'. *The Pakistan Development Review,* vol. 22, no. 3, pp. 129–162.

Khan, M.J., 1981. *Economics of Farm Mechanization and Water Development Policies in Pakistan: a Case Study.* Lahore: Punjab Economic Research Institute.

Khan, M. Ul Haq, 1972. *Purdah and Poligamy. A Study in the Social Pathology of the Muslim Society.* Peshawar: Nashiran-e-Ilm-o-Taraqiyet.

Khan, S.A. and F. Bilquees, 1976. 'The environment, attitudes and activities of rural women: A case study of a village in Punjab'. *The Pakistan Development Review,* vol. 15, no. 3, pp. 237–71.

Khan, N.S., F. Shaheed, Y. Mitha and S. Rehman, 1989. 'Income generation for women: Lessons from the field in Punjab Province, Pakistan'. *South Asia Bulletin,* vol. 9, no. 1, pp. 26–46.

Khurshid, A.s, 1982. 'Input of Migration on the Traditions and Values: A Case Study of Village Behkri, Tehsil Chakwal, District Jhelum'. Unpublished MSc thesis, Department of Anthropology, Quaid-i-Azam University, Islamabad.

Kishwar, S., 1966. *Rural Women's Participation in Farm Operations.* Lyallpur: West Pakistan Agricultural University Press.

Kolenda, P.M., 1963. 'Toward a model of the Hindu *jajmani* system'. *Human Organization,* vol. 22, no. 1, pp. 11–31.

Krishnaraj M. and K. Chanana (eds), 1989. *Gender and the Household Domain. Social Cultural Dimensions.* New Delhi: Sage Publications.

Kuhnen, F., 1968. *Agriculture and Beginning Industrialization: West Pakistan.* Opladen: C.W. Leske Verlag.

Kureshi, K.U., 1978. *A Geography of Pakistan.* Karachi: Oxford University Press.

Kurin, R., 1983a. 'Modernisation and traditionalisation: Hot and cold agriculture in Punjab, Pakistan'. *South Asian Anthropology,* vol. 4, no. 2, pp. 65–76.

—— 1983b. 'Indigenous agronomics and agricultural development in the Indus Basin'. *Human Organisation,* vol. 42, no. 4, pp. 283–94.

Kurin, R. and C. Morrow, 1985. 'Patterns of solidarity in a Punjabi Muslim village'. *Contributions to Indian Sociology,* vol. 19, no. 2, pp. 235–49.

Laporte, R., 1985. 'Urban groups and the Zia regime', in C. Baxter (ed.): *Zia's Pakistan: Politics and Stability in a Frontline State.* Boulder: Westview Press, pp. 7–22.

Latif, S.M., n.d. *History of the Punjab. From the Remotest Antiquity to the Present Time.* Lahore: People's Publishing House.

Lefebvre, A., 1984. 'Punjabi village women and international labour migration from Pakistan', in K. Ferdinand and B. Selmer (eds): *Islam: Family and Society.* Conference report, pp. 173–91. Copenhagen: The State Research Council for the Humanities.

—— 1985. 'International manpower migration from a Punjabi village in Pakistan', in A. Guha, J. Prabhu and F. Vivekananda (eds): *Immigrant Women and Children in Industrial Europe.* Oslo: Institute for Alternative Development Research.

—— 1989. 'Tea Has Taken the Place of Love. The Political Economy of Honour in Pakistani Villages'. Copenhagen: The Danish International Development Agency, unpublished research report.

—— 1990a. 'International labour migration from two Pakistani villages with different forms of agriculture'. *The Pakistan Development Review,* vol. 29, no. 1, pp. 59–90.

—— 1990b. 'Women, honour and money in Pakistani villages. An example of the strengthening of traditions through economic development'. *Den ny Verden,* vol. 23, no. 4, pp. 84–99.

Lefebvre, A. and A. Zragevsky, 1980. 'Les luttes de la communauté pakistanaise de Paris (1972–1977)'. *Peuples Méditerranéens/Mediterranean Peoples,* no. 13, pp. 127–144.

Legassick, M., 1974. 'South Africa: capital accumulation and violence'. *Economy and Society,* vol. 3, no. 4.

Lewis, O., 1958. *Village Life in Northern India.* New York: Vintage Books.

Liu, X., 1982. 'Small land-holdings in the Punjab. The historical perspective'. *The Punjab Past and Present,* vol. 16, no. 32, pp. 386–97.

Longuenesse, E., 1986. 'Migrations et société dans les pays du Golfe'. *Monde Arabe Maghreb-Machrek,* no. 112, pp. 8–21.

MacShane, D., 1990. 'The Gulf's forgotten foreign legions'. *South Asia Bulletin,* vol. 10, no. 2, p. 66.

Maddison, A., 1971. *Class Structure and Economic Growth: India and Pakistan since the Moghuls.* London: George Allen & Unwin.

Mahmood, S., 1976. *Muslim Family Laws.* Lahore: Legal Research Centre.

Mahmood, T., 1981. 'Stratification in a Punjabi Village: A Case Study of Chak Jani, District Gujrat'. Unpublished MSc thesis, Department of Anthropology, Quaid-i-Azam University, Islamabad.

Malik, I.A., 1970. *A Book of Readings on the History of the Punjab. 1799–1947.* Lahore: Research Society of Pakistan, the University of the Punjab.

Malik, I.H., 1967. *A Survey of Socio-economic Changes in Rural Areas of the Punjab Region*, part 2. Lahore: The Board of Economic Inquiry, West Pakistan.

Marriott, McKim, 1959. 'Interactional and attributional theories of caste ranking'. *Man in India*, vol. 39.

—— 1960. *Caste Ranking and Community Structures in Five Regions of India and Pakistan*. Poona: Deccan College Monograph Series, no. 23.

Marriott, McKim and Ronald B. Inden, 1977. 'Towards an ethnosociology of South Asian caste systems'. In K. David (ed.): *The New Wind: Changing Identities in South Asia*. The Hague: Mouton.

Martinussen, John, 1980. *Staten i perifere og post-koloniale samfund: Indien og Pakistan* [The state in peripheral and post-colonial society: India and Pakistan]. Århus: Forlaget Politica, 4 vols.

Maududi, S.A. Ala, 1972 (1939). *Purdah and the Status of Women in Islam*. Lahore: Islamic Publications Ltd.

Meer, Hassan Ali, [1917] 1978. *Observations on the Mussulmauns of India*. Karachi: Oxford University Press.

Mehdi, R., 1984. *The Legal Position of Women in Pakistan: An Essay*. Copenhagen: Humanistic Centre for Women's Studies.

—— 1993. *The Islamization of the Law in Pakistan*. London: NIAS/Curzon Press.

Meillassoux, C., 1975. *Maidens, Meal and Money. Capitalism and the Domestic Community*. Cambridge: Cambridge University Press.

—— 1979. *Les derniers blancs. Le modèle sud-africain*. Paris: F. Maspéro.

Merip Reports, 1984. *Migrant Workers*, no. 123.

Mernissi, F., 1983. *Sexe, idéologie, islam*. Paris: Tierce Editions.

Mines, M., 1972. 'Muslim social stratification in India: the basis for variation'. *Southwestern Journal of Anthropology*, vol. 28, no. 4, pp. 333–349.

Mishra, S.C., 1982. 'Commercialisation, peasant differentiation and merchant capital in late nineteenth-century Bombay and Punjab'. *The Journal of Peasant Studies*, vol. 10, no. 1, pp. 3–51.

Morris, M., 1976. 'The development of Capitalism in South African agriculture: class struggle in the countryside'. *IMRA*, vol. 2, no. 2–3.

Mubasher, M.Y., 1983. 'Paradox of tractorization in Pakistan'. *Agricultural Mechanization in Asia, Africa and Latin America*, vol. 14, no. 1, pp. 69–76.

Mumtaz, K. and F. Shaheed, 1987. *Women of Pakistan. Two Steps Forward, One Step Back?* Lahore: Vanguard.

Nabi, I. (ed.), 1986. *The Quality of Life in Pakistan. Studies in Social Sector Economics*. Lahore: Vanguard.

Nadvi, K., 1989. 'Pakistan: Rural Change and Structural Adjustments of Town and Country Relationships'. Paper presented to conference on 'Muslims, Migrants, Metropolis', Berlin.

Naveed-i-Rahat, 1981. 'The role of women in reciprocal relationships in a Punjabi village', in T.S. Epstein and R.A. Watts (eds): *The Endless Day. Some Case Material on Asian Rural Women.* Oxford: Pergamon Press, pp. 47–81.

—— 1986. 'Meharabad, a Punjabi village: Male outmigration and women's changing role', in F. Selier and M.S. Karim (eds): *Migration in Pakistan: Theories and Facts.* Lahore: Vanguard Books, pp. 139–60.

Netton, I.R., 1992. *A Popular Dictionary of Islam.* London: Curzon Press.

Nijjar, B.S., n.d. *Punjab under the British Rule, 1849–1947.* Lahore: Book Traders.

Nisa, A.U., 1984. 'Impact of Out-country Migration on the Social and Economic Life of the Village Mohra Bhuttian'. Unpublished MA thesis, Department of Anthropology, Quaid-i-Azam University, Islamabad.

Noman, O., 1991. 'The impact of migration on Pakistan's economy and society', in H. Donnan and P. Werbner (eds): *Economy and Culture in Pakistan. Migrants and Cities in a Muslim Society.* London: Macmillan, pp. 77–96.

Owen, R., 1981. 'The Arab economies in the 1970s'. *Merip Reports,* vol. 11, no. 8–9, pp. 3–13.

Papanek, H., 1971. 'Purdah in Pakistan: seclusion and modern occupations for women'. *Journal of Marriage and the Family,* vol. 33 no. 3, pp. 517–30.

—— 1973. 'Purdah: separate worlds and symbolic shelter'. *Comparative Studies in Society and History,* vol. 15, no. 3, pp. 289–325.

—— and G. Minault (eds), 1982. *Separate Worlds. Studies of Purdah in South Asia.* Delhi: Chanakya Publications.

Pastner, C.McC., 1972. 'A social structural and historical analysis of honor, shame and *purdah*'. *Anthropological Quarterly,* vol. 45, no. 4, pp. 248–61.

—— 1974. 'Accommodations to Purdah: a female perspective'. *Journal of Marriage and the Family,* vol. 36, no. 2, pp. 408–14.

Perwaiz, S., 1979. *Pakistan: Home Remittances.* Islamabad: US Agency for International Development.

Premachandra, A., 1993. *Enhancing Developmental Impact of Migrant Remittances: A Review of Asian Experiences.* New Delhi: ILO-ARTEP.

Qayyum, A., 1980. 'Policies and implementation of land reforms: macro level study for Pakistan', in I. Inayatullah (ed.): *Land Reform. Some Asian Experiences,* vol. 4. Kuala Lumpur: Asian and Pacific Development Administration, pp. 61–89.

Qazi, Z.I. and S. Mohammad, 1973. *Farm Accounts and Family Budgets of Cultivators in the Punjab, 1970–71.* Lahore: The Board of Economic Inquiry, Punjab (Pakistan), publication no. 154.

Qureshi, J.M., 1951. *Livestock Survey in the Punjab.* Lahore: The Board of Economic Inquiry, Punjab (Pakistan), publication no. 103.

Rajput, A.B., 1977. *Social Customs and Practices in Pakistan.* Islamabad: Pakistan Branch, R.C.D. Cultural Institute.

Rashid, J., 1980. 'Political economy of manpower export from the Third World'. *Journal of Contemporary Asia,* vol. 10, no. 4, pp. 423–433.

—— 1985. 'Economy under Martial Law Government in Pakistan. Emphasis on Manpower Export', in W.P. Zingel and S.Z.A. Lallemant (eds): *Pakistan in the 80s. Ideology, Regionalism, Economy, Foreign Policy.* Lahore: Vanguard Books.

—— 1986. 'Pakistan and the central command'. *Merip Reports,* vol. 16, no. 4, pp. 28–33.

Rashid, S.M., 1985. 'Land reforms in Pakistan'. *Social Scientist,* no. 148, pp. 44–52.

Rauf, M.A., 1982. 'Labour emigration and the changing trend of family life in a Pakistani village', in S. Pastner and L. Flam (eds): *Anthropology in Pakistan: Recent Socio-Cultural and Archaeological Perspectives.* South Asia Occasional Papers and Theses, no. 8. Ithaca, NY: Cornell University South Asia Program, pp. 114–20.

—— 1984. *Rural–Urban Migration and Rural Emigration in Pakistan. (A Socio-economic Impact Study).* Islamabad: Department of Anthropology, Quaid-i-Azam University.

Raza, M.R., 1969. *Two Pakistani Villages. A Study in Social Stratification.* Lahore: University of the Punjab.

Rey, P.P., 1976a. *Les alliances de classes.* Paris: F. Maspéro.

—— (ed.), 1976b. *Capitalisme négrier. La marche des paysans vers le prolétariat.* Paris: F. Maspéro.

Richards, A. and P.L. Martin, 1983. 'The laissez-faire approach to international labor migration: The case of the Arab Middle East'. *Economic Development and Cultural Change,* pp. 455–74.

Richter, W.L., 1984. 'Pakistan in 1984. Digging in'. *Asian Survey,* vol. 25, no. 2, pp. 145–54.

Rosen, L. 1984. *Bargaining for Reality. The Construction of Social Relations in a Muslim Community.* Chicago: University of Chicago Press.

Rouse, S., 1983. 'Accelerated capital penetration into agriculture and changing class formation: A case study from a large landlord-dominated village in Pakistan Punjab'. *South Asia Bulletin,* vol. 3, no. 1, pp. 1–15.

Rouze, S.J., 1983. 'Systemic Injustices and Inequalities: *Maliki* and *Raiya* in a Punjab Village', in H. Gardezi and J. Rashid (eds): *Pakistan: the Roots of Dictatorship.* London: Zed Press, pp. 311–27.

Russell, S., 1986. 'Remittances from international migration: a review in perspective'. *World Development,* vol. 14, pp. 677–96.

Saeed, K. 1966. *Rural Women's Participation in Farm Operations.* Lyallpur: West Pakistan Agricultural University Press.

Sarmad, K., 1985. *Pakistani Migration to the Middle East Countries.* Islamabad: Pakistan Institute of Development Economics.

Sassen-Koob S., 1978. 'The international circulation of resources and development: the case of migrant labour'. *Development and Change,* vol. 9, pp. 509–45.

—— 1980. 'The internationalization of the labor force'. *Studies in Comparative International Development,* vol. 15, no. 4, pp. 3–25.

Selier, F., 1988. *Rural–Urban Migration in Pakistan.* Lahore: Vanguard Books.

—— 1991. 'Family and low-income housing in Karachi', in H. Donnan and P. Werbner (eds): *Economy and Culture in Pakistan: Migrants and Cities in Muslim Society.* London: Macmillan Academic and Professional Ltd, pp. 35–61.

Selier, F. and M.S. Karim (eds), 1986. *Migration in Pakistan: Theories and Facts.* Lahore: Vanguard Books.

Sen, S., 1979. *Agrarian Relations in India, 1793–1947.* New Delhi: People's Publishing House.

Shafqat, S., 1990. 'Political culture of Pakistan: A case of disharmony between democratic creed and autocratic reality'. *South Asia Bulletin,* vol. 10, no. 2.

Shah, N.M., 1983. 'Pakistani workers in the Middle East: volume, trends, and consequences'. *International Migration Review,* vol. 17, no. 3, pp. 410–24.

Sharma, U., 1980. *Women, Work and Property in North-West India.* London: Tavistock Publications.

—— 1985. 'Caste, class, and gender: production and reproduction in North India'. *The Journal of Peasant Studies,* vol. 12, no. 4, pp. 57–88.

—— 1989. 'Studying the household: Individuation and values', in J.N. Gray and D.J. Mearns (eds): *Society from the Inside Out. Anthropological Perspectives on the South Asian Household.* New Delhi: Sage Publications.

Shaw, A., 1988. *A Pakistani Community in Britain.* Oxford: Blackwell.

Siddiqi, A.H., 1984. 'Nineteenth century agricultural development in Punjab: 1850–1900'. *The Indian Economic and Social History Review* vol. 21, no. 3, pp. 293–312.

Siddiqi, R., 1981. *Analysis of Household Consumption Patterns in Pakistan.* Islamabad: Pakistan Institute of Development Economics, Research Report Series no. 121.

Singh, G.Z., 1975. *The Social and Economic History of the Punjab. Including Haryana & Himachal Pradesh (1901–1939).* Delhi: Ess Ess Publications.

Singh, S., 1980. 'Agricultural development in the Punjab (1849–1947)'. *Journal of Regional History,* vol. 1, pp. 88–106.

—— 1982. *Agricultural Transformation in the Punjab under the British Rule, 1849–1947.* Proceedings of the Punjab History Conference, 16th. session, pp. 204–12.

Slater, M., 1979. 'Migrant development, recessions, and return migration: some consequences for migration policy and development'. *Studies in Comparative International Development* vol. 14, no. 3–4, pp. 3–22.

Slocum, W.L., J. Akhtar and A.F. Sahi, 1960. *Village Life in Lahore District. (A Sudy of Selected Sociological Aspects).* Lahore: Social Sciences Research Centre, University of the Panjab.

Smith, M.W., 1978 (1955). 'Social structure in the Punjab', in M.N. Srinivas (ed.): *India's Villages.* Bombay: Media Promoters and Publishers, pp. 161–79.

Souza, A. de (ed.), 1980. *Women in Contemporary India and South Asia.* Delhi: Manohar.

Spear, P., 1965. *A History of India.* Harmondsworth: Penguin.

Srinivas, M.N., 1984, *Some Reflections on Dowry.* Delhi: Oxford University Press.

—— [1987] 1994. *The Dominant Caste and Other Essays.* Oxford: Oxford University Press.

—— *et al*, [1955] 1962. *Caste in Modern India and Other Essays.* Bombay: Asia Publishing House.

Standing, G., 1981. 'Migration and modes of exploitation: social origins of immobility and mobility'. *The Journal of Peasant Studies,* vol. 8, no. 2, pp. 173–211.

Stevens, R.D., H.A. Alavi and P.J. Bertocci (eds), 1976. *Rural Development in Bangladesh and Pakistan.* An East-West Center Book, Honolulu: The University of Hawaii.

Tan, T.Y., 1994. 'Maintaining the military districts: Civil-military integration and district soldiers' boards in the Punjab, 1919–1939'. *Modern Asian Studies,* vol. 28, no. 4, pp. 833–874.

Tehseen, R., 1981. 'Socio-economic and Political Implications of the *Biraderi* System'. Unpublished MSc thesis, Department of Anthropology, Quaid-i-Azam University. Islamabad.

Terzian, P., 1977. 'OPEC surpluses: myth and reality'. *Merip Reports,* no. 57, pp. 21–24.

Thorburn, S.S., [1886] 1983. *Musalmans and Money-Lenders in the Punjab.* Delhi: Mittal Publications.

Tinker, H. 1977. *The Banyan Tree: Overseas Emigrants from India, Pakistan and Bangladesh.* Oxford: Oxford University Press.

Tsakok, I., 1986. 'The export of power from Pakistan to the Middle East, 1975–85', in S.J. Burki and R. Laporte (eds): *Pakistan's Development Priorities.* Karachi: Oxford University Press, pp. 224–36.

United Nations Economic Commission for Western Asia, 1982. *International Migration in the Arab World,* vols 1 and 2. Beirut: Proceedings of an ECWA Population Conference, Nicosia, Cyprus, 11–16 May 1981.

—— 1982. *Population and Development in the Middle East.* Beirut.

Van den Dungen, P.H.M., 1972. *The Punjab Tradition. Influence and Authority in Nineteenth Century India.* London: George Allen and Unwin.

Van der Linden, J., 1991. 'Security and value: Squatter dwellings in Karachi', in H. Donnan and P. Werbner (eds): *Economy and Culture in Pakistan:*

Migrants and Cities in Muslim Society. London: Macmillan Academic and Professional Ltd, pp. 62–76.

Vreede-De Stuers, C., 1968. *Parda. A Study of Muslim Women's Life in Northern India.* Assen: Koninklijke Van Gorcum.

Walkil, P.A., 1970. 'Explorations into the kin networks of the Punjabi society: A preliminary statement'. *Journal of Marriage and the Family,* vol. 32, no. 4, pp. 700–07.

—— 1972. '*Zat* and *Qaum* in Punjabi society: A contribution to the problem of caste'. *Sociologus,* vol. 22, pp. 38–48.

Watson, J.L., 1977. *Between Two Cultures: Migrants and Minorities in Britain.* Oxford: Blackwell.

Weiner, M., 1982. 'Migration and development in the Gulf'. *Population and Development Review,* no. 8, pp. 1–35.

Weiss, A.M., 1985. 'Women's Position in Pakistan. Sociocultural Effects of Islamization'. *Asian Survey,* vol. 25, no. 8, pp. 863–80.

—— 1990. 'Benazir Bhutto and the future of women in Pakistan'. *Asian Survey,* vol. 30, no. 5, pp. 433–45.

Werbner, P., 1989a. *The Migration Process: Capital, Gifts and Offerings among British Pakistanis.* Explorations in Anthropology Series. Oxford: Berg.

—— 1989b. 'The ranking of brotherhoods: The dialectics of Muslim caste among overseas Pakistanis'. *Contributions to Indian Sociology (NS),* vol. 23, no. 2.

Wilber, D.N., 1964. *Pakistan: Its People, Its Society, Its Culture.* New Haven: Human Relations Area Files.

Wickramasekara, P. (ed.), 1993. *The Gulf Crisis and South Asia: Studies on the Economic Impact.* New Delhi: ILO, Asian Regional Team for Employment Promotion (ARTEP): United Nations Development Programme.

White, L.J., 1974. *Industrial Concentration and Economic Power in Pakistan.* Princeton, NJ: Princeton University.

Wiser W. and C. Wiser, 1967. *Behind Mud Walls, 1930–1960.* Berkeley: University of California Press.

Wolpe, H., 1972. 'Capitalism and cheap labour power in South Africa: from segregation to apartheid'. *Economy and Society,* vol. 1, no. 4.

Yasin, M.G., 1965. *The Economics of Tube Well Irrigation.* Lahore: The Board of Economic Inquiry, publication no. 133.

—— 1975. *Private Tubewells in the Punjab.* Lahore: The Punjab Board of Economic Inquiry, publication no. 159.

Zahlan, A.B., 1984. 'Migratory labour in the Arab world'. *Third World Quarterly,* vol. 6, no. 4, pp. 981–92.

Zingel, W.P. and S. Zingel Ave Lallemant (eds), 1985. *Pakistan in the 80s. Ideology, Regionalism, Economy, Foreign Policy.* Lahore: Vanguard.

INDEX

The Nordic Institute of Asian Studies (NIAS) is funded by the governments of Denmark, Finland, Iceland, Norway and Sweden via the Nordic Council of Ministers, and works to encourage and support Asian studies in the Nordic countries. In so doing, NIAS has published well in excess of one hundred books in the last three decades, most of them in co-operation with Curzon Press.

Nordic Council of Ministers

For Product Safety Concerns and Information please contact our EU representative GPSR@taylorandfrancis.com
Taylor & Francis Verlag GmbH, Kaufingerstraße 24, 80331 München, Germany

www.ingramcontent.com/pod-product-compliance
Ingram Content Group UK Ltd.
Pitfield, Milton Keynes, MK11 3LW, UK
UKHW040623240926
475702UK00027B/1224/J
* 9 7 8 0 7 0 0 7 0 9 8 4 7 *